Abstracts of Wills Chatham County Georgia

- 1773-1817 -

Abstracted and compiled by:
Mabel Freeman LaFar
&
Caroline Price Wilson

Southern Historical Press, Inc.
Greenville, South Carolina

This volume was reproduced
from a personal copy located in
the Publishers private library

Please direct all correspondence and book orders to:
SOUTHERN HISTORICAL PRESS, Inc.
PO Box 1267
Greenville, SC   29602-1267

Originally published 1933 by:
        Lachlan McIntosh Chpt. DAR
ISBN #978-1-63914-253-8
Printed in the United States of America

ABSTRACTS OF WILLS, CHATHAM COUNTY, GEORGIA

FOREWORD

If one wishes to become acquainted with his ancestors, let him read their wills. It is amazing to find between the lines, the personality, the attitude towards life and people, that is conveyed through these post mortem letters.

Herein may be found wisdom, love, esteem, and gratitude - also hate, revenge, and subtle injustice. One can read the records of broken hearts and desperate unhappiness; of bitter disappointments and loss of hope.

It would be interesting history if it had been possible to include the full text of these testaments, but this was not possible within the limits of this undertaking.

The records of Christ Church Parish have suffered loss by fires, as well as the vandalism of several wars, but this volume contains all of the wills on record from the year 1773 to 1817, and includes Books A, B, C, D, and E.

Among these wills are those of Gen. Lachlan McIntosh, Gov. Button Gwinnett, Gov. Edward Telfair, Gen. Samuel Elbert, Maj. Gen. James Jackson, Anthony Wayne, Lady Sarah Wright, widow of Colonial Governor, Sir James Wright, Sir Patrick Houstoun, Peter Tondee, Josiah Tatnall, Jr., and others who were prominently connected with the earlier history of this state.

As a means of adding additional value to these abstracts, the compilers have noted the locality of lands, estates, places, and that of adjoining property, as such points are often means of establishing facts, otherwise unproven.

While the work has been very intriguing and of great interest, it has been beset by difficulties, as in many instances the penmanship was poor, with ink faded or blurred with age, or the manuscript in such condition that a magnifier was in constant use.

But this is true of nearly all old records, and it is a pleasure to feel that the result will prove of value to its readers.

                                        Mabel Freeman LaFar
                                        Caroline Price Wilson

Savannah, Georgia,
October 1, 1933

Key to Arrangement

Wills are arranged alphabetically under names, all A's in book A, listed under that book, all A's in book B, listed under that book, et cetera.

The name of the testator is in capital letters.

Date of drawing is first, followed by date of probating.

Nunc., placed after the dates, indicate that the will is a nuncupative one.

Key to Abbreviations

Gr. son	Grandson
Gr. dau	Granddaughter
Gr. neph	Grandnephew
Gr. niece	Grandniece
Bro	Brother
Dau	Daughter
Neph	Nephew
Chil	Children
Exr	Executor
Extx	Executrix
Gdn	Guardian
Adm	Administrator
Wit	Witness
Ref	Reference
In re	In reference to
Gene	Genealogy
Dist	District
Dec	Deceased
Prob	Probate

ABSTRACTS OF WILLS, CHATHAM COUNTY, GEORGIA

A

Will Book "A"

1 ANDERSON, ELIZABETH
   Feb. 24, 1793; Mch. 11, 1793.
   Aged widow.
   Gr. dau: Elizabeth Tillinghast, the wife of Stuhley Tillinghast, my sole heir.
   Exrs: John Poullen, Stuhley Tillinghast, Elizabeth Tillinghast.
   Wit: Ben Lloyd, John Haupt, James Whitefield.

   ALEXANDER, CHARLES
   Sept. 21, 1794; Sept. 26, 1794.
   Exr. and friend: Agnus Marmion, sole heir.
   Wit: Etienne Mavis Guidon, Margaret Marshall.
   Prob. in Charleston, S.C.

Will Book "B"

   ARDIS, MATHIAS, SR.
   Oct. 29, 1774; Sept. 9, 1782.
   Of township of New Winsor in Ninety-six Dist., S.C.
   To wife and extx: Christian.
   To daus: Elizabeth, Mary, and Sarah.
   To sons: Mathias, John, Isaac, Jacob, Abraham, Daniel, and David.
   "Eight younger children."
   Wit: James Thompson, John Bedenfield, Ninian Petrie.
   By oath of James Thompson, merchant of Augusta, Ga.

   ALLMAN, PHILIP   Carpenter
   Apr. 21, 1781; June 14, 1781.
   To son: Philip.
   Former wife: Jane.
   Mentions: three negroes who ran away in the year 1779 at the time of the siege
2 of Savannah, and refers to 360 lbs. which the government allowed for loss of his
   buildings torn down at the siege.
   Lands in St. Philip's Parish.
   Wife and Exrs: Ann, and William Ross, merchant.
   Wit: J. Artrobus, George Miller, James Meyers.

   ANDERSON, JOHN   Gentleman.
   Sept. 11, 1783; May 31, 1785.
   All to dear and blessed mother, Elizabeth Anderson, who is extx.
   Mentions: his lands in St. George's Parish and in Savannah.
   Wit: Andrew Johnson, John Poullen, James Whitefield.

Will Book "C"

   ALLEN, ROBERT H.
   Nov. - 1790; Jan. 15, 1791.
   Legatees: Mrs. Watlington, her son, John Watlington.
   To Thomas and Lueza, son and dau. of Clarissa Moultree.
   Remainder to Ann Jordine.
   Exrs: Solomon Shad, Matt Clark, William Clark.
   Wit: Peter S. Lafitte, T. Netherclift, John N. Watlington.

Will Book "D"

ALLEN, ROBERT   Stone-cutter.
Sept. 28, 1805; Feb. 4, 1806.
Of New York City.
To neph: Robert Robertson, stone-cutter, sole heir and exr.
Wit: Robert Elliott, John Crow, John Montgomery.

Will Book "E"

ADAMS, NATHANIEL, SR.
Mch. 7, 1806; Nov. 14, 1808.
Of Dist. of White Bluff.
3   To wife: Ann.
To sons: Nathaniel, Jun., Thomas Adams.
To daus: Margaret and Susan Adams.
Mentions: his lands purchased from - - - Bullinger and Webley, which lands border on lands of Michael Densler and the estate of Elbert; gift of deed for a plantation to his son, Thomas, where Thomas now lives, bearing date Jan. 24, 1799; property in Vernonburgh and Savannah.
Exrs: wife, Ann; Nathaniel Adams, Jun.; William M. Evans.
Wit: Jane Adams, Robert Newell, Michael Densler.

ALGER, JAMES
June 11, 1808; Mch. 8, 1809.
To wife: Sarah, her mother dec.
To neph; Preserved Alger, son of Preserved Alger, of Warren, R.I.
To the Misses: Mary Deveaux, Margaret Irvine, and Sally Ann Lanier, dau. of Clement Lanier.
Mentions: his "Oakeland Hill Plantation," and lot in Yamacraw.
Exrs. wife; Sarah; John Milledge; Charles Harris.
Wit: Margaret Irvine, Clement Lanier.

ACHORD, LEWIS   Planter.
Feb. 27, 1809; July 10, 1809.
To sons: Lewis D. and John S.
To daus: Ann and Jane.
Exrs: Wife, Jane, and son, Lewis D. Achord.
Wit: Joseph Ball, Bennett Webber, Walten Stewart.

ABENDANONE, JOSEPH
Sept. 25, 1815; Jan. 4, 1816.
"Mrs. Eliza Swain can furnish information, etc."
Mentions: rents due to Mr. Kopman and Mr. Starr, the hatter.
"Dr. Moses Sheftall to take charge of my affairs."
Wit: William Starr.

B

Will Book "A"

4   BARNWELL, JOHN, SR.
Nov. 17, 1773; Jan. 30, 1784.
Residence, Ladies Island, St. Helena's Parish, Granville Co., S.C.
To dau: Catherine, wife of Andrew Deveaux, and their son Andrew.
To dau: Ann Deveaux, and her dau. Ann.
To daus: Martha Guerard, Elizabeth Deveaux, Bridget Guerard, Mary and Phoebe Sarah.

ABSTRACTS OF WILLS, CHATHAM COUNTY, GEORGIA

To son: John Bernis Barnwell (minor).
To gr. son: James, son of Wm. Deveaux, and his dau. Martha.
To gr. son: John Bernis Barnwell.
To gr. dau: Hannah Deveaux.
Mentions: lands bought from Richard Guerard, Miss Gibion Wright, John Gordon, Adam Daniel, Daniel Blake, Mr. Blakeway in Beaufort town; the island of Warsaw from Kinnaway Norton; and a small tract of Scott's trail, running to Thomas Wigg's land.
Mentions: land his father left him, and plantation called "Scotts."
Exrs: wife, Martha, and son, John Bernis Barnwell.
Wit: D. Dessaussure, Thomas Hughes, L. Rivers.
Codicil dated Nov. 26, 1773.
"Wrote with my own hand."
Married daus: Catherine, Ann, Martha, Elizabeth, and Bridget.
Youngest daus: Mary and Phoebe Sarah.
Testator appoints Lewis Reives, John Barnwell, Jr., Joseph Jenkins, and William Waight to sign titles.
Wit: Daniel Dessaussure, Thomas Hughes, Archer Smith.
Codicil #2 dated April 15, 1775.
Bequeaths property recently bought to some of his children already named.
Wit: John Rhodes, John Williamson, D. Dessaussure.

5 BUCHENAU, NICHOLAS
June 25, 1793; June 4, 1796.
Of Skidaway Island.
Extx. and wife: Margaret, sole heir.
Wit: Edmund Griffith, Peter Papot, James Clark.

BEATTY, JOHN (DR.)
Nov. 12, 1792; Dec. 6, 1792.
To wife: Eleanor, late Patton.
To chil: Eleanor and John Patrick Beatty.
To Miss Ruth Patton, dau. of my wife.
Mentions: lands in little Ogeechee, lot in Trustee's Garden, and an island in the Savannah River, near Purysburg, S.C.
Exrs: wife, Eleanor, and Richard Wylly.
Wit: Benj. Lindsay, Nicholas Turnbull, J. Whitefield.

BROWNHILL, THOMAS   Planter.
Apr. 14, 1786; June 13, 1796.
To son: Thomas Brownhill.
Testator manumits slave, and refers to negro mortgaged to David Murdock, now in the hands of Nathaniel Pendleton.
Exr: Bro-in-law, Nathaniel Stanhope.
Wit: Wm. Stephens, Abm. Jackson, James McGowen.

BELL, WILLIAM   Shoemaker.
Sept. 1, 1800; Mch. 3, 1801.
All to John Harrison, shoemaker.
Exrs: John Harrison, Robert Stratham.
Wit: F. S. Miller, John Kozsburg, Samuel Kinsley.

BELL, JOHN
Sept. 10, 1792; Oct. 3, 1792.
"Mate of ship America," John Connolly, master.
To sister: Elizabeth Bubia, widow, of Marblehead, Mass.
Exr: John Whitley, of Savannah, butcher.
Wit: James Nelson, John Clark, Joseph Welscher.

BELL, DAVID   Merchant.
Mch. 3, 1794; Mch. 31, 1794.
To daus: Mary Griffith and Jane McConkey.
To wife: Jane, and sons, Robert, David, and John Bell, who are exrs.
6 Sons-in-law: Edward Griffith and Andrew McConkey.
Wit: Slaughter W. Cowling, Andrew McConkey, Mary Griffith.

BECK, SOPHIA
May 9, 1796; Nov. 13, 1797.
Of St. Peter's Parish, S.C.
Child in esse.
Mentions: her lot in village of St. Gall, bought by her father of Daniel Shupart; and property bordering on lands of John Ball, Mingledorph, and Villards.
Exr: husband, John Beck.
Wit: Ebenezer Parker, Elizabeth Parker, Jane Griggs.

BUCKLEY, PHILIP
Oct. 30, 1796; June 15, 1798.
Of Charleston, S.C.
On ship Eagle, bound to the coast of Africa.
Exr: Edmund Welch, sole heir, of the ship Augusta.
Attested by James Armstrong, mariner, and Thomas Dollaghan.

BULL, ABSALOM   Gentleman.
Sept. 20, 1791; Sept. 24, 1791.   Nunc.
"A few hours before his death, by word of mouth." "That Dr. William Gale sell negroes, and send wench, Serena, to whom I now give freedom, with my little son, Thomas, to my father Thomas Bull, in Ulster Co., N.Y." My estate to be equally divided among my chil. "All half-pay officers of His Britanic Majesty, to attend my funeral if consistent with laws of this country."
Exr: Dr. William Gale.
Wit: Ezra Plumer, carpenter, and his wife Mary Plumer, and Dr. William Gale.

BOTTOMLEY, MICHAEL
Dec. 24, 1792; Mch. 27, 1793.
of Winton Co., S.C.
Exr: John Cunningham, merchant, sole heir.
Wit: F. T. Smithson, John Shick, Alexander Norris.

BRISBANE, JAMES
Jan. 17, 1794; July 25, 1794.
To present wife Margaret.
To sons: William and Robert.
7 To son: John Stanyarne Brisbane, and his aunt, Susannah Stanyarne, my sister-in-law.
To son: Adam, my present wife's son.
"Considerable property by former wives."
Mentions: his seals, with coat of arms.
Exrs: Thomas Forbes, John Stow, Thomas Wm. Burley Hall.
Wit: John Ferguson, Sr., John McNaughton, Patrick Brown.
Will was prob. in Providence, Bahama Islands, before Hon. John, Earl of Dunmore, and James Armbrister, Deputy Register.

BOURQUIN, JANE JUDITH   Widow.
Feb. 23, 1799; Mch. 11, 1799.
Of little Ogeechee.
To sons: Benedict, Henry, and David Francis.
To dau: Mary Ann.
To gr. dau: Ann Sophia, dau. of my son David Francis.

ABSTRACTS OF WILLS, CHATHAM COUNTY, GEORGIA

Exr: son, Benedict.
Wit: Ben Raynes, Mary S. Raynes, Sarah McKinley.

BOIFEUILLET, MARY ANNA LARMANDIE
Jan. 31, 1801; No prob.
Native of Bergerac in Paigne*, aged 39 yrs. 6 mos., born from Armand De Larmandie, dec., and Henrietta De Lavardie, my father and mother, widow of Charles Peter Caesar Picot De Boifeuillet.
Residence, Sapelo Island.
Four chil: Jeanne Mary, wife of Mr. Ralph Clay.
Charlotte Angelique Sersanne**, Michael, and Joseph Balthazar. (Minors)
Appoints as Guardian, cousin, Mr. Marie Joseph Emile De Charon and his wife, and in lieu of him Mr. Jacques De Chessa and John Lafond, the latter with Margaret Archer as maid, having come with testator from France.
To Mr. Dumont, money for voyage if he desires to return to France.
To Mr. Picot, bro. of my husband.
Exr: Mr. Marie Joseph Emile De Charon.
Wit: John de Laval, J. P. Prignet, Pr. Guinan.
* Note: Perigard, France.
** Note: Servanne.

8   BOISFEILLET, CHARLES PIERRE CESAR (PICOT) DE
Mch. 30, 1799; Sept. 6, 1800.
Of Sapelo Island.
Born at St. Malo, France, age 58 yrs.
Four minor chil: Jean Marie, Sersanne, Michael, Joseph Balthazar Charles.
Extx: wife, Marie de Lamardie, sole heir.
Wit: Jacques Aubert Dechessa, Joseph Deleval, Charles Hammond.

Will Book "B"

BAILLOU, JAMES   Hatter.
June 16, 1777; Sept. 24, 1777.
Extx: wife, Mary Elizabeth Baillou, sole heir.
Wit: George Dressler, Dennis Mahoney, Adrian Loyer.

BOWLES, JOHN   Vintner.
Aug. 30, 1776; Nov. 25, 1777.
Extx: wife, Phillippa, sole heir.
Wit: William Stewart, Thomas Mills, Peter Papot.

BOWEN, SAMUEL, ESQR.   Planter.
May 31, 1774; Sept. 12, 1778.
Residence "Grenwich" purchased from Hon. Grey Elliott, Esqr.
Mentions: a near by island called Macas Island, purchased from John Mulryne, Esqr.
Extx: wife, Jane, sole heir.
Wit: William Belcher, Samuel Farley, Samuel Stirk.

BALLOW, ELIZABETH   Widow.
Dec. 16, 1782; Nov. 10, 1783.
All to niece Sarah Bacon, extx., and her son Joseph Bacon.
Wit: Hannah Gibbons, John McMahon.

BOURQUIN, HENRY, ESQR.
Nov. 23, 1775; Apr. 30, 1785.
Of Little Ogeechee.
To gr. chil: David Huginnin, the younger, and Susannah Maria Huginnin.
To gr. chil: Peter Henry, John, and Mary, chil. of John Morel, Esqr.

To gr. chil: Henry, David, John, and Lewis, chil. of John Keal, dec.
To dau: Harriet, widow of Henry Lewis Bourquin.
To dau: Frances, wife of John Fox.
To Mary McNish, wife of -- McNish.
To Katherine Reims (Rheims), wife of Frederick Reims of Purysburg.
Mentions: his plantation called "Good Hope".
Extxs: Harriet Bourquin, Frances Fox, Katherine Reims.
Wit: James Robertson, Thomas Ross, John Wood.

BROWN, JOHN   Mariner.
Oct. 10, 1785; Nov. 17, 1785.
To son: Thomas, and dau: Frances, both minors.
To Mordecai Sheftall, one negro, now in the possession of Thomas Hamilton,
planter, of Richmond Co., in trust for use of Polly, dau. of Mrs. Mary Curtis,
widow.
Wit: Benjamin Butler, Jacob Waldburge, Joseph Welscher.
After the death of Mordecai Sheftall, exr., Peter Oates and Thomas Brown as
nearest of kin were made Adms.

BULLOCH, ARCHIBALD, ESQR.
Feb. 11, 1775; Mch. 1, 1786.
To "all my children".
Exrs: wife, Mary; James DeVeaux; Joseph Clay.
Wit: Henry Young, Jr., Stephen Haven, Mary Yonga.

BARD, PETER   Merchant.
July 21, 1785; Jan. 4, 1786.
To wife: Ann.
To sister: Susannah Bard, the White House at the village of Yamacraw; also tract
at fork of Great Ogeechee and Canonchee Rivers.
Mentions: the firm of Bard and Thompson; and his accts. with William Pierce &
Co., "of which I am one"; and money which may be due me from the state of Georgia.
Request a division of the estate "given by House of Assembly to John Tubly and
myself."
Exrs: wife Ann; Nathaniel Pendleton; William Pierce.
Wit: Wm. Stephens, Dr. John Brickell, Nich. H. Bugg.

10 BUTLER, ELIZABETH   Widow.
Nov. 21, 1775; Oct. 23, 1780.
Of Great Ogeechee in province of Ga. but now of Charleston, S.C.
To Miss Butler, 500 pounds of S.C. money, subject to above remainder of estate in
S.C. and Ga.
To Jeremiah Savage, Thomas Savage, and Jeremiah Parsons, Esqrs., of Charleston,
S.C.
To bro: William Elliott.
To nephs: William, Ralph, and Stephen Elliott, and George Parsons.
To dau: Mary Elliott Savage.
Mentions: her plantation called the "Farm" on Charleston Neck; tract of land on
the east side of Ponpon River, "my plantation on which I formerly lived in Ga."
called "Silk Hope"; lands on Fort Argyle.
Exr: Jeremiah Savage.
Wit: Dorothy Drayton, James Smith, J. Ewing Calhoun.

BRYAN, JONATHAN, ESQR.
Dec. 15, 1783; Mch. 27, 1788.
Of Brampton plantation called "Union" in Purysburg Township, S.C.
To son: James.
To daus: Mary Morel, Hannah Houstoun, the wife of John Houstoun, atty-at-law.
To gr. sons: Bryan Morel and Joseph Bryan, the son of my dec. son, Josiah.

ABSTRACTS OF WILLS, CHATHAM COUNTY, GEORGIA

Mentions: 2000 acres above Matthew Bluff on Savannah River, originally granted to my bro., Hugh Bryan, Esqr.
Exrs: dau., Mary Morel; son-in-law, John Houstoun; sons, William and James Bryan.
Wit: Ben Lloyd, Esqr., John Wanden, James Port.

BUTLER, SHEM
July 30, 1787; Jan. 17, 1789.
To wife: Elizabeth.
To sons: John, Shem, Jr., Joseph, Thomas, and James.
To daus: Elizabeth, Edith, and Ann.
Mentions: his lands between Ogeechee and Cannochee "where I formerly lived"; 2000 acres formerly granted to Joseph Butler on the Salkehatchie in S.C., and 500 acres bought of William Harn.
Exrs: Benj. Stiles, Esqr., Samuel Harn, John Butler.
Wit: Edward Harden, William Harn, Thomas Smith.

BOLTON, ROBERT, SR., ESQR.
July 24, 1786; May 22, 1789.
To wife; not named.
To son: Robert, Jun.
To daus: Rebecca Nevill, Ann Adams.
To gr. sons: Thomas Nevill, Jun., Robert Nevill, Nathaniel Adams, Jun.
To adopted orphan child: Rebecca Feaveaux.
To neighbors: John Womack, Jacob Ties.
Mentions: his lot in Savannah; lands in St. Paul's Parish; lands in Hampstead between the high gate and White Bluff roads four miles from Savannah; lots in Brunswick and Hardwick.
Exrs: son, Robert Bolton, Jun., merchant in Savannah; son-in-law, Samuel Adams of White Bluff, planter.
Wit: John Hamilton, John Richards, John Nevill.

BEAL, HELENA
Sept. 27, 1787; Jan. 6, 1791.
To son: Ulrich Tobler.
To dau: Mary Gray, wife of James Gray of Augusta, Ga.
Exr: son, Ulrich Tobler.
Wit: George Basil Spencer, Herman Herson, William Lewden.

Will Book "D"

BEECROFT, SAMUEL   Surgeon.
Sept. 20, 1800; Oct. 7, 1801.
To wife: Elizabeth Ann, formerly "Miss Elizabeth Ann Bowen".
To Samuel Hemingway of Liverpool in trust for use of sister, Catherine Maria Leonard of London, and Mrs. Sarah Stephenson.
To father: Robert Beecroft.
To Henry Bourquin, Jun.
To my adopted dau: Jane Elizabeth, dau. of James Flint Bowen, Sr., and the niece of my wife.
To James Flint Bowen, Jun.
Mentions: his plantation called "Sans Souci", at Grenwich.
Exrs: wife, Elizabeth Ann; dau., Jane Elizabeth; and William Henry Spencer.
Gdns: wife, Elizabeth Ann Beecroft; William Henry Spencer, Mary Bowen, sister of my wife.
Wit: James Wallace, William Smith, F. T. Flyming.

12 BOSWOOD, JAMES   Planter.
June 20, 1800; Mch. 5, 1805.
All to Peter Alter, planter, and Daniel Megarven.
Attested by William Chauvin.

BOLTON, ROBERT   Merchant.
Nov. 19, 1802; Feb. 7, 1803.
From the concern of "Robert & John Bolton".
To wife: Sarah.
To daus: Sally, Nancy, Frances Lewis Bolton, and Rebecca Newell Bolton.
To sons: Robert and James McLeah Bolton.
To neph: Thomas and Robert Newell.
To cousins: Curtis and Edwin Bolton.
To - - Newell of Woodstock, in trust for his son, Bolton.
To John Bolton, in trust for my sister, Rebecca Newell, and her sons, Thomas and Robert Newell.
Son-in-law: John Jackson.
Sister-in-law: Ann Gibson.
(John Bolton, bro. of Curtis Bolton.)
Mentions: his lands bought from Thomas Newell, the elder; and Samuel Stiles by the firm of "Newell & Bolton"; "and was afterwards bought wholly by myself"; lands in Savannah, which lands border on lands of Joseph Clay, Sr., Esqr., bought at sale being the property of John Summerocle, dec.; wharf lot in Trustee's Garden bought of Miss Flyming.
Mentions: his plantation in Burke Co.; lot in village of St. Gall; one half rope walk in Baltimore, held jointly with my friend James Peper.
Desires that titles be given to the heirs of Henry Addington for a lot in Hampstead.
Exrs: wife, Sarah; friends, John Bolton, William Wallace, George Woodruff; sons, Robert and James Bolton.
Wit: Nathaniel Adams, Sr., Benjamin Brooks, John Habersham.

BLOUNT, STEPHEN
July 17, 1804; Nov. 5, 1804.
To son: Stephen William Blount*, minor.
To daus: Jane and Elizabeth Ann.
13 Possible child in esse.
Exrs: wife, Charlotte; David Robertson, Fredk. Schewbart.
Wit: Adam Cope, J. Cuyler, John Cline.
   *Note: possibly son by former marriage.

BRITON, STEPHEN, SR.   Planter.
Mch. 17, 1804; May 7, 1804.
To daus: Ann Mills and Mary Thompson.
To sons: John and Stephen.
To gr. son: George Clark, the child of my dau. Mary, now Mary Thompson.
"I desire Mr. Thomas Pitt and Ann Mills to take charge of the chil. of the estate of William Oakman, of which I am exr."
Exrs: David Brady Mitchell; dau., Ann Mills.
Wit: Thomas Robinson, James D. Brownson.

BRISBANE, ROBERT
June 12, 1804; July 31, 1804.
To Miss Eunice Hog and Miss Martha Stevens.
To bro: Adam.
To Theodore Carlton.
To Joseph Davis.
"I devise to the trustees of the Baptist Church in Savannah, my real estate in S.C. for the benefit of the first college which may be instituted by the Baptists

ABSTRACTS OF WILLS, CHATHAM COUNTY, GEORGIA

of Georgia, and my fellow named Prince, they to require of him no other service
than sweeping out the said Church and ringing its bell on the usual occasions."
Exrs: John Bolton, Benjamin Brooks.
Wit: Elias Robert, Henry Holcombe, F. Holcombe.
Codicil dated June 12, 1804.
To bro: John.
To aunt: Esther Bellemy.
Rev. Henry Holcombe to be added to the names of the exrs.
Wit: S. Woodhouse, Thomas Dixon, Elias Robert.

BOWEN, OLIVER
July 20, 1789; Oct. 3, 1800.
Native of Rhode Island.
Resided in Ga., but now at Providence in R.I.
Exr: bro., the Hon. Jabez Bowen.
Wit: John Jenckes, Obadiah Brown, Benjamin Bourn.
At bottom of Page:
To my good friend: Mrs. Jane Watts, widow, of Savannah.
Rec. in book 7 page 296, etc. of the records of the Court of Probate in town of
Providence, Providence Co., R.I.

Will Book "E"

BRAILSFORD, ELIZABETH
July -- 1800; Apr. 17, 1807.
Of Charleston, S.C.
Widow of Samuel Brailsford.
To dau. and extx: Elizabeth.
Wit: Mr. Bee Holmes, Sarah H. Savage.

BOYD, CHARLES   Planter.
May 29, 1807; Dec. 7, 1807.
To wife: Barbara.
To sons: Charles and James.
To dau: Mary Camp, wife of Thomas Camp.
Exrs: wife, Barbara, son, Charles.
Wit: Charles Cope, Alexander Young, F. T. Flyming.

BUFFETT, GEORGE
Nov. 9, 1806; Feb. 8, 1808.
Extx: wife, Mary Ann Buffett.
Wit: Jeremiah Cuyler, John Davies, Dinah Davies.

BRICKELL, JOHN   Physician.
Dec. 5, 1809; Jan. 2, 1810.
To bro: James Brickell.
Exrs: bro., James Brickell; friends, Edward Swarbreck, and Richard Leake.
Wit: Walter Taylor, Joseph Maxwell, William Green, Richard W. Habersham, John Shaw.

BEATTY, ELEANOR   Widow.
July 26, 1810; Dec. 3, 1810.
To bros: Alexander, and Jessey Carey and his children.
To sister: Mary Chesnut.
To Ann and Jane E. Johnston, daus. of Thomas Johnston, dec., and to their bro.
Thomas Johnston.
To Elizabeth Simpson, dau. of James Simpson, dec.
To Mary Ann McKain, William Davies, Edwin Robert, land on Iron Monger's Creek in
the former Parish of St. Philips, granted to Daniel Saxe.

To Richard T. Keating of Bryan Co.
To John Lindsey, son of the Rev. Benjamin Lindsey.
To friend: Nicol Turnbull.
Mentions: his lands in district of White Bluff known as "Farm Plantation"; lot in the Trustee's Garden.
Exrs: Richard T. Keating, William Davies, Nicol Turnbull.
Wit: Susannah Simpson, George Glen, John Davies.

BRYAN, JOSEPH
In Sept. 1812; Feb. 2, 1813.
Of Wilmington Island.
To wife, two sons, and two daus. not named.
Father-in-law: Gen. Thomas M. Foreman of Maryland.
Exrs: Maj. John Screven, Col. David McCormick, Charles Harris.
Wit: Charles Harris, atty-at-law.

BUCKHALTER, JOSHUA   Planter.
Dec. 22, 1812; Feb. 2, 1813.
To neph: Jacob Buckhalter.
To Elizabeth Nungazer.
Mentions: his lands in Savannah and in Wilkinson Co.
Exrs: wife Catherine; friend Henry Nungazer.
Wit: Theodocius Barton, Jun., Ann Duke, Green R. Duke.

BRIERE, JEAN FRANCOIS
Sept. 18, 1812; Feb. 14, 1814.
Age 39, born in the Parish Couree Boeufs, now called the department of Sarte, formerly the diocese and election of Mans.
Son of the late Jean Briere and of the late Julienne Pean.
"My father and mother died in the Parish of Champagne."
To wife: Jeanne Margueritte Cazeaux-Briere, my only heir.
Mentions: his property in France.
Exrs: wife, Jeanne, and uncle, Julien Briere.
Wit: Paul P. Thomasson, Gabriel L. Colmesnil, E. Rodott, S. B. Berthelos.
Translated from the French by Miss Martha Youngblood, Savannah, Ga.

16 BEECROFT, ELIZABETH ANN
Apr. 26, 1815; June 6, 1816.
Relict of Dr. Samuel Beecroft.
To sister and extx: Mary D. Bowen.
Wit: Ann Johnston, Henry Bourquin, Jun., Joseph K. Carr.

BROOKS, BENJAMIN
Mch. 20, 1817; June 2, 1817.
To son: Robert, left in care of Francis H. Welman.
To son: Charles, left in care of R. Richardson.
Exrs: bro., Charles Brooks; Francis H. Welman, co-partner.
Wit: Dr. Benjamin A. White, Benj. W. Dela Mater, Thomas P. Chairs.

BARNARD, MARY
July 15, 1815; July 17, 1815.
To Jane Williams, wife of D. D. Williams.
To Philip Minis, son of Isaac Minis.
To -- Wells, son of Elijah Wells, dec.
Mentions slaves belonging to: Mrs. Benjamin Wall, Nicholas Fox, Captain Kennedy of Augusta.
Exr: Isaac Minis.
Wit: William Habersham, John A. Casey, Moses Herbert.

ABSTRACTS OF WILLS, CHATHAM COUNTY, GEORGIA

BECU, ABRAHAM   Baker.
Feb. 2, 1815; Jan. 4, 1816.
To wife: Mary.
To step-dau: Lydia Broughton.
To step-gr. dau: Elizabeth Mary Judith Bryan.
Mentions: his lands in Savannah, and in Wilkinson Co.
Exrs: wife, Mary; Elijah Broughton; Samuel Bryan.
Wit: Nathaniel Lewis, John Furches, Lewis Myers.

C

Will Book "A"

17 CHAPPEDELAINE, JULIEN JOSEPH HYACINTHE DE
Oct. 25, 1793; Dec. 1, 1794.
To John Baptiste Mark Michael de Chappedelaine, legitimate son of Rene Ann Mary Caeser de Chappedelaine, one third of Island of Sappelo; one quarter in Jaeckell Island; one quarter in St. Catherine's Island. Said heir now living in Parish D'hillifore de Dole, in Bretania. Should he leave no heirs, the property to next branch of family residing at Mayenne.
Mentions: his mill near Morristown, N.J.; debt due from Mr. Boisfeuville.
"Have affixed my seal and arms, at Sappelo Island."
Wit: Elisha B. Hopkins, John Griffin.
Codicil bequeaths to: Mad. Shueter, Faux Bourg Saverne a Strasburg.
To Antoinette Lafalloise.
To Mrs. de Loemaride.
To Mrs. LaMettrie La choux.
Exr: Mr. Doumoussay, who was afterwards replaced by Thomas Decheneaux, Sept. 13, 1794.
Papers in connection with this will show that the legatee had received no notice of this will previous to 1801. He was then in France, but came to Ga. in 1802, June 18, and found that the island had been sold at auction, etc., and signed by his bro-in-law, Picot de Clorriviere, Adm., who with Gabriel Yromet and -- Mirante, give bond Apr. 5, 1803. One of the codicils was wit. by John Parker and Samuel Meers, and another was wit. by William Lawrence.

CRANE, MATHEW   Carpenter.
Nov. 11, 1797; Jan. 10, 1798.
To the chil. of bro., Patrick Crane of Ireland.
Exrs: Christopher Hall, John Newton Fry, John Dillon.
(Fry & Dillon, shopkeepers.)
Wit: Furney Hickman, Thomas Lawson, Joseph Welscher.

18 CHAPMAN, JAMES
Oct. 30, 1793; Jan. 4, 1794.
By deposition of Miss Isabel and James Mossman.
Ref. is made to accts. against the estates of George Cuthbert, Sir Patrick Houstoun, and John Simpson, these to be divided among the chil. of sister, Ann Grant; other accts. in hands of Messrs. Simpson & Davidson of London, to be paid to Lewis Grant, minister at Cromdale, and Alexander Grant, minister at Caldermure.
To Ann McGillen, dau. of my sister, Elizabeth McGillen.
Exr: James Mossman.

CURRIE, JOHN
Sept. 26, 1799; Mch. 3, 1800.
(Died Sept. 26, 1799.)

To bros: Alexander, Joseph, and John Currie.
To sisters: Jane, Elizabeth, and Catherine Currie.
To uncle: William Crostwaite.
To Joseph, son of my friend, Col. Ferdinand O'Neal.
To godsons: Robert, son of William Delony, and -- Dews.
To friends: Thomas and Joseph Miller, John Cunningham, Patrick Crookshanks, Col. Ferdinand O'Neal.
Mentions: a bill of sale from Mr. Bulloch; and that he wishes the freedom of a negro girl, now in the possession of Mrs. Houstoun.
Exrs: George Parker, Joseph Millar, Andrew McCredie, merchants.
Attested by Dr. James B. Young, Cunningham Newall.
(Physician in charge, Dr. Beecroft.)

CHAVENET, SENIOR
Nov. 20, 1799; May 4, 1801.
Mentions: his bros. and sisters, not named.
(A refugee from St. Domingo.)
Exr: O. Duhigg, Sr., "husband of my niece Miss Beynard."
Will translated by Thomas Decheneaux.

COURSE, DANIEL   Merchant.
May 6, 1794; Mch. 28, 1796.
To wife: Elizabeth.
To aged mother, "now in Charleston, S.C."
To dau: Charlotte Rebecca.
To bros: John and Isaac Course.
Child in esse.
Extx: wife, Elizabeth.
Wit: Ezra Dennison, Robert Lawton, Thos. Golphin Holmes.

CLARK, JONATHAN
Aug. 5, 1793; Aug. 16, 1793.
To wife: Herodias, sole legatee.
To bro: William Clark, sailmaker.
Mentions: his lands in Dist. of Ninety-six, and Winton Co., S.C.
Exrs: wife, Herodias; Ebenezer Hill, merchant.
Wit: James Belcher, Abraham Leggett, William Ewing.
Will attested in N.Y. before Peter Ogilvie, by Abraham Leggett of City of N.Y., blacksmith.

CLARK, LEMUEL   Merchant.
Oct. 24, 1797; Nov. 18, 1797.   Nunc.
Exr: Nathaniel Sturdivant, to deliver to wife and children, now in Halifax, Plymouth Co., Mass.
Wit: Susannah T., wife of Willar Sears, storekeeper, and Gordon Isaac Seymour, printer.
Nathaniel Sturdivant qualifies as exr. May 10, 1798.

Will Book "B"

CATER, STEPHEN
Aug. 23, 1779.
Of St. George Parish, S.C.
To neph: Dr. John Cater.
Wit: W. McGillivray, Stephen Baker.
Taken from the original, Register's Office Oct. 20, 1782.

ABSTRACTS OF WILLS, CHATHAM COUNTY, GEORGIA

CATER, JOHN   Physician.
May 23, 1782; Oct. 10, 1782.
At present of Savannah.
Mentions: "property received from my uncle, Stephen Cater, of the Parish of St. George in S.C., deed bearing date Aug. 23, 1779."
Extx: wife, Susannah, sole heir.
Wit: David Montaigut, Joseph Farley, F. Brooks.

CHRISTOPHER, JACOB   Planter.
May 5, 1776; June 12, 1777.
Of St. Philip's Parish, S.C.
To son: George, minor.
Exrs: John Jones of Sunbury, John Kell, merchants.
Wit: James Beverly, John Kell of Sunbury.

CLARK, HENRY
Oct. 18, 1783; Nov. 13, 1783.
To wife: Margaret.
To chil: Archibald and Mary.
Exrs: wife, Margaret, and James Storey.
Wit: David Montaigut, John Poullen, John Strong.

CUTHBERT, GEORGE
Apr. 10, 1767; Nov. 4, 1786.
Ref. is made to marriage contract.
To wife: Mary.
To cousin: James Chapman.
To George and Joseph, sons of Dr. James Cuthbert.
Exrs: James Cuthbert, Alexander Inglis, merchants of Savannah.
Wit: Grey Elliott, David Brydie, Jonathan Evans.
Samuel Stirk and Edward Lloyd were bondsmen with Joseph Cuthbert of Drakies, in Ga., for the estate of George Cuthbert, dec., dated Nov. 4, 1786.

Will Book "C"

CLARK, WESTON
Apr. 10, 1786; Oct. 23, 1788.
Of Philadelphia.
To Rev. George Duffield, for use of Presbyterian Meeting in Pine St., his residence to be in house in front between Skipper and Almond Sts.
To cousins: James and Jane Clark, son and dau. of William Clark; William J. Donaldson; Margaret Donaldson, dau. of Arthur Donaldson; and James Senoile.
To father-in-law: Capt. Samuel Wilson.
To -- Arthur Fullerton, minor.
To aunt: Margaret Treo.
To Miss Sally Thorne, Archibald Brown, A. Campbell, Isaac Donaldson, William P. Donaldson, William Thorne, Eleanor Fulerton, John Garrett, and Arthur Campbell, shoemaker.
Mentions: his mother, dec.
Exr: Capt. William Brown of Southwark.
Wit: William Knox, Arthur Donaldson.

COPP, JOHN
No date; Aug. 31. 1789.
Residence the "Filature".
Mentions: three chil., not named.
Exrs: sister, Esther Seabury; friend, Dr. James Brown.
Wit: F. T. Smithson, William Nornent.

COHEN, PHILIP JACOB   Merchant.
Sept. 16, 1790; Nov. 18, 1790.
To Elizabeth Stronach?; a negro wench, "for her care of me during my long sickness."
Exrs: friends, Adam Tunno, Israel Joseph of Charleston, S.C., John Glen, atty-at-law.
Wit: Levi Sheftall, Isaac Poloch, James Glen.

CLYATTE, JAMES
Jan. 23, 1790; Jan. 26, 1790.
To wife: Saragh.
My chil: James, David, Samuel, Ann, and Rebecca Clyatte.
Mentions: lands bought of James Hines.
Exrs: wife, Saragh; friend, James Habersham.
Wit: Jonathan Arnets, David Delh, Penny Barber.

Will Book "D"

CORKER, WILLIAM
July 5, 1802; Dec. 15, 1802.
Chil: Mary, Charles, and Susannah.
Extx: wife, Leah, sole heir.
Wit: Thomas Young, Dianna Clyatt, Benjamin Collier, Henry Johnston.
Attested by William Davies and Moses Sheftall.

CROPP, SARAH
May 15, 1803; Apr. 27, 1805.
Mentions: husband, John Cropp, dec., and two youngest chil., Sarah and Benjamin Cropp.
Exrs. and Gdns: sons-in-law, John B. Jones and John Watters.
Wit: Charles Odingsells, George Heisler, George W. Allen.

CRAVELLIER, WILLIAM   Baker.
May 10, 1807; June 2, 1807.
Of Lacrotal, France.
Mentions: parents, bros., and sisters living in France.
Mentions: "two tenements belonging to me on the lot, the property of Mrs. Stebbins in Bryan St."
Exrs: friends, Desire Lambertoz and Paul Dupon.
Wit: James M. Wilson, Alexander Low, I. A. Morrice.

CHEW, BENJAMIN   Planter.
Oct. 25, 1806; Jan. 5, 1807.
Of St. Peter's Parish, S.C.
Will made while in Savannah.
To wife: Obedience.
Only son: Benjamin Chew, age about nine yrs.
Richard Pelot of S.C., Adm. of the estate of Caleb Chew, "of which I am an heir".
To sister: Elizabeth Garvin.
Exr. and Gdn: William Cornelius Barton.
Wit: William H. Spencer, James Platt, Elizabeth Barton, William Wiggins.

Will Book "E"

CUTHBERT, LEWIS G.
Aug. 30, 1803; Jan. 7, 1811.

ABSTRACTS OF WILLS, CHATHAM COUNTY, GEORGIA

Extx: wife, Martha Wood.
Wit: Joseph L. Bridges, Benj. Langley, John Keller.

COURVOISIE, JOHN FRANCIS WILLIAM   Planter.
Aug. 27, 1810; Dec. 2, 1811.
A native of the City of Vivey Pays de Vaux Canton of Bern, Switzerland.
To wife: Mary.
To son: John Francis Courvoisie.
To gr. dau: Mary Fox Courvoisie.
To sisters: Louisa and Charlotte.
To James D. Courvoisie Fox, son of James Fox.
To Mary Ann Fox, dau. of William B. Fox.
To William B. Fox, land known as Matthew Mauve's old field, where he now resides.
Mentions: his estate called "Devillare" near the City of Vivey.
Exrs: wife, Mary, and friend, Charles Harris, Esqr.
Wit: William Craig, Alexander Habersham, Thomas Edward Lloyd.
Codicil dated August 27, 1810.
"My body to be interred on a plot of ground where the chil. of William B. Fox are buried."

CAMPBELL, MARTHA GADSDEN.   Spinster.
Jan. 21, 1813; Feb. 6, 1815.
To niece: Sarah Fenwick Jones, dau. of my sister Sarah Jones.
Mentions: land n Richmond Co. known as "Canoe Creek Plantation".
Extx: sister, Harriet Campbell.
Wit: E. Jackson, Edward F. Tatnall, George Jones.

CUTHBERT, JAMES   Physician and Planter.
Dec. 23, 1806; Mch. 23, 1807.
To bro: Lewis Cuthbert.
To Mary Cowper, widow of the late Basil Cowper, Esqr.
To Ann McQueen, wife of John McQueen, Esqr., of E. Florida.
To Jane Bourke, widow of Thomas Bourke, Esqr.
To Miss Elizabeth Smith, dau. of John Smith.
Mentions: property from my mother, Mrs. Annie Cuthbert, and George and James Cuthbert.
Exrs: John McQueen, Jun., Robert Mackey, William Mein.
Wit: Charles Harris, Robert Scott, Charles Roberts.

CRANE, JOHN
Nov. 2, 1783; Feb. 12, 1785.
Of S.C.
My bro: James Crane of St. Mary Islington in the Co. of Middlesex.
To Mrs. Sarah Cleaver of the same Parish as my bro.
To Mr. Joseph Barron of Clarkenwell Parish in the same Co.
To John Perry.
To John Groves.
To Mrs. Elizabeth Wood.
To the poor living in the late Rev. George Whitefield's Chappel yard in Totenham Court Road.
Exr: Rev. Thomas Hill.
Wit: John Mitchell, Charles McDonald, Joseph Dunlap.

CRAWFORD, WILLIAM   Planter.
June 20, 1809; Nov. 11. 1809.
Of Little Satilla in Glynn Co.
To bro: D. John Crawford.
To sisters: Barbara Crawford of Scotland and Betty Crawford Nicol ("whom I believe is married to Mr. M. Nicol").

Exrs: John Couper of St. Simons, planter, and Richard M. Stites.
Wit: Samuel Miller Bond, Washington Gale, S. Mordecai.

COCHRAN, JANE
Aug. 14, 1793; May 2, 1809.
Wife of James Cochran, Esqr., planter.
Testator was Jame Delegal before marriage. Josiah McLean was trustee for her property and slaves.
To chil. of niece, Sophia, the wife of Josiah McLean.
Exrs: Peter Deveaux, Joseph Habersham, William Stephens, friends.
Wit: John Fox, Francis Fox, James Taylor.
Wit. certified by David Francis Bourquin.

D

Will Book "A"

25 DAY, WILLIAM
Sept. 23, 1773; July 10, 1777.
Of St. Bartholomew's Parish, Colleton Co., S.C.
To sons: William, Joseph, and Thomas, minors.
To sister: Elizabeth Day.
Mourning to friends, Patrick Turnbull and Miss Rebecca Hunt.
Mentions: "the plantation where I now reside, willed me by Elijah Hartee"; and grants of June 2, 1769.
Exrs: sons, and friends, John and James Miles, James Hamilton, Esqr.
Wit: Patrick Hues, John Ladson, Patrick Turnbull.

DAWSON, THOMAS
July 20, 1779; Jan. 19, 1789.
Of St. Helena's Parish, Granville Co., S.C.
Bequeaths a large family Bible to wife, Mary.
Mentions: a deed of gift to wife from Mrs. Samuel Wright, of cattle and land; and his property bordering on lands of John Dawson, Nathaniel Wardly, George Allison, Joseph Baker, John Francis Williams; and his lands in Augusta.
Exrs: wife, Mary; Charles Bealer; George Allison.
Wit: Thomas Cater, Joseph Dawson, Henry Patterson.

DEMERE, RAYMOND   Planter.
Oct. 14, 1788; June 1, 1791.
To wife: Mary.
To dau: Mary Elizabeth Demere.
To two daus. of James Gwin by his first wife, Margaret.
To Morris Miller, son of Samuel Miller, dec.
To Capt. John Mercier.
To my kinsman: Raymond Demere, Jr., of St. Simon's Island.
Exrs: Col. Joseph Habersham, Maj. John Habersham, Capt. John Mercier, Charles Harden.
Wit: J. Whitefield, Alex. Watt, James White.
Codicil dated Mch. 29, 1790.
26 Testator makes dau. Frances equal heir with her sister Mary Elizabeth.
Wit: Mary Forsythe, William Rogers, Joseph Norton.

DUNLAP, JOSEPH
Apr. 20. 1797; Dec. 27, 1798.
To kinsman: John Patterson.
Remainder in trust to Robert Bolton, for use of his (Bolton's) sister, Rebecca Newell, and her sons, Thomas and Robert.

ABSTRACTS OF WILLS, CHATHAM COUNTY, GEORGIA

Exrs: Robert Bolton, John Bolton, merchant.
Wit: Mathew Hill, Curtis Bolton.

DAY, SARAH MARY
July 6, 1797; Feb. 21, 1799.
Relict of Maj. Joseph Day, late of Ogeechee, planter.
Extx: mother, Elizabeth Box, sole heir.
Wit: Sarah Davies, Thomas Galphin, W. John Davies.

DEVILLE, JOHN ANTHONY MARY
Dec. 1, 1798; Dec. 12, 1798.
Native of Guillestre, Dept. of Alpes, Bishopric of Embrun, now of Savannah.
To sisters: Mion and Henrietta Deville.
Mentions: property in France to other sisters and bros.
Freedom to slave, Colon, and $50 should he return to St. Domingo.
Exr: Mr. Thomas Decheneaux.
Wit: John McMahon, Henry Darnell, J. B. Goupy.
Codicil dated Dec. 9, 1798.
In event of death of exr. appoints Mr. John Poullis Adm.
Wit: James Teague.

DODER, EMANUEL
Nov. 8, 1798; Nov. 26, 1798.
Born at Genes, Italie, and some fifty yrs. in City of Marseilles, "where I had a wife named Martha Gamelle Dodere and dau. Maria, married to a Mr. Chapus".
Exr: Mr. John Blane, born in Dept. des Boucher du Rhone, now in Savannah.
Wit: Charles Verguen, John Deville, James Schmuber.
Translated by Aime Coppat.

27 DAVIS OR DAVIES, FRANCIS
Sept. 2, 1798; Oct. 17, 1798.
Of Cherokee Hill.
To son: Edward Davies.
To my other six chil: Peter, Thomas, Sarah, Mary, John, and William.
Mentions: "buying the plantation where I now live from Martha and Isaac Young."
Exr: son, Peter.
Wit: Jane Goodall, Justus H. Scheuber, Thomas Palmer.

DUMOUSAY, FRANCIS MARIA LOYS DE LAVAURE
Dec. 7, 1793; Sept. 20, 1794.
To every child of Mrs. Elizabeth Grantell, widow of Bernard Lefils..
To godson: Francis Stort, legacy in care of Mrs. Grantell, Thomas Decheneaux, or Poullain, or Trubert.
Mentions: bro-in-law, Estevan Trubere, at Paris.
Exrs: John Poullain and Thomas Decheneaux, merchants.
Wit: John Haupt, John Lemoyne (Roman priest) and Robert Greer.

Will Book "B"

DAVIS, EDWARD
July 2, 1783; May 17, 1787.
To son: Edward Thomas Lloyd Davies, being born on March 14, 1781.
Extx: wife, Rebecca.
Wit: Samuel Stirk, Benjamin Lloyd, Edward Lloyd.

DAWSON, MARY   Widow.
Feb. 16, 1786; Apr. 7, 1786.
Exrs: and heirs, son, Richard Dawson, and dau., Mary Hatcher Dawson.
Wit: William White, Charles Milledge, Joseph Welscher.

DARTHIANGUE, JOHN   Mariner.
Jan. 1, 1786; Jan. 18, 1786.
To wife: Jean Marie Galat Darthiangue, and dau., Clarissa, of the city of Nantz in France.
Mentions: "debts due me from sale of cargo of slaves imported by me in the Polaire Magdalaine, myself commander, from Africa."
Exr: friend, Benjamin Gobert of Savannah.
Wit: David Montaigut, John Poullen, John Haupt.

DRESLER, GEORGE   Gentleman.
July 26, 1782; Jan. 11, 1787.
To wife: Elizabeth, one shilling.
To Mary, the widow of my son, one shilling.
Exr: everything to friend Jacob Casper Waldhauer.
Wit: Michael Readick, Philip Miller, Dr. John Martin.

DELEGAL, GEORGE, ESQR.
June 3, 1778; Apr. 1, 1783.
Of Christ Church Parish.
To wife: Jane.
To niece: Sophia Deveaux.
Mentions: his lands on Little Ogeechee.
Extx: wife, Jane.
Wit: William Stephens, Mary Anderson, John Becket.

DIXSEE, JAMES   Planter.
Nov. 5, 1785; Nov. 30, 1785.
Of Burnpot Island, Chatham Co.
To Susannah, wife of Nicholas Miller, and dau. of my late wife, Isabella.
To the chil. of my bro. William.
To neph: James Dixsee, son of my bro. William.
Exrs: William Stephens, Thomas Mills, neighbors, and friends.
No wit.

DEVEAUX, JAMES, ESQR.
June 27, 1771; Dec. 7, 1785.
Of Shaftsbury, Island of Argyle, Christ Church Parish.
To sons: William and Peter.
To dau: Mary, wife of Archibald Bulloch, Esqr.
Son, Peter, and dau. Margaret, under age.
Mentions: his bro. Andrew, dec.
Mentions: his lot on Ellis Square; two small islands in the Savannah River; wharf lot under the Bluff in Savannah; lot in Hardwicke on Great Ogeechee; Island of Great Wassaw; lands in St. Mathews Parish, lands on Skidaway, which lands border on lands of Henry Young, Sr., and John Milledge (the land was granted by the Government).
Mentions: lands purchased from Bartholomew Zuberbuhler and Matthias Roche, Esqr.; lands on Skidaway Island called "Springfield", purchased from Messrs. Harris and Habersham. It was originally allotted to Richard Palmer and "purchased by me" from William Palmer.
"My late father had a land grant in S.C. on the forks of the Salcacha."
Exrs: dau., Mary; sons, William and Peter; friends, Archibald Bulloch, Esqr., James Read, James Mossman, Henry Young, Sr.
Wit: John Irvine, G. Houstoun, Henry Young, Jr.
Codicil dated Nov. 20, 1774.
Refers only to monies.
Wit: Charles Wm. McKinnen, Richard Davis, Henry Young, Jr.
Codicil dated Nov. 5, 1785.
Mentions: his dau. Margaret, who is now the wife of William Stephens, Esqr.

ABSTRACTS OF WILLS, CHATHAM COUNTY, GEORGIA

Testator paid money to Mr. Kelsall.
Wit: James Chapman, Margaret Somerall.

Will Book "C"

DAVIS, WILLIAM   Cordwainer.
Apr. 15, 1790; Apr. 21, 1790.
To Moses Sheftall, "for his attention to me in my present sickness".
Mentions: 200 acres on the Ogeechee in Washington Co., the title of which land is in the possession of Eli Cummings, Esqr.; and "all the property left to me by Garrett Allen in will, and also my right to bounty land due me by this State, as also my pay due me by this State as a State soldier."
Exr: Moses Sheftall.
Wit: John Nixon, David Ross, Denbo Cable, William Irvine.

DENEAUX, WILLIAM, ESQR.
Sept. 5, 1786; Sept. 20, 1790.
To wife: Ann.
To sons: John Bermers DeNeaux, James, and William Fairchild DeNeaux.
To daus: Sarah Martha and Mary Olivia DeNeaux, Ann Brown, wife of James Brown.
Mentions: his stock on Port Royal Island; town lot in Beaufort, S.C., bought from William Gilbert; lands on Argyle Island, which lands border on lands of Dr. Houstoun; lands on Savannah back river; lands on the Salkehatchie in S.C.; lands in Purysburg, S.C.; lands up the Savannah River left by my father; lots in Hardwicke; lot in Savannah opposite the Market, and wharf lot under the Bluff; plantation called "Shaftesbury".
Exrs: bro., Peter DeNeaux; James Mossman, Esqr.; William Stephens; and my sons as they shall reach the age of twenty-one yrs.
Wit: William Harris, Peter Henry Morel, Abraham Jackson.
Codicil dated Apr. 1, 1789.
To gr. son: James DeNeaux Brown, son of Dr. James Brown and my dau. Anne.
Wit: Walter Maxwell, Fredk. Herb, Jun., John Storie.

DENSLER, HENRY   Planter.
Aug. 4, 1787; Jan. 25, 1790.
To wife: Catherine Barbary.
To oldest son: Michael, three other sons not named.
To youngest child: Susannah (minor).
Exrs: sons-in-law, John Verrage, Christian Dasher.
Wit: George Nungazer, Thomas Dowl, Peter Thies.

Will Book "D"

DAVIS, RICHARD
Died on the 19th, of Oct. 1801, at the house of Mrs. Rachel Walker, about four o'clock in the afternoon.
Bequeaths all property to the son of Mrs. Rachel Walker, William Walker, who is a cripple and an orphan.
Sworn to by Mrs. Rachel Walker and Sarah Hill.
Before Robert Bolton on Oct. 21, 1801.

DAVANT, JAMES   Planter.
Dec. 13, 1801; Feb. 7, 1803.
Of S.C.
To wife: Elizabeth.
To eldest dau: Mary Kicklighter.
To daus: Elizabeth Ficklen, Leddy Webb, and Rebecca Davant.

To sons: John and James.
Mentions: his lands on Hilton Head, and slaves bought from Mr. Nunigate.
Desires to be buried at the Church on Hilton Head, S.C.
Exrs: Samuel Ficklen, John and James Davant.
Wit: Robert, John, and Curtis Bolton.

DILLON, CHRISTIANA
Dec. 12, 1802; Apr. 1, 1805.
Wife of Robert Dillon.
Acquired property in S.C. in 1791.
To Anna Alecea and Thomas Chiffell, chil. of my bro., Philothews Chiffell of S.C.
To sister: Sophia Stole (Stull?).
Exrs: husband, Robert Dillon; friend, Elizabeth Brabant; Sophia Stole.
Wit: S. G. Bourquin, George Allen.

Will Book "E"

DOTSON, CELIA
No date; Dec. 7, 1807.
To gr. chil: Ann Dotson and William Gibbons.
To Daniel Joiner.
Chil. are left in care of Robert Bowman.
Wit: William Harrison.

DANSLER, BARBARA   Spinster.
Oct. 17, 1804; Jan. 4, 1808.
Dau. of Henry Densler.
To sister: Susannah Densler.
Exr: bro., Fredk. Densler.
Wit: J. Keale, Fredk. Shaffer.

DENSLER, MICHAEL   Planter.
Nov. 15, 1807; May 10, 1808.
To sons: Michael, David, and John.
To daus: Ann Margaret and Sophia Densler.
Exrs: wife, Anne; David Densler (son); John Dillon.
Wit: Henry Nungazer, Peter O'Connor, George Nungazer.

32 DAVID OR DAVIS, JOSEPH   Merchant.
Sept. 15, 1811; Oct. 28, 1811.
To sisters: Berenin Isaac Davis, Hannah Isaac David.
To bro: Samuel Isaac Davis, all of Konigsburgh.
Mentions: payment obtained against me in Federal Court by Philip Cohen; notes given me by Samuel Solomon & Co., which notes I have endorsed to David Leion, said notes to be put in hands of Jeremiah Cuyler, Esqr.; my stock of goods which are in the store lately occupied by Levy Hart & Co., be sent to Charleston to be sold at auction by Campbell; the goods in the store I now occupy to be taken by Sampson Mordecai, also my furniture by Howe & Dimon, auctioneers of Savannah. Jeremiah Cuyler, Esqr., to be atty. for my estate.
Exr: David Leion.
Wit: Fleming Aiken, S. Mordecai.

DOON, JOHN   Shopkeeper.
Oct. 10, 1813; Feb. 14, 1814.
To wife: Ann.
To son: John.
To dau: Mary Ann.
To bros: Patrick and Michael Glasgow, natives of the Parish of Ballyrone, Queens Co., Ireland.

ABSTRACTS OF WILLS, CHATHAM COUNTY, GEORGIA

Extx: wife, Ann.
Wit: Robert W. Pooler, Charles Atkins, John Pooler.

DIXON, JOSEPH   Mariner.
Oct. 1, 1814; Nov. 14, 1814.
To friends: James W. Stewart, Martin Gilbert, Thomas Carlton, Charles Jameison, John Scott.
To my friend, Simon Jackson, a legacy left me by my friend, Jordan Williams.
Mentions: wages due me for services on U. S. Frigate Essex, Commodore Porter.
Exr: Simon Jackson.
Wit: Levi S. D'Lyon, John Nolan.

DRISCOLL, MARGARET
Sept. 9, 1814; Apr. 4, 1815.
To son: Thomas.
To bro: Lawrence Mahoney.
To sister: Elizabeth Mahoney, both of the town of Yanghal, Co. of Cork, Ireland.
To Mary Flyn (an orphan girl).
Testator owns a Sloop and property in Savannah.
Exrs: Timothy Driscoll (husband), Dr. Bourquin, John Pettibone.
Wit: Christian Moies, John Pooler.

DAWSON, JOSEPH
Mch. 11, 1814; May 1, 1815.
To bros: John, Thomas, Richard, James.
To nieces: Mary Elizabeth and Martha Shereman, daus. of my sister Elizabeth.
To neph: Joseph Humbert, youngest son of William Humbert and my sister Esther.
Mentions: his landed estates, and slaves sold to Mr. Mein.
Exrs: John Dawson (bro.), James Roberts.
Wit: L. H. Feay, Arch. M. Cleran, Henry McAlpin.

DEUBELL, JOHN H.   Planter.
June 21, 1815; July 20, 1815.
To Ann Elizabeth Christ and her chil.
To the chil. of Elizabeth Berge.
To Ann Sackman.
To the poor of the village of Elbenrath.
Exrs: wife, Ann; Fredk. Herb; Jeremiah Cuyler.
Wit: John A. Casey, Andrew Knox, John B. Norris, Benj. Sheftall.

DAVIS, ELIZABETH
Aug. 13, 1816; Mch. 3, 1817.
Relict of Rezin Davis.
To daus: Desdemona Pickles, Cynthia O. Bannon, Lucy Caves.
Wit: Laban Wright, William Walters, Green R. Duke.
Codicil dated Aug. 13, 1816.
Dau: Desdemona Pickles, extx.
Same wit. as in will.

DEAKINS, WILLIAM, JUN.   Merchant.
Mch. 2, 1798; July 9, 1799.
Of George Town, Maryland.
To wife: Jane.
To bros: Francis and Leonard Marbury Deakins.
To Paul Hoye.
Mentions: his lands in George Town where James Clark lives; lands at or near the mouth of Seneca Creek, Co. of Montgomery, Md., called "Seneca Landing", and one called "Fortune".
Exr: Francis Deakin.

Wit: Benj. Stoddert, Charles Worthington, John Weems, John Thompson Mason.

D'ESPINOSE, JEROME FRANCOIS
July 12, 1808; July 2, 1810.
My three chil: Jerome Jules Joseph Jean Genevieve D'Espinose, Jean Jaques D'Espinose, Caroline Victoire Adelaide D'Espinose.
My wife to take the advice of my friends, Jean Andre Barbarroux and Antoine Jacques Dufaura.
Mentions: his property in the U. S. and St. Domingue.
Extx: wife, Claire Adelaide Armaignac.
Wit: A. J. M. J. Dufaure, J. P. Rossignol de Grandmont, U. Tobler.
Translated from the French by Miss Martha Youngblood, Savannah, Ga.

E

Will Book "A"

35 EIRICK, CATHERINE   Widow.
June 4, 1793; July 22, 1793.
To gr. daus: Catherine, Isabella, and Ruth Eirick.
To gr. son: John Adam Eirick.
Mentions: his lands in the village of Highgate, bought from John Shack; lands in St. Philip's Parish; and money due me from Alexander Watt.
Exrs: Fredk. Rester, John Armour, Herman Herson.
Wit: William Davis, John Armour, --- Whitefield.

EVANS, MARTHA   Gentlewoman.
June 30, 1788; Feb. 15, 1793.
To gr. chil: William and Sarah Evans.
Exrs. and Gdns: John Ruppert and William Lewden.
Wit: Peter Kerr, D. Moses Vollotton, Edmund Dillon.

EVANS, JONATHAN
Aug. 10, 1794; July 25, 1796.
"Heretofore of Savannah, but now a trader on the banks of the River Gambria on the coast of Africa."
All to neph. and niece, William M. and Sarah, who are Exrs., chil. of my dec. bro. William Evans, merchant.
Wit: Francis Tighe, James Anderson, both of Gambria.
Testified by Francis Hauthwat.

Will Book "B"

EWEN, WILLIAM
Sept. 30, 1776; June 20, 1777.
To wife: Margaret.
To Richard, son of my eldest bro., Richard Ewen.
To Priscilla Jones of S.C.
To Mary Saunders of Savannah.
Wife's bro., Jacob Walthour of Ebenezer.
36 Mourning rings to: Mary, dau. of Col. Noble Jones; Priscilla, wife of John Holman; Mary, wife of William Saunders.
To the Charity School in St. Andrews, Holborn, London.
Mentions: his land grants in St. George's Parish, Brunswick, Ewensburgh, and Savannah; lands in St. Matthews Parish from deed of conveyance from James Read, lands in Savannah from Francis Goffe and David Gray.
Exrs: wife, Margaret; Archibald Bulloch; Wm. O'Bryan.

ABSTRACTS OF WILLS, CHATHAM COUNTY, GEORGIA

Attested by Edmund Longworthy and Nehemiah Wade.
Testator appoints Jacob Waldhauer in the room of Archibald Bulloch, Esqr., dec., to act with Wm. O'Bryan.
Note: William Ewen is referred to in Eff. Co. records as a potter.

Will Book "C"

ELLIOTT, THOMAS   Planter.
June 2, 1786; Feb. 19, 1789.
Of Hilton Head, S.C.
To wife: Eliza Ann.
To mother: Elizabeth Elliott.
To sister: Eliza Drayton.
Bro-in-law: Glen Drayton, Esqr.
Mentions: his house on King St., Charleston, left in will by my gt. gr. mother, Mrs. Hunt.
Exr. and bro: Benj. Elliott, Esqr.
Wit: Zachariah Horskins, Thomas Webb, Israel Andrews.
Codicil dated Sept. 27, 1786.
Child in esse.
Wit: Benj. Elliott, Sr., Henry Harvey, Samuel Elliott.

EPPINGER, JOHN
Aug. 31, 1790.
Qualified as exr. under his father's will in addition with his mother, Barbarah.

Savannah Record Room, Book R, page 58. June 1, 1797.
Heirs of Barbara and John Eppinger:
John Eppinger, bricklayer.
James Eppinger, taylor.
George Eppinger, carpenter.
Mathias Eppinger, carpenter.
Balthazer Shaffer, taylor, wife dec., Margaret Eppinger.
Joseph Roberts, taylor, wife, Winifred Eppinger.
James Jones, planter, wife, Sarah Eppinger.

ELBERT, SAMUEL
July 2, 1788; Sept. 15, 1789.
To chil: Catherine Rae, Elizabeth, Sarah, Samuel Emmanuel De LaFayette, Matthew, and Hugh Rae Elbert.
Exrs: wife, Elizabeth, and friend, William Stephens.
Wit: Joseph Clay, Hugh Scott, D. Macleod.
Codicil dated July 6, 1788.
Testator appoints Joseph Habersham as an additional exr.
Wit: Joseph Clay, Hugh Scott, G. Wilson.

Will Book "D"

ELLIOTT, RALPH E.   Planter.
June 7, 1805; Jan. 5, 1807.
Of Beaufort, S.C., now of Savannah.
To son: Ralph.
To the chil. of my bros., William and Stephen.
To Thomas, William, and Benj. Savage.
To Mary and Susan E. Clay, daus. of Joseph Clay, Jun.
To Eliza, Thomas, and James Heywood, chil. of Thomas Heywood.
To Thomas S. and Ann Clay, chil. of Rev. Joseph Clay.

Mentions: his property in Beaufort; and plantation on Port Royal Island called "Cedar Grove".
Exrs: bros., William and Stephen Elliott; neph., William Elliott; Thomas and William Savage.
Wit: George Woodruff, Robert Habersham, Esqrs., Eliza S. Pomeroy.

Will Book "E"

ENOE, GEORGE
July --, 1806; Apr. 6, 1810.
To my only child and son, William.
38 To sister: Mrs. Mary Schweicoffer.
Mentions: his mother-in-law, Mrs. Mary Sanders.
Exrs: sister, Mrs. Catherine Hartstene of Ga.; nephs., Jacob Hartstene of Ga.; Benj. Hartstene of S.C., planter.
Wit: James Watts, Fredk. S. Fell, Benj. Jacols, Jun.

F

Will Book "A"

39 FAHM, FREDERICK
Apr. 27, 1796; May 2, 1796.   Nunc.
To son: Jacob.
To daus: Mrs. Catherine Long and Mrs. Sophia Gugel.
Exrs: William Lewden, Peter Samuel Lafitte.
Testified by Herman Herson, Justus Scheuber, Jacob Fahm, Betsy Oglesby, Peter S. Lafitte.

FOX, JOHN   Planter.
Sept. 20, 1795; June 12, 1797.
Exr: friend and cousin, Henry Bourquin, the elder, and sole heir.
Attested by John Hamilton, Thomas Hogg, James White, Benedict Bourquin.
Caveated by John Morel, "for himself and other first cousins".

FLOYD, MARGARET
Apr. 5, 1792; Oct. 18, 1793.
"My estate in Scotland."
To Mary, Charles, Eston, Ann, and James, chil. of Charles Boyd.
Exrs. and sons: Charles Boyd, Sr.; and Richard Floyd.
Wit: John Trevor, George Ritter, Elizabeth LaRoche.

FULFORD, JAMES HAVILAND   Cordwainer.
Oct. 3, 1794; Mch. 24, 1795.
Of the village of Acton.
Mentions: his lands in St. Philip's Parish; property in Providence, Island of Bahama; lands bordering on lands of Mary Harbeck, widow, Henry Harbeck, John Green, and Mrs. Jones; and a negro on the estate of William Wylly, Esqr.
Extx: dearly beloved friend, Ruth Patton, sole heir.
Wit: Alexander Weitt, Paul H. Wilkins, Nath. Dowdy.

40 FOX, DAVID
Nov. 18, 1799; Mch. 3, 1800.
To sons: Josiah and Elijah.
Exrs: wife, Susannah, and bro. Josiah Fox.
Wit: John Bull, Elizabeth Butler.

ABSTRACTS OF WILLS, CHATHAM COUNTY, GEORGIA

Will Book "B"

FOX, JOSEPH
Dec. 5, 1783; Jan. 14, 1784.
To the chil. of bro. William Fox.
To neph: Charles, son of bro. William.
To Mrs. Quarterman, sister of my late wife.
To sister: Mrs. Turner.
To the chil. of the late John Stewart, Esqr., of Newport, my late wife's father.
Mentions: his lands on Little Ogeechee, formerly the residence of his father; lot in Sunbury (from wife).
Exrs: friends, William Quarterman, Thomas Gibbon, Jr., and William Fox.
Wit: Ann Gibbon, Peter Dowl, Esther Gibbon.

FOX, ANN   Spinster.
May 27, 1773; Nov. 29, 1784.
To bros: John, William, Jonathan, James, and George.
To niece: Elizabeth, dau. of bro. Benjamin, dec.
To niece: Elizabeth, dau. of bro. George.
Exrs: bros., John and George Fox.
Wit: John McMahon, Joseph Raynes, John Wilson.

FOX, JOHN, SR.   Planter.
Apr. 6, 1775; Aug. 21, 1783.
Of Little Ogeechee.
To sons: David and John Fox, minors.
Exrs: wife, Frances; bro., William Fox; James Habersham, Jr.
Wit: Jonathan, Joseph, and John Fox.

FERGUSON, JOSHUA   Planter.
Dec. 28, 1777; Jan. 2, 1778.
To sons: John and James.
Exr: friend, Thomas Cooper.
Wit: Thomas Carter, John Hoggatt, Benjamin Sheffield.

FINDEN, WILLIAM
Sept. 26, 1783; Sept. 20, 1785.
"Late of Carshalton, County of Surrey, but now of London."
Extx: wife, Mary, sole heir.
Wit: S. Burton, Joseph Powell of London.

FARLEY, BENJAMIN   Planter.
Jan. 3, 1781; May 24, 1786.
To wife: Ann.
To sister: Mary Winn.
Mentions: his lands on St. Tilly's in St. David's Parish, Glynn Co.; lands in St. Philip's Parish bordering on lands of Mr. Butler; lands in St. Matthew's Parish bordering on lands of Joseph Clay; lot in Yamacraw.
Exrs: wife, Ann, David Francis Bourquin, John Wallace, Peter Winn.
Wit: Thomas Gibbons, Jun., Thomas Brownhill, Joseph Gibbons.

FOX, WILLIAM, SR.   Planter.
Jan. 21, 1783; Dec. 14, 1784.
Of Christ Church Parish.
To wife: Elizabeth.
To dau: Mary Ann.
To sons: Benjamin, David, Richard, Josiah, and youngest son, Jacob.
Mentions: his lands on the south side of the Altamaha and St. Mary's.

Exrs: bros., John and Jonathan Fox, and son, David.
Wit: Alexander Crighton, Elizabeth Crighton, Elizabeth Fox.

FOX, RICHARD   Planter.
Apr. 15, 1771; Mch. 27, 1772.
Of Christ Church Parish.
To bros: William, George, Benjamin, John, Jonathan, and James.
To sister: Ann Fox.
To Richard, son of bro. William, planter.
To James and Mary Ann Fox, chil. of bro. James.
To David, son of bro. John.
Mentions: his lands in St. David Parish, on Buffalo Swamp.
Exrs: bros., William and George Fox.
Wit: -- Baillow, Hugh Sym, Samuel Clark.

Will Book "C"

42 FURSE, JAMES   Mariner.
May 27, 1774; July 10, 1790.
Of City of Bristol.
To friend, James Loehier, upholsterer, of Bristol, in trust for wife, Herodia, and small children "as may be living at my dec."
Extx: wife, Herodia.
Wit: Catherine Greethead, J. Greethead, Jas. Hanikswell.
Deputy Registers: John Stevens, Henry Stevens, George Gostling, Jun.

FARLEY, JOHN   Cabinet-maker.
Jan. 29, 1781; Mch. 10, 1781.
To wife: Sarah.
To only son: John Farley.
To dau: Ann.
To sister: Elizabeth Farley.
Mentions: money due from James Habersham.
Exrs: wife, Sarah; bro., Joseph Farley; John Tebeau.
Wit: D. Zubley, Jun., David Moses Vollotton, John Lawrey.
Footnote: Elizabeth Spencer, widow, qualified as Admx. of said estate, Aug. 23, 1792.

Will Book "D"

FORSYTH, BENJAMIN
Feb. 10, 1802; Mch. 1, 1802.
To William Forsyth, now in school at St. Mary's. (Son)
"All my chil. to have suitable education."
Extx: wife, Margarett.
Wit: James Hemphill, William Royston, Charles Cope.

FOX, SUSANNAH
Nov. 2, 1806; Feb. 5, 1807.
To sons: Josiah and Elijah.
To friend: Andrew Bird.
Extx: sister, Elizabeth Fox.
Wit: John Purcell, Elizabeth Butler, Ann Matthews.

ABSTRACTS OF WILLS, CHATHAM COUNTY, GEORGIA

Will Book "E"

43 FARLEY, GRACE
Oct. 2, 1809; July 2, 1810.
To dau: Ann Johnston, wife of Alexander Johnston.
To gr. dau: Ann Farley Johnston.
To neph: William Parker.
Extx: dau., Ann Johnston.
Wit: Sarah Johnston, Joseph Maxwell, David Matthew.

FRETOT, CHARLES EUSTAKE
Oct. 7, 1811; Nov. 11, 1811.
Formerly of St. Domingo.
To chil: Charles John Baptiste Nicholas and Michael Thomas August Fretot.
To Eliza and Eugena Roma, daus. of Francis Roma.
Mentions: his property in Europe and America.
Extx. and Gdn: wife, Mary Margaretta.
Wit: P. Thomasson, F. Gigant, H. Midy, Thomas Decheneaux.

FIDD, BENJAMIN
Nov. 2, 1811; Dec. 8, 1812.
Of Effingham Co.
To friend: David Davies Williams of Chatham Co.
Wit: William F. Port.

FRASER, MARY   Widow.
Apr. 25, 1810; Apr. 3, 1812.
Of Port Royal Island, S.C.
To daus: Caroline Ann and Harriott Maria Fraser.
Mentions: her lands on Port Royal called "Springfield", where Mr. John Richardson now resides; property in Beaufort; the silver marked with the family crest.
Extx: daus., Caroline Ann and Harriott Maria Fraser.
Wit: William Joyner, Joseph Porter, James Caven.
Codicil dated Jan. 7, 1812, in Beaufort.
"My sons, George, John S., and Alexander G. Fraser (when he is of age) to be made exrs. with their sisters."

44 FARLEY, SARAH
Feb. 14, 1812; Apr. 21, 1812.
To Eliza J. Drysdale.
To John Drysdale, in trust for Laleah H. Watts, wife of Robert Watts, Esqr.
Extxs. and aunts: Sarah Drysdale, Eliza Irvine, and Rachel Johnston.
Wit: Laleah Wood, W. Stephens, William Parker.

FEAY, OBADIAH M.
Jan. 18, 1815; Apr. 3, 1815.
Of St. Paul's Parish, S.C.
To wife: Esther.
To son: William.
Exrs. and Gdns: bro., Launcelot H. Feay; Henry McAlpin.
Wit: Archibald McCleran, Duncan McMillan.

FERGUSON, MARY   Widow.
Apr. 3, 1816; Nov. 19, 1816.
To gr. chil: Benjamin and Richard Morel.
Mentions: her property in Savannah; and an account against the estate of Richard Morel, dec.

Extx: dau., Ann Morel.
Wit: William Lucas, Robert Towers, Abner Ross.

FRASER, JOHN L.
May 15, 1816; June 7, 1816.
Mentions: his bros., George, Alexander, and William, dec., of S.C.; mother, dec., sister, Caroline Fraser, dec. of S.C.
Mentions: his property in Savannah; and interest in the property of Richard Russel Ash of S.C., dec., as left in will.
Extx: wife, Caroline.
Wit: Rebecca M. Pooler, William C. Daniell, Robert H. Petigru.

G

Will Book "A"

45 GILBERT, WILLIAM   Planter.
Feb. 10, 1795; Apr. 23, 1796.
Of Wilmington Island.
To wife: Ann.
To daus: Elizabeth and Mary Ann.
Bro: John Gilbert, dec.
Exrs: John Tebeau, Solomon Shad.
Wit: Michael Germain, John Lyon, Peter Miller.

GILZEAN, JOHN   Merchant.
Jan. 19, 1798; Feb. 21, 1798.
Of Parish of St. James, County of Cornwall, Island of Jamaica.
To Peter Roth, of same island for many kindnesses.
To aunt: Margaret Thompson, alias (nee) Saunders, wife of --- Thompson, schoolmaster of Wick in Caithness.
To cousin: Mary Sparks, alias (nee) Mary Gordon, wife of George Sparks, watchmaker in Elgin, County of Murray, and to her sister, Ann Gordon, who was unmarried in 1787.
Exrs: John Shand, Esqr., of Spanish Town, Jamaica, and Messrs. Simpson and Davidson of London, merchants.
Wit: Robert Noble, David Duff, William Mills.
"This testator took passage on brig 'William', Thomas Clark, commander, and was taken ill" -- directed that his will be put in the hands of John Cunningham, merchant in Savannah, to be sent to John Shand, but John Cunningham had left the continent and his affairs were with Crawford Davidson who attests the handwriting and declares the wit. absent from the state.

GIBBONS, ANN
Nov. 10, 1799; Mch. 4, 1800.
To daus: Esther Stallings and Martha Fox.
To gr. chil: Martha Stallings, Thomas Gibbons Stallings, James Stallings, John
46 Stephen Miller, Thomas G. Miller, Rebecca, Catherine Elizabeth, Joseph William, and Charles Fox.
Exrs: son, John Barton Gibbons; gr. son, Charles Fox; Col. James Stallings.
Wit: Andrew McLean, Margaret W. McLean, Margaret Bourquin.

GIBBONS, WILLIAM
June 14, 1799; Nov. 26, 1800.
Of Morton Hall.
To wife: Valaria.
To sister: Ann Hall.
To bro: Joseph, and his chil.

ABSTRACTS OF WILLS, CHATHAM COUNTY, GEORGIA

To cousin: Barack Gibbons.
To Eliza Anciaux, niece of Mrs. Gibbons.
To Ann, wife of Joseph Gibbons.
To Lydia, my wife's sister.
To William and Ann, chil. of my bro. Thomas.
Mother: the late Hannah Gibbons.
Joseph Gibbons had a dau. Sarah.
Mentions: his lot in Yamacraw adjoining the property of the late John Shick; bro. Joseph inherited land from Joseph Gibbons.
Exrs: wife, Valaria, and her sister, Lydia Anciaux; bro., Thomas; cousin, Barack Gibbons, friend, Andrew Turnbull.
Wit: Lemuel Kollock, Joseph Deleval, De La Croixe.

GIBBONS, JOSEPH   Atty-at-law.
July 15, 1794; May 5, 1795.
Of Liberty Co.
To sister: Sarah, wife of Edward Telfair, and their daus., Sarah and Mary.
To bros: Barach and William Gibbons, the younger.
To niece: Sarah, dau. of George Jones, and wife, Mary, dec.
To his sister he gives a tray now at the house of Mrs. Anciaux.
Father: dec.
Mentions: his lands in Franklin Co., granted to William Gibbons; and the suit of the exrs. of William Young, brought in by James Jones.
Exrs: bros., William and Barach Gibbons; George Jones; Joseph Clay; Edward Telfair.
Wit: Nicholas Anciaux, Lydia Anciaux, John Davis.

47 GIBBONS, HANNAH
Sept. 17, 1796; July 11, 1798.
Of Mulberry Hill.
Relict of Joseph Gibbons.
To sons: Joseph and Thomas.
To son: William Gibbons, and his wife, Valaria.
To dau: Hannah, wife of Mathew McAllister.
To dau: Ann, wife of Nathaniel Hall, dwelling next to John Lowrey, chairmaker.
To sister: Ann Gibbons.
To Mrs. Sarah Sym.
To Mrs. James Smith.
Exrs: son, William; William Gibbons, Jun.; Wimberly Jones.
Wit: John Glen, Sarah Glen, James Cox.
Codicil dated Apr. 28, 1798.
Mentions: her gr. son, William Joseph, son of Joseph Gibbons.
Testator revokes as exrs. son and gr. son, both William Gibbons, and appoints James Mossman and George Jones.
Wit: Susannah Ring, Michael Spahn, John Glen.

Will Book "B"

GWINNETT, BUTTON
Mch. 15, 1777; May 30, 1777.
"I'm sound in Body and Mind for which I am under the highest obligation to the Supreme Being. How long I shall remain so God only knoweth. I therefore dispose of my property both real and personal in the following manner."
One half of real and personal estate to wife and dau.
The other half to the Rev. Mr. Thomas Bosomworth. This is only to convey my estate in America.
Exrs: Thomas Savage, Lyman Hall.
Wit: John Farley, William Hornby, Thomas Hovenden.

Note: Wife, Ann; dau., Elizabeth, the wife of Peter Belin.
Ref: Savh. Rec. Room, Box G, Apr. 21, 1779. C. P. Wilson.

GRIFFIN, MATHEW   Planter.
Dec. 8, 1786; May 4, 1787.
To stepson: John Warner Smith, now residing in Penn.
To the chil. of Mr. Thomas Mills.
Exrs: Gen. James Jackson, Mr. Thomas Mills, shopkeeper.
Wit: George Rolfes.

48 GIBBONS, WILLIAM   Planter.
Mch. 6, 1769; Feb. 28, 1771.
To wife: Sarah.
To daus: Sarah and Mary.
To sons: Barach, James Martin, Joseph, Josiah, William (minor).
Mentions: lands sold to James Habersham, Esqr.; purchased land from Joseph Parker; lands adjoining Newington Village belonging to the estate of Bartholomew Zouberbuhler, dec.; lands on Great Satilla River, S.C., granted to Benjamin Singleton; lands on New Port River in St. Andrew's Parish; wharf lot under the Bluff.
Exrs: wife, Sarah; sons, William and Josiah; kinsman, John Martin.
Wit: Noble Jones, Thomas Gibbons, Jr., J. J. Zubly.
Codicil dated Feb. 8, 1771.
Child in esse.
Mentions: bros., Joseph and John, dec.
Gdns: wife and John Martin.
Exrs: nephs:, Joseph and William Gibbons; John Winn, Esqr.; Rev. John Osgood; Rev. John Joachim Zubly.
Wit: William Young, John Davis, William Brabant.

GERMAIN, PRISCILLA   Widow.
Nov. 10, 1775; May 15, 1783.
To three chil: Michael and Ann Germain, Priscilla, wife of Jeremiah Camphor, planter.
Mentions: an original grant to bro., George Peters, west of the town of Savannah; town lot in Hardwicke.
Exr: friend, Mordecai Sheftall.
Wit: George Randolph, David Cardoza, William Jones.

GIONIOLEY, JOHN
Feb. 22, 1770; Sept. 2, 1771.
To my six chil: Hannah, Joseph, Benjamin, John, Jonathan, and Helena.
Mentions: his wife, dec.
Exrs: sons, David, Nicholas, and Samuel; "Mester Zuble' si parson."
Wit: Jonathan Peat, Thomas Flyming, John Van Rensselvai.
(A John Gionovle of Beaufort gives bond for adm.)
Note: Also spelled Giovansle.

49 GUINN, RICHARD   Planter.
Jan. 15, 1785; Jan. 26, 1785.
To wife: Elizabeth.
If no heirs, to bro. John's three sons, bro. George's dau., and my sister Mary Wonderly's six chil.
To neph: John, and his two bros., and their cousin, Sarah Guinn.
To Miss Elizabeth Bonett, bed and furniture.
Exrs: wife, Elizabeth, Thomas Mills.
Wit: Dr. John Brickell, Rebecca Hammond, Samuel Brownson.

ABSTRACTS OF WILLS, CHATHAM COUNTY, GEORGIA

GIRARDEAU, JOHN BOHUN
June 13, 1777; Nov. 22, 1784.
To sons: John Bohun, my eldest son, and Peter Girardeau.
To daus: Elizabeth and Mary Ann.
Child in esse.
Exrs: wife, Hannah; friends, Andrew Maybank; Henry Hyrne of S.C.
Wit: James Cochran, Thomas Ledbetter, Jain Ledbetter.
Note: For the will of John B. Girardeau, Jr., see "Annals of Georgia," vol. 1, by Caroline P. Wilson.

Will Book "C"

GIBSON, ROBERT   Planter.
Mch. 4, 1790; Mch. 8, 1790.
To wife: Sarah.
To sons: Robert Stewart Gibson, Daniel, and William.
Exr: son, Daniel Gibson.
Wit: George Dunn, Michael Ritton, Joseph Welscher, Esqr.

GUGEL, JOHN   Shoemaker.
June 25, 1786; May 27, 1788.
To wife: Ann Mary.
To my nine chil: Hannah Ash, Dorothea Resser (Reisser), Christopher, Joshua, Daniel, David, Salome Millen, Christian, and Samuel Gugel.
Exrs: sons, Christopher and Samuel Gugel.
Wit: Herman Herson, Peter Millen, Jacob Weisenbaker.

50 GIBBONS, SARAH   Widow.
Jan. 7, 1790; Jan. 23, 1790.
To sons: William, Joseph, and Barach Gibbons.
To daus: Sarah Telfair and Mary Jones.
To chil., if any, of Sarah Telfair.
To gr. chil: Noble Wimberly Jones, Rebecca Martin Jones, Sarah Gibbons Jones.
Mentions: her land bought of Peter Boquet in Newington Village.
Exrs: sons, William, Joseph, and Barach Gibbons; sons-in-law, Edward Telfair, George Jones, Esqrs.
Wit: W. Jones, Sarah Glen, John Glen, Esqr.

GABLE, ABRAHAM   Carpenter.
Feb. 15, 1790; Mch. 11, 1790.
To son: John.
To sister: not named.
Exrs: wife, Elizabeth Susannah, and John Richards.
Wit: Justus H. Scheuber, John Shick, Balthaser Shaffer.

GALACHE, JAMES   Planter.
Nov. 10, 1790; Dec. 24, 1790.
Mentions: lands on Little Ogeechee "bequeathed me by my dec. sister, Mrs. Jane Russell."
Exrs: wife, Ann Elizabeth; dau., Ann Galache; son, James, when of age; friend, John Poullin.
Wit: Augustus Mayer, David Moses Vollotton, Hugh Scott.

GOFFE, JANE   Widow.
Jan. 14, 1791; Jan. 29, 1791.
To son: John Goffe.
To Daniel Goffe Fips, neph. of my late husband.
To Elizabeth, the dau. of Daniel Goffe Fips.
To Jane Johnston, dau. of James Johnston.

To Mrs. Rebecca Judah, money due me from John King, for her attention and care of me.
Mentions: money due from Peter Henry Morel, from the firm of Sawyer and Morel.
Exrs: friends, Owen Owens, William Thompson.
Wit: William Coales.
Codicil not dated.
Mentions: son, Benjamin, and two youngest daus., Mary and Susannah; mother, dec.
51 Mentions: her back plantation; money due from Mr. Postel, and bond for which is in the hands of Mr. Heyward.

Will Book "D"

GREER, RICHARD   Inspector of Customs.
Nov. 16, 1801; Aug. 10, 1803.
All to Mrs. Penelope Culberson.
Exr: friend, Edward Griffith.
Wit: John N. Love, Edward White, Edward Griffith.

GLEN, JOHN
Apr. 1, 1799; June 3, 1799.
To wife: Sarah.
To sons: George, James, and Thomas.
To daus: Margaret Hunter, wife of William Hunter, Sarah Bulloch, wife of Archibald Stobo Bulloch.
Exrs: wife, Sarah; father-in-law, Noble Wimberly Jones; bro-in-law, George Jones, Esqrs.; and sons, James and George Glen.
Wit: Ebenezer Jackson, Pheneas Miller, John Howell.

GORDON, AMBROSE   Merchant.
May 13, 1804; July 31, 1804.
To sons: William Washington and Tombigby Gordon.
To daus: Margaret, Elizabeth, Nancy, Mississippi, and Julia.
Mentions: his lands on the Altamaha, and lands in Camden Co.
Exrs: wife, Elizabeth; friends, James Gardner; William Washington; Thomas Gibbons.
Wit: John Twiggs, Abm. Twiggs, J. Mead.

GLEN, SARAH   Widow.
Feb. 9, 1804; Jan. 14, 1805.
To sons: James, George, Thomas, Noble Wimberly Glen.
To daus: Ann M., Mary J., Catherine, Charlotte, Margaret Hunter, Sarah Bulloch.
Mentions: her property on Isle of Hope, originally granted to the Hon. Henry Parker; lands bordering on lands granted to Noble Jones, Esqr., called "Wormslow"; plantation called "Wimberly."
52 Exrs: father, Noble Wimberly Jones; bro., George Jones; sons, George and James Glen, also Gdns.
Wit: William Clarkson, Isabella Hunter, James Hunter.

GIBBONS, WILLIAM
Sept. 21, 1803; Apr. 20, 1804.
To sister: Sarah Telfair.
To bro: Barach Gibbons.
To kinsman: John Gibbons.
To Mrs. Ann B. Gibbons.
To nephs: Josiah, Thomas, Alexander Telfair, and Noble Wimberly Jones.
To neices: Mary, Sarah, Margaret Telfair, and Sarah Gibbons Jones.
To sisters: Rebecca, and sister Jones.
Mentions: his mother, Sarah Gibbons, dec.
To Joseph Clay Habersham and John Bolton Habersham, sons of my dec. friend, John Habersham.

ABSTRACTS OF WILLS, CHATHAM COUNTY, GEORGIA

Mentions: his lands bought from John Joachim Zubley; Mr. Cartan Campbell; Maj. Habersham in Louisville; John Wereat, dec.; James Bulloch and Charles Irvine exrs. for Elizabeth Powell, dec.; with Matthew McAllister, the property of David Montaigue; and slaves from Mein and Mackey; land grants in Franklin Co., but now the Co. of Jackson; land grants in Camden Co. on Great Satilla River.
Mentions: his lands in Savannah; lands in Glynn Co., original grant to John Gibbons; lands in Jefferson Co., original grant to James Habersham, dec.; plantations called "Retreat" and "Beech Forest"; lands in St. Gall, Brunswick, and Newington Village; lands bordering on lands of John Gorham, George Ogg, Joseph Martin, Mrs. Ann Gibbons, and John Houstoun.
Exrs: bro., Barach Gibbons; Edward Telfair; George Jones; John Gibbons; nephs., Josiah Telfair, Noble Wimberly Jones.
Wit: U. Tobler, John William Shaffer, William McClane.

GIBBONS, VALERIA
Aug. 9, 1801; Aug. 11, 1801.
Widow of William Gibbons, Sr.
To the chil. of Matthew McAllister and wife, Hannah, now living; husband buried in Rhode Island.
53 To niece: Eliza Anciaux.
Exr: Barach Gibbons.
Wit: Richard M. Stites, Thomas Young, Jr., Susannah Clark.

GLASS, JOHN
May 6, 1805; May 30, 1805.
To "each of my chil."
Exrs: wife, Mary; Paul Vollotton, Jeremiah Cuyler.
Wit: Frederick Shaffer, Thomas D. Norton, Robert Christie.

GUY, GEORGE WILLIAM
-- 1802; Sept. 2, 1805.
To father: Richard Guy.
To bro: Benjamin.
To sisters: Mary and Elizabeth Guy.
To Lydia, dau. of Mrs. Mary Parker, formerly Sauls.
Exrs: James Wilson, Benjamin Wilson, James Rosser.
Wit: Maturin Neil, Benjamin R. Guy, Josiah Gotear.

Will Book "E"

GERMAIN, MICHAEL
Nov. 15, 1806; Feb. 8, 1808.
Testator leaves money to Baptist Church in Savannah in trust for Mount Enon College.
Exrs: dau., Ann Amelia, and friend, Thomas F. Williams.
Wit: Henry Holcombe, Priscilla Scheuber, Benjamin Brooks.

GUNN, JAMES
Sept. 17, 1807; May 10, 1808.
Of Richmond, Va.
Extx: mother, Sarah Gunn.
Wit: George Scherer, Francis Howard.
Codicil dated at Savannah Mch. 25, 1808.
Mentions: money due him from Col. Ferdinand O'Neal, and James Gunn O'Neal.
Wit: Ebenezer Stark, George L. Low.

GIBBONS, JOHN BARTON   Planter.
Nov. 27, 1807; Mch. 10, 1809.

         To bro: John Gibbons.
         To Jack and Tom Miller.
54   Extx: wife, Charlotte S. Gibbons.
         Wit: Francis Courvoisie, Sr. and Jun., William McNatt.

         GRANDMONT, JACQUES PHILIPE ROSSIGNOL DE
         Nov. 4. 1808; Oct. 2, 1809.
         Of St. Domingo.
         To wife: Marie Madeline Henrietta Rossignol de Belleanse.
         Mother: not named.
         Mentions: his lands on the Island of St. Domingo, France; lands in the U.S.;
         money due to Mr. Picot de Cloriviere.
         Wit: Ant. Carles, Francis Mondonville, U. Tobler, John Francis Ponyat.

         GADDY, JAMES
         Jan. 4, 1811; May 6, 1811.
         To Sally, William, Murriah, and Sinia Hollinger, heirs of Martha Hollinger.
         Exrs: Martha Hollinger, Reason Davis.
         Wit: friends, Jonathan B. Bacon, Robert Sibley, Joseph Wiggins.

         GUNN, CHRISTOPHER
         Dec. 9, 1816; Jan. 10, 1817.
         To son: John C. C. Gunn.
         To neph: Christopher S. Gunn.
         Exrs: friends, Capt. Joseph Davis, Abraham Delyon.
         Wit: Benjamin Wall, Esqr., Isaac Wall.

         GINOVELY, MARY   Widow.
         Nov. 20, 1812; Aug. 2, 1813.
         To son: George Atkerson.
         To gr. chil: Joseph Lee Atkerson, William John Atkerson, Mary Susannah Atkerson.
         To Margaret Atkerson, widow.
         To Elizabeth Key, niece of Susannah Atkerson, first wife of George Atkerson.
         Exr: son, George Atkerson.
         Wit: William Jones, Thomas Wilson.

55   GIBBONS, BARACH
         July 28, 1814; Oct. 17, 1814.
         To sister: Sarah Telfair, relict of Edward Telfair, Esqr.
         To nieces: Mary, Sarah, Margaret Telfair, Sarah Gibbons Jones.
         To George Jones, Esqr.
         Mentions: the lands granted to William Gibbons, James Baillou, Joseph Stanley;
         his lot in Savannah occupied by Andrew Knox; lots in Newington; plantation called
         "Sharon".
         Exrs: my four nephs., Thomas, Josiah Gibbons Telfair, Alexander Telfair, Noble
         Wimberly Jones.
         Wit: John Lawson, Stephen Crafts, Paul Keller.

         GIBSON, ROBERT S.
         Apr. 15, 1812; June 5, 1815.
         To wife: Sarah, dau. of Richard Turner.
         To chil: Louisa Catherine, Joseph Robert, Richard Turner, Robert Stewart Gibson.
         Mentions: his plantation on Whitemarsh Island.
         Gdns: Richard Turner, Solomon Shad, Sr., Lewis Turner, David Bell.
         Exrs: John Bolton, James Barnard, George Herb, and son, Joseph Robert Gibson,
         when he reaches the age of eighteen yrs.
         Wit: John Eppinger, James Eppinger, Edmund Jarvis.
         Codicil in three parts:
         Part one:

ABSTRACTS OF WILLS, CHATHAM COUNTY, GEORGIA

Wit: David Bell, J. Marshall.
Part two, dated June 16, 1814.
In part one and two, testator requests that his chil. be educated.
Wit: George Jones, John P. Williamson, Moses Sheftall.
Part three:
To William and Edward Barnard.
Same wit. as in part two.

GIBBONS, JOHN
Feb. 2, 1816; Mch. 4, 1816.
To niece: Catherine Eliza Clanton of Columbia Co.
To nephs: John Stephen and Thomas Glen Miller of Natches, and James G. Stallings of Columbia Co.
56 Mentions: a pair of silver waiters marked "A.B.G."; two soup ladles, one marked "Benfield" and the other marked "G.M.F."
Requests all slaves about fifty-two in number to be set free.
Exrs: Thomas and Alexander Telfair, John P. Williamson, Esqrs.
Wit: William Davies, atty-at-law.

H

Will Book "A"

57 HANNER, NICHOLAS   Planter.
June 1, 1791; July 8, 1791.
Of White Bluff.
To wife: Elizabeth, formerly Mrs. Morgan, widow, one third of estate.
To Ann Morgan, dau. of my wife.
Remainder to Nicholas Hanner, Jun., Catherine Timmons, Elizabeth Buckholter.
Mentions: his plantation called "Acton".
Exrs: George Nungazer and John Poulen.
Established by Elizabeth Hanner, Catherine Timmons, William Morgan, John Timmons.

HOUSTOUN, JAMES   Planter.
June 25, 1791; Sept. 27, 1793.
"About to depart to Great Britain."
To sons: James Edmund and Mossman Houstoun.
To "each of my dear daus."
Mentions: his plantation called "Greenwich"; plantation on Argyle; plantation named "Colerain"; land on Hog Island; lands purchased from Mary Warnock.
Exrs: bros., Sir George and John Houstoun; James Hume of Great Britain; James Mossman.
Wit: John Glen, J. and T. Netherclift, Jun.
Codicil refers to slaves, and wit. by William Jones and John McIntosh.

HOUSTOUN, JOHN
May 2, 1796; July 22, 1796.
To goddaus: Ann Priscilla and Joanna Houstoun, Harriet Louisa Bailie, now in Scotland.
To adopted dau. and niece: Harriet Thompson Houstoun.
To bro: William and wife, now in N.J.
To wife: not named, has a claim to negroes by a certain deed executed by her
58 father bearing date Mch. 25, 1782, and wit. by Peter - - - and Davice Douglas.
Mentions: his lands at White Bluff.
Exrs: my three nephs., Patrick and James Edmund Houstoun, and John McIntosh.
Wit: Andrew Johnston, James Armstrong, John Glass.

HIGGINS, ICHABOD
Oct. 18, 1798; Dec. 3, 1798.
To wife: Martha.
To dau: Kethea Collings.
To gr. son: John, son of dec. son, John Higgins.
Exrs: Robert and John Bolton.
Wit: Green Simpson, James Hemphill, James Johnston.

Will Book "B"

HADRICK, ALEXANDER
Dec. 24, 1777; Feb. 9, 1778.
All to Andrew Stirk, who is exr. and sole heir.
Wit: Ambrose Wright, Peter Papot, --- Noble.

HARRIS, FRANCIS HENRY
Apr. 27, 1777; May 14, 1783.
To James and Catherine (goddau.), chil. of my esteemed friend, Joseph Clay, Esqr. Remainder to sister, Elizabeth Harris.
Exrs: Joseph Clay, Joseph Habersham, John Habersham, Esqrs.
Wit: Thomas Ross, William Maconchy, William Stephens.

HERBOCK, MICHAEL   Planter.
June 12, 1782; Sept. 28, 1782.
Of Christ Church Parish.
To sons: Jacob, Michael, and John.
Exrs: wife, Mary; sister, Catherine Reddy; George Basil Spencer.
Wit: Francis Paris, William Hoskins, Henry Herbock.

HOWLEY, RICHARD   Atty-at-law.
Dec. 26, 1784; Jan. 4, 1785.
To daus: Catherine Ann Howley and Sarah Powell Gibball.
Extx: wife, Sarah.
Wit: Hugh Bourk, William McIntosh, Jun., James Whitefield.

HOUSTOUN, SIR PATRICK   Baronet.
May 10, 1784; Nov. 29, 1785.
To bros: George, James, John, and William.
To neph: John McIntosh.
To eldest dau. of bro., George.
Exr: bro., George Houstoun.
Wit: Dr. John Irvine, John Moodie, Peter S. Laffitte.

Will Book "C"

HARN, SAMUEL   Planter.
Dec. 4, 1788; Mch. 19, 1789.
To bro: Henry Harn. (another bro. not named)
To cousins: John Butler, Jun., James, John, and Henry Hunter Harn, sons of James Harn.
Exr: Henry Harn, Sr.
Wit: Thomas Harn and John Butler.

HARRIS, MORDICA
May 17, 1791; June 3, 1791.
To gr. son: James Mordica Harris.
Mentions: town lot in Leeds near Savannah.

ABSTRACTS OF WILLS, CHATHAM COUNTY, GEORGIA

Exrs: wife, Mary, and friend, John Ruppert.
Wit: Asa Emanuel, John Rents, John Mcfarlen.

HARDEN, WILLIAM   Planter.
Sept. 23, 1783; Apr. 6, 1789.
Of Price William Parish.
To sons: Edmund, William, Charles, Edward.
To dau: not named.
To sister: Rebecca White.
To mother: Mary.
Mentions: his lands on Hutchinson Island; lands purchased from John Keating.
Exrs: wife, Sarah; bros., Charles and Edward Harden; friend, William Ferguson.

60 HERB, FREDERICK   Planter.
May 19, 1788; Nov. 1, 1790.
Of Sea Island of Ga.
To wife: Ursuala.
To sons: Frederic, John, and George.
To daus: Catherine, wife of Rev. Mr. Bergmann, Mary, Rebecca, and Hannah, wife of John Schmit.
Mentions: his lands on the Ogeechee River; lands in Hampstead; house in Savannah where Mrs. Teider used to dwell; lot bought from George Garbet, dec., in Savannah.
Exrs: wife, Ursuala, sons, Frederic and John Herb.
Wit: Justus H. Scheuber, U. Tobler, John Schick, Balthaser Shaffer.

Will Book "D"

HARDEN, EDWIN   Planter.
Aug. 28, 1801; July 14, 1804.
To neph: Thomas Huston Harden.
Mother: Mary Harden, dec.
Exrs: wife, Jane; son, Edwin Harden, Jun.; friends, Robert Reed; Joseph Clay, Jun.; Josiah Tattnall, Jun.; John Pray; Charles Odensells, Esqrs.
Wit: Jeremiah Cuyler.

HALL, WILLIAM LISTER
July 29, 1803; Sept. 26, 1803.
Of Effingham Co., Ga.
All to George Galphin Nowlan.
Exr: William Joseph Spencer.
Wit: Moses Clark, John N. Fordham, William T. Bysam of Saggharbour Pro. in Suffolk Co., N.Y.

HAIST, GEORGE   Gentleman.
Oct. 16, 1799; Dec. 11, 1801.
To son: George.
To dau: Elizabeth Haist.
Mentions: his plantation called "Wakefield"; property in Savannah; lands bought from Catherine Gordon.
Exrs: David Johnston of White Bluff, William Greenwood, Jun. of Charleston, Joseph Machin of Savannah.
Wit: Thomas Gibbons, George Parker, John Caig.

61 HARN, MARY ELIZABETH   Spinster.
Nov. 23, 1801; Jan. 4, 1802.
To aunt: Martha Heron or Harn.
To cousin: John Harn.
To the chil. of Henry H. Harn.

Mentions: money in the hands of Alexander D. Cuthbert.
Wit: Richard M. Stites, Richard Stuart, Manus Lemle.

HELBERT, MARY MAGDELEN
Feb. 1, 1802; Mch. 1, 1802.
To Mrs. Eliza Fox.
To Mrs. Isabella Bird, dau., infant (sic) of Andrew Bird.
To Mrs. Elizabeth Fox.
To Mrs. Ann Fox.
To John Henry and Thomas Elbert Robert, sons of the late J. H. Robert of Savannah.
Exrs: friends, David Francis Bourquin and Andrew Bird.
Wit: Alice Coleman, Susannah Fox, Thomas H. Coleman, Mary Fox, Mary Neasman.

HOBBS, JOHN   Planter.
Aug., 1801; Oct. 6, 1801.
To wife: Rebecca.
To Mary Heisler, dau. of John Heisler.
To William Henry Cuyler, son of Jeremiah Cuyler.
Exrs: friends, Matthew McAllister, Jeremiah Cuyler.
Wit: Edw. Swarbreck, Robert Greer, John Swarbreck.

HORSKINS, ZACHARIAH
July 4, 1796; July 1, 1805.
Of St. Luke's Parish.
To wife: Henrietta Catherine Horskins.
To sister: Martha Cook, wife of Samuel D. Cook.
To neph: John Cook.
To niece: Mary Ann F. Cook.
To Mr. Joseph Clay.
Mentions: his mother and dau., not named.
Exrs: father, John Horskins, friend, Joseph Bryan.
Will proved by Thomas Rhodes.

62 HARSTENE, JOACHIM   Planter.
Feb. 26, 1803; July 28, 1803.
To wife: Catherine.
To sons: Jacob and Benjamin.
To daus: Anna, Catherine Bonner, and Mary King.
To gr. chil: Joseph, Benjamin, Thomas, and Elizabeth King, chil. of William King of Effingham Co., planter; David, Joachim, and Gabriel Saussey, chil. of David Saussey, planter, and dau., Catherine; Peter and Eliza Bonner.
Mentions: his dau. Catherine's former husband, David Saussey.
Mentions: his lands in Beaufort Dist., lying between lands of Lewis Lanier and Mrs. Heyward; lands bordering on lands of Rev. Mr. Smart; lands bought from John Dillon and William Holzondorf; lands known as Erherts, Waldsher, Keall's, Pellins, and Yamasee; lands originally granted to Adrian Meyers, Henry Bourquin, Caspar Meyers, Gamble & Flowers.
Exrs: wife, Catherine, sons, Jacob and Benjamin.
Wit: James Ross, George Enoe, Joseph Welscher.
Codicil dated Mch. 2, 1803.
Mentions: his lands on Whitemarsh Island, Chat. Co.
Same wit. as in will.

HERSON, HERMAN   Shipwright.
June 24, 1801; Aug. 3, 1801.
To wife: Johanna Christianna Herson.
To the chil. of my full bro., Henry Herson, living at Oldenberg, Germany.
To my half bro: Claus Jacobs.

ABSTRACTS OF WILLS, CHATHAM COUNTY, GEORGIA

To sister: Wuckpt Margaretta Derkson.
To the chil. of John and Matthias Wisenbaker of Effingham Co., planters, and Jacob Wisenbaker, late of same Co., planter.
Mentions: a lease in Savannah dated May 1, 1793, on the property of the German Lutheran Congregation for thirty-three yrs. -- bequeaths money to the poor of the same congregation, and to the poor at Ebenezer in Effingham Co.; and his property in Savannah.
Exrs: wife, Johanna Christianna; John Wisenbaker; John Herb of Savannah, blacksmith.
Wit: John Y. White, Christopher Frederick Triebner, Joseph Welscher.

63 HUNTER, WILLIAM   Merchant.
Aug. 18, 1802; Feb. 7, 1803.
To wife: Margaret.
To "my children".
To sisters: Isabella and Lydia Elizabeth Hunter.
Exrs: wife and Gdn., Margaret; bro., James Hunter; friends, Ebenezer Jackson, George Jones.
Wit: Richard Dennis, Lemuel Kollock, George Barnes.

<u>Will Book "E"</u>

HOGG, THOMAS
Aug. 8, 1810; Dec. 3, 1810.
To daus: Ann Rebecca and Maria Frances Hogg.
To son: John.
To Mary Anderson, the mother of Ann and Maria Hogg.
Mentions: his lots on Ellis and Johnson Squares; lots on the South Commons, formerly owned jointly with John Currie, dec.
Exrs: friends, George Anderson, James Johnston.
Wit: Robert Fair, Samuel M. Bond, S. Mordecai.

HARPER, ANN
Dec. 7, 1807; Jan. 8, 1808.
To niece: Elizabeth Cornelius.
To Thomas Harper.
Mentions: lands bought from John Harryson.
Exr: cousin, Daniel Joiner.
Wit: Patrick W. and John M. Kenty, Esqrs.

HARTSTENE, BENJAMIN   Planter.
Jan. 27, 1808; July 23, 1808.
Of South Carolina.
To mother: Catherine Hartstene.
To bro: Jacob.
To Jacob and Ann M. Hartstene.
Mentions: his lands in S.C.; lands on Whitemarsh Island, Ga.; lot in Savannah.
Exrs: bro., Jacob Hartstene, and Joseph A. Scott, Esqr.
Wit: Henry Bourquin, Jun., Joshua Dasher, George Enoe.

64 HABERSHAM, JAMES, THE ELDER, ESQR.
May 8, 1775; Nov. 23, 1775.
To sons: James, John, and Joseph.
To sister: Mary Bagwith of Whitby in Yorkshire, in Great Britain.
To neph: Joseph Clay and Ann, his wife.
To Joseph, son of my neph., Joseph Clay.
To James, son of Joseph Clay.
To gr. son: Alexander, son of my son, James.

To gr. dau: not named, dau. of my son, James.
To bro-in-law: Robert Bolton.
To dau-in-law: Hester, wife of my son, James.
To my son James, "a gold repeating watch which was bequeathed to me by my dear friend for thirty-three years, the Rev. George Whitefield, dec."
Mentions: his lands called "Dean Forest"; plantation called "Silk Hope", the land granted him Mch. 5, 1756; lands in St. George, St. Philips, St. Mary, and St. David Parishes; lands on Great and Little Oggechee; lot in Savannah on Ellis Square; lots in Brunswick and Hardwicke; lands purchased from Jonathan Bryan, Esqr., James Miller, dec., Miss Esther Rasberry, Elizabeth Deveaux, Henry Bourquin, Noble Wimberly Jones, Henry Ellis, Esqr.; lands bordering on lands of Lachlan McGillivray, Rudolph Pury, Alexander Wylly, Richard Fox, Philip Delegal, the elder, William Gibbons, Jun., Peter Guerard, James Tebbeau, Charles Watson, Daniel McKay, Capt. Goldsmith, James Lunier, James Wright, Esqr., Charles Burnet. "Whereas Daniel Demetre, late of this province, dec., in and by his last will and testament bearing date July 20, 1758, bequeathed property to my three sons, James, John, and Joseph, with Francis Harris, Esqr., and me, James Habersham, the elder, as exrs. for the estate, I gave up the rights of several negroes and other effects to Thomas Harris, son-in-law of Daniel Demetre, sold some of the land to John Gisnovoly, dec., Mordecai Sheftall, Thomas Burrington, dec., James Wright, Esqr., and Alexander Crighton."
Exrs: sons, James, John, and Joseph Habersham.
Wit: John Jamieson, John Storrs, John Fox.

65 HALL, NATHANIEL, ESQR.
July 29, 1805; Sept. 1, 1807.
Of Nassau, New Providence.
To wife: Ann.
To sister: Sarah Powell.
To bros: not named.
To nephs: Samuel and George Webb Hall, Esqrs., of Bristol.
To friends: Josiah Tattnall, Sr., Thomas Forbes, William Telfair, Henry Moreton Dyer, Hannah McAllister.
Mentions: his affairs in the hands of Chambers Langston & Co. of London, and Thomas and John Moss of Liverpool; lands in the Bahamas.
Exrs: wife, Ann; bro., Joseph Hall of Bristol; friends, John Armstrong of New Providence; Mathew McAllister of America.
Wit: John McCartney, James Kerr, Jun., John Garey.
Codicil dated July 17, 1807.
At my wife's death all property in Georgia to revert to her sister, Hannah McAllister, wife of Mathew McAllister, Esqr., and to her chil., Mathew Hall McAllister and Harriot Hannah McAllister.
To my friend; Harry Webb, Esqr.
Testator names Henry M. Dyer, Esqr., and Robert Thompson of New Providence as additional exrs.
Wit: Thomas Forbes, William Stephens, Andrew LoCroix.

HENDLEN, JOHN M.
Nov. 22, 1810; Feb. 18, 1811.
To bro: James.
To James McLaren, son of my bro-in-law, Archibald McLaren, sole heir.
Exrs: John Thompson of Colerain, Archibald McLaren.
Wit: William Mein, Joseph Dawson, William H. Taylor.

HUGENIN, DANIEL   Confectioner.
Sept. 28, 1811; Oct. 7, 1811.
Has no relations in this country.
To John Lawson, Esqr., in trust for a negro man, Simon Jackson, "for his kindness to me."

ABSTRACTS OF WILLS, CHATHAM COUNTY, GEORGIA

Exr: John Lawson.
Wit: Richard M. Stiles, Esqr.

66 HEBERE, PETER   Gunsmith.
One Sunday which I believe to be the 14th of Mai, 1809; May 20, 1809.
At Bonnabella.
Mentions: that he owes money to Mr. Thomas Decheneaux for a house purchased at the sale of the late Robilliard "of which I intended to pay the interest to his dau., Katy, now living with Mr. Deneaux"; that he owes money to Mr. Pazaret, Mr. Sague, Andrew Surcy (meaning Sorcy), my frield Riffault, Isadore Stouf, Nazaret & Co.; that he owes ground rent to Mathurin Reingeard, to Lewis Marchand for gin bought from John Feather, and a quarter of a dollar for two lbs. of bacon "to my friend, Francis Morel."
Mentions: that Larogue is the son-in-law of Isadore Stouf.
Testator made a key for a chest of drawers for Isadore Stouf, bought from the plantation "Asselin".
Mentions: his lands at Bonnabella.
Exrs: Richard Mary Stague (meaning Stites), Thomas Decheneaux.
Wit: Peter Dupont, merchant.

HARRISON, EDWARD
Mch. 25, 1812; Feb. 1, 1813.
To wife: Cynthia.
To sons: William Bolding and Edward Lawson Harrison.
Exr: bro., William Harrison.
Wit: John Smith, Sr. and Jun.

HULSE, JUSTUS   Shopkeeper.
Mch. 12, 1812; Mch. 23, 1812.
To father: Justus Hulse of N.Y.
To sister: Amey Hulse.
To the chil. of my bros., George and Daniel Hulse.
To the chil. of my sisters, Mary, Experience, and Amey.
Mentions: his property on Broughton St.
Exrs: wife, Hannah; Patrick Duffy; John Tillman.
Wit: Samuel Brant, Patrick Duffy, John Tillman.
Note: Also spelled Hultz.

HUTCHISON, ELIZA
May 25, 1812; Dec. 8, 1812.
To son: James.
67 To dau: Eliza Morrison, wife of James Morrison.
Wit: William Davies, Sarah Johnston, M. A. Johnston.

HUGHES, OWEN
Aug. 31, 1812; Sept. 9, 1812.
To Eliza Maria Hughes, stock of cattle left me in will of John Bonnell of Screven Co.
To William Wilkie.
To Ann Duke, dau. of Green R. Duke.
To Dr. Michael W. Hughes.
To bro: Edward Hughes of Phil., address by letter to Phillip Smith.
Mentions: his lands in Wilkinson Co., and half part of a negro girl called Harriet, in which Mrs. Winefred Bonnell has a life estate.
Exrs: friends, Dr. Michael W. Hughes, and Green R. Duke, Esqr.
Wit: Anthony Butler, T. Hall, John Pettibone, Esqr.

HARBOCK, JOHN
Mch. 23, 1814; Aug. 1, 1814.

To James Boyd.
Exrs: Patrick Duffy, James Boyd.
Wit: John T. Sefetre, Jonathan Vickers, William Killpatrick.

HOGG, EUNICE
June 5, 1815; Jan. 19, 1816.
To neph: Thomas Dixon.
Exrs: niece, Ann Stephens Norton of St. Luke's Parish, S.C., and George Allen, Esqr., atty-at-law of Richmond Co.
Wit: Frederick Densler, S.G. Bourquin.

HAIG, GEORGE   Planter.
Dec. 3, 1816; Dec. 10, 1816.
To the chil. of my bro., Dr. Maham Haig.
Child in esse.
Mentions: his slaves purchased from Emanuel Wambersie.
Exrs: wife, not named, Dr. Maham Haig, Alexander Telfair.
Wit: Sarah Telfair, William Davies, Charles Harris.

68 HILL, JOSEPH
Oct. 11, 1808; Feb. 25, 1815.
Of Ogeechee.
To dau: Maria Hill.
To godchild: Susannah Statham, dau. of Robert Statham.
To Pharo Mabry's eldest dau., not named.
To John Lyon, an orphan child, a tract of land in Liberty Co. called "Crack Tick"; land in Sunbury, property owned by his mother.
"I have twelve or fourteen bros. in the Brazils, Portugal, and other western isles, and one sister in a Nunnery, all well off in circumstances."
Mentions: his right and title to Ogeechee Ferry and Bridge; lands in Savannah back of the property of Thomas Young and near William McFarlane.
To the commissioned officers of the Chatham Artillery in Savannah for the use of the company.
Exrs: Richard M. Stites, John Bolton, Jeremiah Cuyler.
Wit: Benjamin Stites, T. Mann, Joseph Stillwell, Joseph Maxwell.

HOUSTOUN, RICHARD D.   Tailor.
Oct. 1, 1814; Oct. 12, 1814.
"I make my will with the consent of my Gdn. and trustee, James M. Wayne, Esqr."
To wife: Nancy.
To infant dau: Sarah.
To mother: Dolly Houstoun.
To the chil. of my sister, Esther, Lloyd, and Elizabeth Gordon.
Child in esse.
Mentions: his property in Savannah on Carpenter Row.
Exrs: George Anderson, Jeremiah Cuyler, Esqrs.
Wit: Levi S. D'Lyon, Thomas Glen.

HOLMES, JOSEPH B.
Division of estate, May 16, 1816; Adms. appointed were John Waters, Adam Cope, Barna McKinne, John Eppinger, James Morrison.
To mother: Mrs. Elizabeth Holmes.
To sister; Mary M. Holmes.
To David Taylor, Jun., and his chil.
69 To the chil. of my bro., David G. Holmes, dec.
Gdn: the Rev. Charles O. Screven who hath intermarried with the widow of David G. Holmes.
This estate consisted of considerable personal property.
Wit: W. M. Kelley, Thomas W. Davies.

ABSTRACTS OF WILLS, CHATHAM COUNTY, GEORGIA

HERB, JOHN
Division of estate, May 11, 1816; Adms. appointed were John Eppinger, William M. Evans, Frederick Densler, John H. Ash, Esqrs.
To wife: Catherine.
To chil: John F., Hannah, Mary, and Catherine.
Mary and Catherine being infants.
No wit.

I

Will Book "A"

70 IRVINE, JAMES
Oct. 10, 1798; Sept. 1800.
Of Craven Co., N.C.
Exr: James Blanks, sole heir.
Wit: John Blanks, William Kinsey.

Will Book "E"

IMFELD, ANTHONY   Gunsmith.
Oct. 8, 1814; Oct. 12, 1814.
Exr. and friend: in trust to Julien Desmouliens.
Wit: Joseph Charrier, John Delberghe, Paul P. Thomasson.

IRVINE, ANN ELIZABETH
Apr. 28, 1807; Oct. 29, 1807.
Wife of John Irvine, Practitioner of Physics.
To sons: Alexander, wife, Sarah; Kenneth; and Charles.
To daus: Ann Bulloch, widow, Margaret Irvine, Elizabeth Baillie, wife of Thomas Baillie, Sophie Evans, wife of William Evans, Esqr., and Isabella Irvine.
To gr. son: James Stevens Bulloch, son of my dau., Ann Bulloch.
Mentions: her landed estates in Camden Co.; town lot in Sunbury; plantation called "Dunane".
Exrs: sons, Alexander and Kenneth Irvine; friends, John Elliott, William B. Bulloch.
Wit: Mary Bulloch, William G. Box; William B. Bulloch.

J

Will Book "A"

71 JONES, LEWIS
Nov. 5, 1793; Dec. 4, 1793.
"Certificates sent to England for services in piloting the British Fleet in the war with America."
Extx: Amy Scranton, widow, and sole heir.
Wit: David Squires, David Bruston, Sheftall Sheftall.

JORDAN, WILLIAM
Nov. 8, 1791; Mch. 2, 1792.
Of South Carolina.
To the chil. of sister, Mary Timmons.
Exr: Plowden Weston, Esqr., planter of S.C.
Wit: John McDowell, Jacob Sass, Richard Gilbert Watt.

JARVIS, JOHN   Planter.
Dec. 10, 1795; Jan. 5, 1796.
Of Skidaway Island.
To sons: Edmund and John, minors.
Exrs: Edward Harden, Robert Bolton, Hampton Lillibridge, Charles Odingsells.
Wit: William Harvey, Henry O'Brien, Edward Buys.

JONES, JAMES
Nov. 11, 1800; Mch. 3, 1801.
To dau: Alethia M. Jones.
To sister: Alethia A. Stark.
To cousins: Nancy (or Ann) and Elizabeth Marbury, daus. of Leonard Marbury.
To two stepdaus: not named.
To friends: Ebenezer Stark, John Milledge, Ferd. O'Neal, in trust for my cousins, Leonard, William, and James Jones Marbury.
Mentions: his plantation in Bryan Co.
Exrs: wife, not named; friends, Ebenezer Stark, John Eppinger, John Milledge.
Wit: James Johnston, Jun., Owen Jones, A. G. Walter.

72 JONES, HENRIETTA B.
Aug. 12, 1788; July 12, 1800.
Wife of William Jones, atty-at-law.
Refers to marriage settlement with William Jones, Aug. 1779, late of Talgarth Co., Brecon, South Wales.
Will drawn in London, "while on a visit, but shortly bound on voyage to New Providence, Bahama."
Estate in three parts: to husband one part, the other two-thirds to sisters, Jane Judith Bourquin, Catherine Rehm, and Frances Fox.
To nephs: John and Lewis Keall, John Fox, Bartholomew and Jacob Waldburger, atty-at-law.
To niece: Mary, wife of John McNish of S.C., planter.
To William Henry and John, sons of Col. John Lewis Bourquin of S.C.
To Henry, son of my neph., Henry Bourquin, of Little Ogeechee.
To Sophia, wife of --- Hull of S.C., planter.
To Mary White, spinster, of Little Ogeechee.
To niece: Henrietta Hoskins.
Exrs: husband, William Jones, and Jacob Waldburger.
John Young Noel, atty-at-law, was appointed by testator to represent her affairs in Ga., in May, 1794.
Wit: James Ferrier, George Haist, Mary Ashbrook.
At the time this will was prob., William Jones was dec., and Henriette Hoskins (now Almy) applied for letters as "next of kin".
At the request of Bartholomew Waldburger and Zachariah Hoskins the will was delivered to the clerk of the Ordinary's Office.
Mrs. Jones, the dau. of Henry Bourquin and the widow of Henry Lewis Bourquin in 1779, when she married William Jones.

<u>Will Book "B"</u>

JANSAC, JAMES
July 25, 1779; Aug. 24, 1785.
All to dau., Mary Ann Berger, widow of Peter Berger.
Wit: Frederick Fahn, John Curtis, John Daniel Hammerer.

73 JONES, NOBLE
Oct. 12, 1775; Aug. 2, 1777.
To dau: Mary.

ABSTRACTS OF WILLS, CHATHAM COUNTY, GEORGIA

To John, George, Edward, and Catherine, chil. of my son, Noble Wimberly Jones, and his wife, Sarah.
To gr. dau: Sarah, wife of John Glen, Esqr.
To son: Inigo, and his chil., Sarah, Mary, and Noble.
To Margaret, Sarah, and James, chil. of John Glen, Esqr.
Mentions: his plantation called "Wormsloe", original grant Dec. 9. 1756; tract of land conveyed by William Scales and wife, Frances, both since dec., the Island of Redoubt, granted Sept. 15, 1756; lands purchased from Thomas Lee, dec., and Grey Elliott; lands sold to Francis Harris; town and farm lots in Savannah "granted Me" Jan. 16, 1756; lands at Ogeechee, and in St. Matthew and St. Andrews Parishes.
Exrs: chil., Noble Wimberly Jones and Mary Jones.
Wit: Henry Preston, Rebeckah Davis, Alex. Reid.

Will Book "D"

JAMIESON, JOHN
No date; Dec. 5, 1803.
Of Tybee Island, but now of Savannah.
To May Jamieson alias (nee) Mary Warner of New Providence, Island of Nassau.
Adm. and wife: Emelia Jamieson alias (nee) Emelia Fee.
Wit: James Wood, James Hemphill, Edmond Walsh.

JOHNSTON, MATTHEW   Factor.
Nov. 22, 1799; Nov. 7, 1803.
To wife: Elizabeth Mary Evans Johnston.
To two chil: Elizabeth and James Thompson Johnston, minors.
To father: not named.
To bros: James and Andrew William Johnston.
To bro-in-law: James Robertson.
Exrs. and Gdns: James Robertson, Andrew William and James Johnston.
Wit: William Davidson, Thomas Scarbrough, Owen Jones.

JOHNSON, ANDREW   Physician.
Aug. 6, 1800; Jan. 3, 1803.
To sons: Matthew and Andrew William.
To daus: Nisbit and Marion Ann.
Wife: dec.
To sons-in-law: Dr. Thomas Taylor, medical books, and James Robinson, London magazines for year 1772 "and my Eoleon Harp".
To friend: Lady Ann Houstoun.
Mentions: his property on the Altamaha and lot in Hardwick.
Exr: bro-in-law, James Robertson.
Handwriting proved by John J. Gray.

JONES, NOBLE WIMBERLY   Physician.
Jan. 7, 1805; Jan. 14, 1805.
To wife: Sarah.
To son: George.
To gr. son: Noble Wimberly Jones.
To gr. daus: Sarah Gibbons Jones and Catherine Jones Glen.
To gr. son-in-law: Archibald Bulloch, Esqr.
Mentions: his wharf lot and stores under the bluff and "nearly opposite my present residence", and town lot on the Bay "on which I lived previously to the fire of 1796."
Exrs: wife, Sarah; son, George; neph., Dr. James Glen; gr. son, Noble Wimberly Jones.
Wit: James Grimes, Matthew McAllister, Moses Sheftall.

JACKSON, MAJ. GEN. JAMES
Oct. 1, 1805; May 5, 1806.
To wife: Mary Charlotte.
To son: William Henry Jackson, lawyer, "a town lot fronting Oglethorpe Square where I resided before the fire of 1796, half of lot presented me by Legislature for services during the Revolutionary War. I hope it will be the last piece of property he parts with." Also his law library and "the print struck from the subscription engraving of myself and my sword".
To son: James, "who has a philosophical turn, my Encyclopaedia, the picture of crayon of myself at Halscombe."
To son: Jabez, "who has chosen the mercantile profession, my wharf and Bay lot in Brunswick, purchased by me at confiscated sales as the property of Inglis & Hall, my old picture to be copied for my son."
To youngest son: Joseph, "my old picture to be copied for my son and the remaining part of my library."
Mentions: his mother, dec.; his wife's father, the Hon. William Young, and "my aged and afflicted mother-in-law, Mrs. Sophia Young"; bro-in-law, James Box Young; wife's aunt, Mrs. Dillon, dec., wife of Robert Dillon.
To bro: Henry, for whom he had cared during his infancy, and who forfeited his property in England and came to America.
To Thomas W. Whitefield, "whom in a great degree I view him as my own son, having received him from his father on his death bed."
To George and William Whitefield, minors, "I was exr. of their father's estate."
To friends: Thomas de Mattos Johnson, "who rendered service to the state whilst I filled the Executive Chair."
*"Would like for my wife to marry if she can meet an honest and worthy man, deserving of her regard."
Mentions: his lands purchased from Rev. Mr. Rogers of N.Y., "being the garden lot to my town lot near the Bank, and said by Claud Thompson, the surveyor, to adjoin Eppinger's brick yard"; lands near the Jew's burying ground purchased from Matthew Ash; lands in Cedar Hill and Halscombe.
Exrs: wife, Mary Charlotte; bros., Abraham and Dr. Henry Jackson; friends, Thomas de Mattos Johnson, Gen. David Brydie Mitchell, and all my sons when of age.
Wit: Thomas Whitefield, Ebenezer Stark, Archibald Mackay.
*Out of six hundred wills, this statement appears only once.

Will Book "E"

JOHNSTON, JAMES   Printer.
Feb. 14, 1807; Jan. 2, 1809.
Native of Great Britain.
To wife: Sarah.
Mentions: that his property was confiscated.
Wit: Norman McLeod, John Irvine, Jeremiah Cuyler.

JONES, SARAH
Mch. 11, 1796; Apr. 6, 1810.
Wife of George Jones, Esqr., late widow of McCartan Campbell, Esqr., late of Augusta.
"By way of marriage settlement executed by and between Charles Cotesworth Pinckney, Charles Drayton, McCartan Campbell, on Aug. 28, 1790, and by a deed of settlement made previous to my marriage with George Jones of the first, myself of the second part, and Edward Telfair, Josiah Tatnall, Jun., and Ebenezer Jackson of the third part, bearing date Mch. 18, 1795."
To daus: Maria, Sarah, Martha, and Harriett.
To son: Edward.
Mentions: her lands in County of Richmond known as "Goodale Plantation".
Exrs: husband, George Jones, friend, Edward Telfair.
Wit: John Y. Noel, F. T. Flyming, Richard M. Stites.

ABSTRACTS OF WILLS, CHATHAM COUNTY, GEORGIA

JAFFRAY, ALEXANDER
Apr. 3, 1810; July 2, 1810.
To Mr. Thomas Gildchrist.
Wit: Stephen Achors, Esther Cummins.

JOHNSTON, DAVID   Planter.
Aug. 29, 1812; Nov. 16, 1813.
To nephs: James Johnston of Glasgow, and his male chil.; David Johnston of Leslie; Robert Bissett, Esqr., of Prinlans.
To neph: David Johnston, a minor, son of John Johnston of Glasgow.
To the chil. of Wilhelmina Johnston and the Rev. Mr. Kirkland.
To Mrs. Ann Courteny.
Mentions: lands leased from James Johnston, Esqr., on St. Catherine's Island; debts due from Owen Owens, Esqr.
Exrs: James Johnston, Robert J. Houstoun, James Dixon, Esqrs.
Wit: Oliver Sturges, Thomas W. Rodman, Lovell Warden.

JOHNSTON, SARAH
Jan. 23, 1814; July 3, 1815.
Relict of James Johnston.
To son: Lewis.
To gr. chil: James and Sarah Wall.
To James Morrison and John Drysdale in trust for my gr. chil.
Exrs: daus., Rachel, Sarah, and Bellemy.
Wit: Bellemy C. Robertson, J. Cuyler, John Drysdale.

JONES, SARAH
Jan. 27, 1810; Feb. 6, 1815.
Widow of the late Dr. N. W. Jones.
To gr. daus: Margaret Hunter, Sarah Bulloch, Ann Bourke, Catherine Jones Grimes, Mary Milnor, Charlotte Glen, daus. of my late dau., Sarah Glen.
To gr. dau: Sarah Jones, dau. of my son, Dr. George Jones.
Exrs: son, George Jones; gr. son, George Glen; friends, Barack Gibbons, William Stephens.
Wit: Philip D. Woolhopter, Thomas W. Rodman.
Codicil dated May 18, 1813.
To gr. gr. dau: Sarah Jones Grimes, dau. of my gr. dau., Catherine Jones Grimes.
Wit: Mary H. Pomeroy, spinster.

K

Will Book "A"

KERR, ELIZABETH
Mch. 25, 1791; Jan. 28, 1793.
Wife of Peter Kerr, carpenter, formerly Elizabeth, widow of Abraham Gable.
Refers to previous settlement in trust to James Myers and Balthazer Shaffer.
To Elizabeth, Mary, and Amealy Myers, chil. of James Myers.
Mentions: her lands in Savannah and Little Ogeechee.
Exr: son, John Gable.
Wit: Gabriel Leaver, John N. Reynolds, James Myers.

KELLER, GEORGE ADAM   Butcher.
Jan. 20, 1794; Dec. 8, 1794.
To gr. son: John Adam Keller.
Mentions: his lot in Trustees Garden; lands bordering on lands of Abraham Gay.
Exrs: son, George Paul Keller, and dau., Mary.
Wit: Alexander Keith, George Threadcraft, Philip Ulmer.

KIEFFER, DAVID   Planter.
Sept. 14, 1775; Feb. 24, 1783.
Of Vernonburgh.
To wife: Susannah, sole heir.
To son: Frederick, one shilling.
To sister: Mary Apolonia Nungazer.
Wit: John Campbell, Pater Theiss, George Bolinger, George D'Erbage, Deputy
Register.

Will Book "C"

79 KRUTMAN, EDWARD   Musician.
Nov. 21, 1787; May 29, 1788.
Of Westphalia, Germany.
To "my scholars, the daus. of Gen. Elbert, all my music books and music pieces."
To Sapho Mitchell, a silver watch.
To the poor of the Calvanistic religion, belonging to the Brick Meeting Congregation.
Mentions: money due from Joseph Clay for teaching his daus., money due from Mr.
Hearn, the bookseller, and David Duncan; money owed to John Shick, Esqr.,
Balthaser Shaffer, Gabriel Leaver, and Dr. Becroft.
Exrs: Maj. Gen. Samuel Elbert of Colonels' Island and John Shick, Esqr.
Wit: Balthaser Shaffer, Miss Sarah Howe, Justus H. Scheuber.

Will Book "D"

KERN, JOHN PETER   Merchant.
6th. and 9th. days of Sept., 1802.   Nunc.
To sister: sent for from Germany, "also have two other sisters in Germany, one
of them married having chil."
Wit: John Smith, John Henry Deubell, Joseph Hebel.
Committed to writing on behalf of Miss Sophie Kern of Savannah, spinster sister,
Sept. 14, 1802.

KEALL, DAVID   Gentleman.
Nov. 14, 1783; Apr. 3, 1784.
Of St. Peter's Parish.
To sons: John and David Washington Keall.
To bro: Lewis Borquin Keall.
Mentions: his property in Beaufort District; property on Back River, formerly the
property of Henry Keall, dec.; lot in Purysburg; lands bordering on lands of
Waldburg, Meyers, and John Houstoun.
Exr: Lewis Bourquin Keall.
Wit: John Keall, Frederick Rhem.

80 KELSALL, JOHN
No date; May 7, 1804.
"Designating myself Strathie Hall on the Ogeechee River, I possess one moiety with
my sister Ann, spinster, of London, in said plantation, being a British subject,
generally residing at Ezuma, one of the Bahama Islands."
To Ann Kelsall, spinster, of London.
To son: Hodge.
To eldest son: Roger, and four other chil.
Mentions: his lands in S.C. and Ga.; lands left in will of gr. father, James M.
Kayor; Strathie Hall now rented to Mr. Gillivary, Esqr.

ABSTRACTS OF WILLS, CHATHAM COUNTY, GEORGIA

Exrs: wife, Lucretia; son, Roger; friends, James Mossman and M. Kay, Esqr., who is the son-in-law of John McQueen, merchant of Savannah.
Wit: John Leslie, Richard Pearis, John H. Harris.

Will Book "E"

KEIFER, DAVID
Nov. 5, 1812; Jan. 4, 1813.
Of District of White Bluff.
To son: David.
To daus: Elizabeth Catherine and Susannah.
Mentions: his lands in Savannah.
Exrs: son-in-law, John George Heisler (minor); friends, Joshua Buckhalter, William Davies, Esqr.
Wit: Frederick Keifer, David Gnann, Thomas Fisher.

KERBLAY, LEQUINIO, ESQR.
Jan. 1, 1808; Sept. 21, 1813.
Of Edgefield District, S.C.
To wife: Madame de Levis.
To Madame Cecile Vandepere.
Mentions: his plantation called "Good Rest", and negroes sold to Mr. Rainsford.
Exr: Monsieur Petit de Villers.
Will translated by de Villers.

L

Will Book "A"

81 LOWREY, JOHN   Chairmaker.
Nov. 25, 1794; July 13, 1796.
To daus: Rachel, Jane, and Elizabeth, the wife of Daniel Ounsell.
Mentions: his land in Savannah; lot in Yamacraw adjoining the land of John De la Rosques.
Extx: wife, Elizabeth.
Wit: William Norment, Christopher Gugel, Joseph Welscher.

LOYER, ADRIAN   Silversmith.
Feb. 17, 1781; Mch. 17, 1781.
To wife: Christiana.
To dau: Isabella, minor.
Child in esse - if son, to be called Edward.
Exrs: wife, Christiana, David Montaigut, William Ross, merchant.
Wit: Thomas Reid, David Brydie, William Jones.

LLOYD, THOMAS   Planter.
July 11, 1771; May 25, 1772.
Of St. Paul's Parish.
To eldest son: John.
To chil: Elizabeth, Thomas, Samuel, Francis, James, Jane, and Patience.
Mentions: his land where Margaret Proctor now lives.
Exrs: wife, Patience, Hughes Middleton, Mordecai Sheftall.
Wit: Edmund Cartledge, Reuben Blanchard, Mordecai Sheftall.

LESLIE, ALEXANDER   Merchant.
Feb. 24, 1792; Oct. 27, 1792.
To wife: Elizabeth.

To dau: Lucy, by first wife.
82 To chil: Ann, Alexander, Robert, James, Elizabeth, and Charlotte.
Possible child in esse.
Mentions: bond due by Capt. John Stallings, "who lives on the river St. John's in New Brunswick, now in the hands of John Thompson"; his lands in Nova Scotia and New Brunswick.
Exrs: John Cunningham, John Fisher, Alexander A. Leslie.
Wit: Hezekiah Harding, John Greer, George Myers.

LILLIBRIDGE, HAMPTON   Planter.
Aug. 28, 1799; Mch. 3, 1801.
To wife: Ann, was Ann Offutt.
To Mrs. Lettice Offutt.
To Hampton and Oliver Martin Lillibridge, sons of my neph., John Lillibridge.
To dau: Henrietta, minor.
Mentions: his plantation on Skidaway; plantation called "Shandy Hall"; lots in Savannah.
Mentions: his wife and chil. are interred at Shandy Hall, and that he wishes to be buried there.
Exrs: Charles Odingsells, James Jones, Edward Harden, Charles Screven of Chatham Co., Ezekiel Harris of Richmond Co.
Wit: J. Bolton, Jacob Hartstene, Joseph A. Scott.

Will Book "B"

LARKING, EDWARD
July 3, 1777; July 17, 1777.
All to Martin Byrn, who is exr.
Wit: Bruce Wyensly, James Byrns.

LEWIS, OLIVER, ESQR.   Atty-at-law.
June 16, 1784; Jan. 10, 1785.
To eldest bro: Seth Lewis of Conn.
To bros: William and Selah Lewis.
To sisters: Miss Nancy Perry of E. Windsor and Mrs. Anna Jepson of Hartford.
Mentions: his parents, not named.
Exrs: bro., Seth Lewis, Lyman Hall.
Wit: Samuel Bird, Dalziel Hunter, Nathan Williams.
Attest. of Hezekiah Gilbert.

83 LLOYD, REBECCA   Widow.
Apr. 13, 1778; Mch. 8, 1783.
Exrs: sons, Benjamin and Edward, dau., Rebecca.
Wit: Mathew Stewart, Amedius Chiffelle, Ann Eaton, spinster.

LEWIS, FRANCIS
Jan. 16, 1784; Jan. 28, 1786.
To wife: Christiana.
To dau: Ann Lewis
Exr: friend, Thomas Taylor.
Wit: Joel Walker, James Powell, Abram Mordecai.

LEE, THOMAS   Gentleman.
Feb. 11, 1778; No date.
To wife: Mary Ann.
To bro: William Lee.
To sisters: Ann and Rebecca Lee.
To godson: Isaac Weddall.

ABSTRACTS OF WILLS, CHATHAM COUNTY, GEORGIA

To friend: John McLuer, "my bay horse and military sash".
To John Lyon, the younger, in trust for sister, Rebecca Lee.
Mentions: his lands in St. Philips Parish, near the lands of Luke Mann.
Exrs: wife, Mary Ann; father-in-law, William Fox, the elder; friends, John McLuer, and William Stephens.
Wit: Mary McLuer, --- Cuyler, Joseph Goldwire.

Will Book "D"

LEVETT, FRANCIS
July 12, 1802; Oct. 4, 1802.
Of McIntosh Co., Ga.
To wife: Charlotte.
To son: John Levett, minor.
To dau: Charlotte Julia Levett.
Exrs: friends, William Stephens, Matthew Johnston, James Johnston, Jun., all of Savannah.
Wit: Solomon Baisden, planter, John Thompson, planter, John Barrington, surgeon, all of McIntosh Co.

84 LIVINGSTON, JOHN CATTLE
Dec. 29, 1803; Jan. 14, 1804.
Of Daufuskie Island, St. Luke's Parish, S.C.
To sister: Mary Frazer.
To nephs: George, William, John, and Alexander Frazer.
To Henry Richardson, Sr.
To John Richardson.
To Richard Ash Frazer.
To Miss Caroline Frazer.
To Miss Harriett Frazer.
To John L. Hopkins.
Exrs: Charles Odensels and John Bolton of Ga., Paul Hamilton and Francis Hopkins of S.C.
Wit: Mark Duffy, R. Watts, Edward Wooley.

Will Book "E"

LEVETT, JOHN
Apr. 9, 1808; Nov. 17, 1808.
Of the Parish of Marylebonne, in London.
This codicil to be part of my will.
"One copy of the will was left with my bro-in-law, Rev. Thomas Bennett, and one other with William Bell, Esqr., of Russel Square in London, which I have omitted to name in said will."
Exrs: William Stephens, D. B. Mitchell, Thomas Spalding, Esqrs., "these are to be exrs. of my will so far as relates to my property in this country."
Wit: Isham Onales, W. Garbett, C. Stephens.
At Juliantown, McIntosh Co.
Mentions: his mother to be added to the exrs. already named.
John Levett died Oct. 7, 1808, at seven P.M., in McIntosh Co.
Wit: Dr. Joseph Maxwell, Mr. Robert Watts.

LEWIS, CHRISTIANA
Dec. 23, 1786; July 1, 1811.
To bro: Peter Grant.
Mentions: her lands in Frederica.
Exr: friend, Joachim Noel Faning.

Wit: John Poullen, Francis Courvoisie, L. Viaz?.

85 LUCENA, LUCAS   Butcher.
July 17, 1805; Mch. 9, 1812.
To sons: John and Thomas of Charleston, S.C.
To daus: Suckey, Hannah, Isabella, Jane, Lucinda, and Nancy, wife of John Meed.
Exrs: son, Thomas of S.C., and Dr. William Parker.
Wit: Hendk. Fisher, Joseph Spencer, James Watts.

LEION, ANNA
June 10, 1812; Dec. 8, 1812.
Wife of David Leion, Esqr.
To sister: Judith Minis.
Exr: Hon. William Stephens, Esqr.
Wit: Charlotte Stephens, Peter Deveaux, Charles Dunham.

LLOYD, EDWARD
Mch. 28, 1812; May 4, 1813.
Of Oglethorpe Co.
To wife: Sarah A.
To dau: Rebecca Frances.
To Mrs. Mary Lloyd, widow of my dec. bro., Benjamin.
Mentions: his property at White Bluff.
Exrs: wife, Sarah A. Lloyd; Charles A. Redd of Clarke Co.; Thomas Edward Lloyd of Chatham Co.
Wit: Johnson Brickerstuff?, John P. Hightower, George Y. Farrar.

LUBEN, JEAN
May 14, 1813; May 26, 1813.
To John McDermott.
Exrs: Etienne Metivier, Jean D. Sitz.
Wit: --- Truel, Jean B. Lapey, --- Pounia.
Translated from the French by F. D. Petit de Villers, interpreter of Foreign Languages and Notary Public of Chatham Co.

LEWDEN, WILLIAM   Carpenter.
July 31, 1809; Mch. 7, 1814.
Being aged.
To nieces: Dorcas, Isabella, Susannah, and Sarah Miller; Elizabeth Vollotton, wife of Paul J. Vollotton.
To the chil. of my present wife, John Rebecca, and Selina.
86 To Elizabeth Miller, dau. of David Miller.
To nephs: William and David Miller.
Exrs: wife, Mary, Paul J. Vollotton, John Dillon.
Wit: Ant. Carles, John Waters, Thomas Decheneaux.

LATOUR, PETER (PIERRE) GRASSET
Oct. 5, 1815; Mch. 5, 1816.
To son: Alexander Grasset Latour, about eight yrs. old.
Mentions: his property in the U.S. and France.
Exr: friend, Anthony Mellisimo.
Wit: Jean B. Gilbert, Joseph Charrier, Paul P. Thomasson.

LAPEYERE, JOHN B.
Nov. 22, 1815; Mch. 5, 1816.
To friend: Paul P. Thomasson, who is exr.
Wit: John B. Gaudry, Francis Roma, Gabriel L. Colmesnil.

ABSTRACTS OF WILLS, CHATHAM COUNTY, GEORGIA

M

Will Book "A"

87 MURRAY, JOHN   Carpenter.
Dec. 23, 1796; Jan. 4, 1797.
Exr: godson, John Edmund Anderson, son of John Anderson, baker.
Wit: James Johnson, Daniel Miller, Joseph Welscher.

McKEY, JOHN   Mariner.
June 19, 1797; June 29, 1798.
On board ship Eagle.
To bro: Michael Mackey in Ireland.
Exr: James Armstrong.
Wit: Thomas Waugh, surgeon, John Davis, chief mate.

MINIS, ABIGAIL   Aged widow.
Oct. 27, 1789; Dec. 6, 1794.
To five daus: Leah, Esther, Judith, Hannah, and Sarah.
To gr. chil: Abigail, Francis, Abraham, Isaac, Esther, and Philipa, chil. of my dec. son, Philip Minis.
Exrs: daus., Leah and Esther, and William Stephens.
Wit: Joseph Habersham.

MORTIMER, WILLIAM
June 10, 1796; Sept. 12, 1796.
Extx: Clarissa Moultrie, sole heir.
Wit: Thomas Hylton, John Murray.

MONTAIGUT, DAVID
Apr. 4, 1795; June 6, 1796.
Manumits general slaves.
Exrs: John Glen, and John Wallace, British Consul.
Wit: Charles F. Chevalier, James Wallace, Jabez Upham.

Will Book "B"

88 MORGAN, THOMAS
Apr. 17, 1778; Sept. 14, 1778.
To chil: William, Thomas, and Ann.
Extx: wife, Elizabeth.
Wit: Shem Cook, John Gorham, John Lindsay.

McINTOSH, JOHN   Planter.
July 22, 1781; Jan. 17, 1783.
Of St. Andrew's Parish.
"Being under the necessity of being absent from the Parish."
To dearly beloved cousin, Mrs. Winenwood Noble, widow, sole heir and extx.
Mentions: money due him from the estate of George McIntosh, dec., and appoints Mrs. Noble to collect it from Mr. George Houstoun.
The exrs.for the estate of George McIntosh were Robert Bailie, George Houstoun, and Patrick Houstoun.
Wit: Georgiana McIntosh, Hugh Lowrey, Ann Lowrey.

MULLRYNE, CLAUDIA
Dec. 10, 1781; Feb. 6, 1784.
Wife of John Mullryne.
To daus: Catherine Moore, widow, and Mary Tatnal.

To gr. sons: John Mullryne Tatnall, and Josiah Tatnall, Esqr.
To gr. dau: Claudia Cattell Tatnall.
To son-in-law: Josiah Tatnall, Esqr.
To John, Charles, and Margaret, chil. of the/late John Green.
To Thomas Boone, eldest son of Thomas Boone, Esqr.
Mentions: a bond given Dec. 7, 1781, to Thomas Boone of London by Claudia Cattelle Tatnall, spinster; her lands called "Bonaventure" adjoining the lands of Samuel Bowen and Josiah Tatnall; the forty-five acre lots, and a tract purchased of the attorneys of His Excellency, Henry Ellis, Esqr., called "Thunderbolt"; plantation adjoining Thunderbolt called "Placentia" adjoining the lands of Claudia Cattelle Tatnall, Charles Price, Richard Williamson, Benjamin Weddall, Philip Miller, James Galache, and Mrs. Milledge.
Exrs: dau., Mary Tatnall, Josiah Tatnall, Esqr., and gr. sons.
Wit: K. Douglass, George McKensie, George Bailie, Jun.

McLEAN, ANDREW   Merchant.
July 3, 1784; Apr. 18, 1785.
Of Augusta, Ga.
To sons: Andrew Cowper and William McLean.
To dau: Mary.
Mentions: money in hands of James Jackson, Esqr., merchant in London.
Exrs: wife, Catherine, and William Clark.
Wit: Samuel Elbert, David Douglass, Flor. Sullivan.

McFARLANE, SUSANNAH   Widow.
Sept. 10, 1784; Oct. 27, 1784.
To sons: John McFarlane and Benjamin Wilson, merchant in Savannah.
To gr. son: John Jamieson Johnston, son of Mr. Thomas Johnston.
To Mrs. Martha Cook.
Mentions: her lands on Great Ogeechee; money due from James Thompson.
Exrs: Leonard Ciecel, merchant, and Dr. John Irvine.
Wit: Thomas Elfe, Gabriel Leaver.

MARTIN, JOHN, ESQR.
Jan. 3, 1786; Jan. 30, 1786.
To godson: Lucius Quintius Cincinnatus Milton, son of my kinsman, John Milton, Esqr.
To Thomas Comber Walton, son of friend, George Walton, "in testimony of the esteem I have of his father's character, and of my approbation of his public conduct, having gone through many years with him in the warmest and most intimate friendship, and been together in some of the trying scenes of the late war."
Mentions: his lands bordering on lands of James Postell and Mark Carr.
Extx: wife, Mary Debora.
Wit: George Walton, John Milton, James Bulloch.

MAXWELL, JAMES   Planter.
Mch. 13, 1772; July 13, 1780.
Of St. Philips Parish.
To wife: Ann.
To chil. of present marriage.
Exrs: wife, Ann, James Mackay, and William Maxwell.
Wit: James Hardie, Thomas Padden, Lemuel Lanier.
Handwriting attested by Roger Kelsall.

MACKAY, JAMES
June 10, 1785; Jan. 13, 1786.
Of Strathey Hall.
To gr. son: John Kelsall, and his sister, Ann Kelsall.
To gr. chil: Barbara, Ann, Simonds, John, and Stephen Maxwell, chil. of my dec. dau., Ann, and her late husband, James Maxwell.

ABSTRACTS OF WILLS, CHATHAM COUNTY, GEORGIA

To the chil. of Mary Maxwell, dec. wife of John Butler Maxwell, and also a dau. of my dec. dau., Ann.
To Barbara Clark, wife of William Clark.
Mentions: his lands called "Red Bird" (1100); lands on Turtle River called "Buffalo Swamp" in St. David's Parish, Glynn Co., adjoining grants to James Postell and Col. Mark Carr; lands on Green's Creek in Chatham Co.
Exrs: William Maxwell of "Belfast" in Chatham Co., James Mossman of Savannah, Esqrs., and William Clark.
Wit: George Handley, James Jackson, Jacob Waldburger.

Will Book "C"

MURDOCK, DAVID
Apr. 10, 1788; Jan. 6, 1789.
To Peter Karr, carpenter.
Left no chil.
Wit: John Lowrey, John London, John McFarlain.

MANN, JOHN, ESQR.
Jan. 19, 1786; June 29, 1789.
Of Liberty Co.
To son: Luke Mann.
To dau: Mary Sapp.
To gr. sons: Thomas and Luke Mann, sons of Luke Mann.
Mentions: his lands on the north side of the Altamaha River in Washington Co.; lands on little Canuche in Liberty Co.
Exr: son, Luke Mann.
Wit: Sylvanus Robeson, Joseph Warren, Sarah M. Kinley.

91 MOORE, JOHN
Dec. 26, 1786; Aug. 24, 1789.
To sister: Elizabeth Edwards.
Mentions: his lands in Ga. and S.C.
Exr: bro., James Moore.
Wit: John Beatty, William Day, Paul H. Wilkins.

MILLER, ROBERT
Nov. 29, 1773; Feb. 8, 1774.
Of St. John's Parish.
To seven chil: James, Samuel, Daniel Miller, Elizabeth Clark, Judith, Mary, and Hariet Miller.
To gr. daus: Martha and Magdalena Miller.
Exrs: (sons) Samuel and Daniel Miller; friend, Parmenus Way, Esqr.
Wit: Josiah Powell, Esqr., Parmenus Way, Jun.
Foot note: Henry Bourquin as Adm., Cum Testamento Annexo, July 9, 1791.

MOORE, AARON
July 21, 1785; Jan. 2, 1790.
To three chil: William, James, and Elizabeth.
Mentions: that James and Elizabeth are minors, and he wishes Elizabeth to live with Mrs. Greenhow.
Mentions: his lands in Effingham Co., and lands bought from William Mathews.
Exrs: son, William Moore, John Goldwire, Thos. Polhill.
Wit: Thomas Palmer, James White, John Younger White.

MILLS, THOMAS   Merchant.
Jan. 20, 1789; Feb. 4, 1791.
To wife: Sarah.

       To son: Thomas.
       To dau: Sarah Mills.
       Mentions: that in the event his chil. die without issue, his estate real and
       personal to be sold and remitted to the Island of Guensey, and "there to be
       divided in and among my bros. and sisters chil.
       Exrs: wife, Sarah Mills, friends, William Stephens, James Mossman.
       Wit: James Clark, Daniel Course, John Course.
       This will signed by Thomas Mills alias Moullin.

92 MOORE, CATHERINE   Widow.
    July 14, 1790; Jan. 15, 1791.
    To sister: Mary Tattnall, wife of Josiah Tattnall, Esqr.
    To John Mullryne Tattnall, Esqr., and each of his chil.
    To Josiah Tatnale, Jun., Esqr.
    To Maj. John Habersham.
    To niece: Claudia Cattel, the wife of Col. Hamilton.
    To Mary and Claudie Tatnale, chil. of Josiah Tatnale, Jun., Esqr.
    To John and Ann Habersham, chil. of John Habersham, Esqr., of Savannah.
    To Jane Watts, dau. of Jane Watts, widow.
    To friend: Margaret Eustace, widow, and her son, John Shey Eustace, Esqr., (who
    is now abroad) "plantation near Savannah called 'Cattel Park' the property left
    me by my gr. mother and aunt Cattel."
    Mentions: "there is a balance due me from the estate of my aunt Cattels now in
    the hands of Abram Ladson of S.C., Adm. of the estate; the money due me from
    the Hon. Judge Pendleton."
    Exrs: Margaret Eustace, John Shey Eustace, John Habersham, Esqr.
    Wit: John Smith, John Robertson, Dr. James Box Young.
    Codicil dated Jan. 7, 1791.
    Mentions: money due from Major Demere.
    Mentions: her father and mother dec.; and David Brydie Mitchell, Esqr., atty-
    at-law, "to be exr. to my last will instead of John Habersham."
    Wit: Francis Levett, John Milledge.
    Note: Cattle Park near Savannah, derived its name from the family of Cattelle.

                              Will Book "D"

MION, CONGNAEY
Mch. 5, 1796; Aug. 23, 1801.
Of Elizabeth Town.
To wife: Elizabeth, sole heir.
Exrs: Jauvin and Duclos, inhabitants of Jersey, our common friends.
Proved by Thomas Decheneaux, translator, J. A. Dechisse, N. Nazaret.

93 MOORE, SUSANNAH   Widow.
    Apr. 30, 1798; Mch. 1, 1802.
    To dau-in-law: Mrs. Ann Moore, widow of my son, John M. Moore.
    To bro: Robert Bolton.
    To nephs: William M. Evans, and Thomas and Robert Newell, sons of Capt.
    Thomas Newell.
    To niece: Susannah M. Adams, dau. of Mr. N. Adams and Ann Bolton, dau. of my
    bro., Robert.
    Mentions: her property in Savannah, purchased from William Stradman; wharf lot
    under the bluff now occupied by William Belcher and George Lamb.
    Exrs: Robert Bolton, William M. Evans, John Habersham, Nathaniel Adams, Jun.,
    William Belscher, all of Chatham Co.
    Wit: Samuel Newell, Curtis Bolton, W. Stephens.
    Codicil dated Mch. 28, 1800.
    To sister: Rebecca Newell.
    To Ann Riley, "who is living with me."

ABSTRACTS OF WILLS, CHATHAM COUNTY, GEORGIA

To the dau. of my friend, John Habersham.
Mentions: her lands adjoining the property occupied by Mr. Dronico; lands bought from John Exley.
Testator appoints her dau-in-law, Ann Moore, to be added to the exrs.
Wit: William Stephens, Ann Riley, Ann Gibson.

MINIS, LEAH
May 29, 1795; July 5, 1802.
To sisters: Judith, Hannah, and Sarah Minis, who are extxs.
Wit: W. Stephens, John Wallace, George Anderson.

MUIRES, SARAH
Oct. 9, 1799; July 3, 1802.
To daus: Susannah, the wife of Samuel Ihly; Mary, the wife of Thomas Palmer; Elizabeth; and Frances.
To gr. daus: Anna and Eliza, the chil. of my dau., Elizabeth.
To gr. son: Samuel Ihly, Jun.
Mentions: her property in Savannah.
Extxs: daus., Mary Palmer, Elizabeth Anderson.
Wit: Thomas Palmer, Susannah Anderson, William Norment.

94 MACLEOD, DONALD   Planter.
Mch. 16, 1802; July 5, 1802.
To wife: Elizabeth Macleod.
To daus: Catherine and Mary Eliza.
To son: Francis H.
To William Macleod Bannatyne in Scotland in trust for my neph., Donald Macleod, son of my sister Ann Macleod.
Mentions: that he owns slaves jointly with Francis H. Harris, who owes him money; money due to Joseph Clay, Esqr.; his property in Savannah.
Exrs: wife, Elizabeth; son, Francis H.; Joseph Habersham; William Stephens; Matthew McAllister; William Elliott; Stephen Elliott; Andrew Turnbull; Ebenezer Stark, Esqrs.
Wit: George Woodruff, William Maclean, Littleton Hunt.
First codicil not dated, nothing of interest.
Second codicil, dated May 24, 1802.
Mentions: "the lands to be purchased on Ogeechee Neck, the property of John Kane, Esqr., for my son, Francis, I revoke."
To dau: Catherine, his sermons and religious books.
To bro: John Macleod, to (balance of page torn away, cannot find the original will.)
Wit: S. M. Cormick.
Third codicil dated May 26, 1802.
To Rodonick and Norman Macleod, mourning rings.
To Ebenezer Stark, a mourning ring.
To Mrs. Norman Macleod.
Wit: S. M. Cormick.

McALLISTER, RICHARD   Planter.
June 24, 1802; Dec. 30, 1802.
Of McIntosh Co., now of Baltimore.
To wife: Louisa McAllister.
To dau: Louisa Caroline.
To sister: Sarah Orme, relict of John Orme of Montgomery Co., Md.
To nieces: Amelia Mary McAllister and Matilda Maria McAllister, daus. of my bro., Archibald.
Mentions: his father, dec.
Exrs. and Gdns: wife, Louisa, neph., George Washington McAllister, son of my bro., Archibald.

Wit: John Henry Hoskins, Sarah Stellman, Ann Edwards.
Will prob. in Baltimore.

95 MOSSMAN, JAMES   Planter.
June 1, 1801; June 16, 1803.
To wife: not named.
To sister: Margaret Stack, formerly the wife of Christopher Oliver.
To nephs: Philip Young, John, Ralph, and James Oliver, chil. of Christopher and Margaret Oliver.
To nieces: Margaret and Jane Oliver, chil. of Christopher and Margaret Oliver.
To Mossman Houstoun.
Exr: neph., James Oliver.
Wit: John Y. Noel, Sarah C. Noel, Samuel Mordecai.

MOREL, JOHN   Planter.
Mch. 20, 1802; July 5, 1802.
To minor chil: not named.
To neph: John H. Morel.
To bro: Peter Henry Morel.
Mentions: " a settlement made of certain property to John and Alexander McQueen, trustees of my wife's property, (marriage settlement) bearing date June 18, 1789. - I acknowledge void; as some of the slaves, etc., having been sold and through necessity of the exrs. of my father's estate (as the negroes were descended to me) my wife to be paid $1000 a year"; his plantation on Ossabo on Savannah River; Pembroke plantation on the Salts; property in Savannah; lands purchased from Mr. Fisher.
Exrs. and Gdns: John Milledge, George Jones, John G. Williamson, William B. Bulloch, Charles Harris, Esqr.
Wit: Michael Burke, A. D. Abrahams, Sheftall Sheftall.

MACKAY, ADAM
Jan. 2. 1805; Mch. 5, 1805.
Of Co. of Glynn, now living in Savannah.
All to Owen Hughes of Savannah, sole exr.
Wit: Thomas Robertson, William Wilkie, Barnard McCann.

McCORMICK, SAMUEL   Physician.
Sept. 25, 1803; Dec. 5, 1803.
Of St. John's Parish, Berkely Co., S.C., now of Savannah.
96 To wife: Dorothy McCormick.
To son: Robert.
To Emily Walter, dau. of my wife.
Exrs: Thomas U. P. Charlton, Joseph Miller, William Christie, James B. Richardson, John Richardson, Elias Ball, Dr. H. Richardson of Carolina.
Wit: Job T. Bolles, Will Lee Brent, Charles Cooper.

McINTOSH, GEORGE
Oct. 7, 1804; Nov. 4, 1805.
To dau: Clarissa.
Wit: Charles Odingsells, George W. Allen.

McCANN, BARNARD
Oct. 13, 1805; Jan. 6, 1806.
To William Cale, son of William Cale, dec., "who lives with me."
To Elizabeth Robinson, dau. of Thomas Robinson.
Exrs: Owen Hews, Jeremiah Cuyler.
Wit: William A. Moore, Jacob Cunes.

McGARVAN, DANIEL
May 29, 1805; Feb. 5, 1807.

ABSTRACTS OF WILLS, CHATHAM COUNTY, GEORGIA

All to wife: Dorcas, sole extx.
Wit: Charles Slade, Robert Christie.

McKNIGHT, MARY ANN   Planter.
Sept. 26, 1805; Feb. 5, 1807.
To gr. sons: Isaac and Benedict Young.
To gr. daus: Nancy Young, Mary E. Allen.
Exrs: George Allen, William Stephens.
Wit: James Wells, Benjamin Douglas.

MILLAN, JOHN
Jan. 11, 1805; Mch. 5, 1805.
Of S.C., now living in Savannah.
To wife: Martha Millen.
To two chil: Martha Bane Millen and Elizabeth Millen.
Mentions: that his wife's bro., John Simmons, now resides on Ociatey plantation, where he wishes his family to reside.
Mentions: his property on May River in S.C., adjoining the lands of William Pope, Sr., late the property of Henry Middleton; plantation called "Strathboggon" on the Ociatey Creek; lands in St. Peter's Parish bordering on lands of Nathaniel Johnson; bonds in the hands of Caig & Mitchell of Savannah; bonds now in the possession of wife from Josiah William Austin of St. Luke's Parish.
Exrs: wife, Martha, George Edwards of Spring Island, S.C., John Riley of Coosewatchie, S.C., William White of Savannah.
Wit: William McFarland, Abm. Strobart, William W. Simmons, Thomas Robertson.

MILLER, CHRISTIANA   Widow.
Jan. 31, 1805; Mch. 5, 1805.
To two nieces: Rebecca and Mary McGee.
To friend: Mrs. Mary Clark, the wife of James Clark of Savannah, lumber measurer.
To Miss Rebecca Taylor.
To Joseph William Clark, son of James Clark.
Mentions: her lands in St. Andrew's Parish, now Liberty Co.
Exr: James Clark.
Wit: Hardeman Stone, Laban Wright, James Devine, Joseph Welscher.

MALL, MARGARET   Widow.
Oct. 19, 1799; May 5, 1806.
Of Little Ogeechee.
To dau: Elizabeth Rosco.
To gr. dau: Mary Ealy.
Exrs: Henry Bourquin, Benjamin Bourquin.
Wit: Sophia Bourquin, Jane Dollar McCaw Bourquin, Mary Screven Raynes.

McINTOSH, LACHLAN, THE ELDER, ESQR.
Jan. 21, 1802; May 5, 1806.
Age 76 yrs.
To wife: Sarah.
To sons: George, Henry, and Hampden.
To dau: Esther Ward, wife of John Peter Ward.
To youngest dau: Catherine McCauley Harris, wife of Charles Harris, Esqr., of Savannah.
Mentions: his lands in Liberty Co., lands near old Darien; lands on Clapboard Bluff on Cathead Creek; lands in the upper end of McKitchan's Island; lands on Cumberland Island, in the Co. of Camden; lands in Savannah, and property on St. James Square; lands bordering on lands of Joseph Clay on the Augusta Road called the "Glebe lands"; lands on Skidaway Island; lands bordering on lands of the late Abigail Minis; bounty lands given him by grants or otherwise for military or other public service; lands in McIntosh Co., and in McIntoshville so called in honor of

"my worthy father", who was the first inhabitant of that Co.; island of Doboy, at the mouth of the Altamaha, "which I gave to my wife forty yrs. ago."
Exrs: sons, George, Henry, and Hampden McIntosh; sons-in-law, John Peter Ward, and Charles Harris.
Wit: Edmund Bacon, J. Benjamin Maxwell, Joseph Welscher.

McCREDIE, ANDREW
Mch. 12, 1807; Apr. 22, 1807.
To son: James McCredie of Newark, N.J.
To bro: David McCredie of Charleston, S.C., merchant.
To the chil. of my sister, Jane.
To Eliza H. Scoffield, for services during an illness.
Mentions: his property in Savannah, adjoining the lands of William Belscher, purchased from William Thomson and his wife, Harriet Cunningham Thomson, conveyed by their atty., William Mein.
Exrs: bro., David McCredie, friends, David Brydie Mitchell, William Mein, Joseph Miller.
Wit: William B. Bulloch, Thomas Whitefield, William B. Maxwell.

Will Book "E"

McQUEEN, ELIZABETH
Oct. 21, 1796; Nov. 22, 1797.
Wife of Alexander McQueen, Esqr.
To eldest dau: Harriet.
To daus: Maria and Eliza.
Mentions: her father, sister, and bro., William Fuller, dec.
Mentions: "a deed of indenture bearing date of Apr. 21, 1795, made by and between my bro., Thomas Fuller of Beaufort, S.C. of the one part and William Fuller and John Barnwell trustees, a deed of gift of nineteen negroes from my bro., Thomas."
Exrs: Edward Telfair, Thomas Netherclift.
Wit: D. McLeod, Barrack Gibbons, Ebenezer Stark.
Bryan Morel qualified as Adm. Nov. 3, 1807.

MULCASTER, GEORGE
Apr. 9, 1806; May 10, 1808.
To aunt: Elizabeth Box.
Exrs: friends, John Lillibridge, Solomon B. Smith.
Wit: Frederick Reynolds, Oliver M. Lillibridge.

MENDELHALL, THOMAS
Mch. 3? 1808; Nov. 14, 1808.
To dau: Sarah, wife of Henry Hall.
To sons: Thomas and John.
To sister: Hannah Pastorius, and her dau., Sarah Ann Pastorius.
Mentions: his mother, dec.
Exrs: sons, Thomas and John, son-in-law, Henry Hall.
Wit: Griffin L. Lamkin, George A. Port, James Armstrong, John N. Brailsford.

McQUEEN, ANN
Dec. 2, 1807; July 10, 1809.
To sons: John and William.
To Isabella and Elizabeth Hunter.
Mentions: her islands of Oatlands.
Exrs: son, John McQueen, daus., Eliza and Sarah McQueen.
Wit: Charles Harris, Benjamin Whitehead, John Hunter.

MUTER, ROBERT   Grocer.
Jan. 5, 1812; Jan. 30, 1812.

ABSTRACTS OF WILLS, CHATHAM COUNTY, GEORGIA

To Richard M. Stites.
Exr: friend, Joseph Parker, shopkeeper.
Wit: R. M. Dimon, Patrick Duffy, Thomas U. P. Charlton.

100 McKENTY, PATRICK
Apr. 8, 1813; June 23, 1813.
To wife: Catherine.
To Catherine and Peggy Remshart.
To Thomas Gribben.
To Peter Deveaux.
To Daniel McCarty of Co. of Antrim, town of Larne, Ireland.
Mentions: his property in Savannah; land near Pipe Makers Bridge, bordering on lands of Thomas Gibbons.
Exrs: Daniel Remshart, Thomas Gribben.
Wit: D. D. Williams, N. W. Glen, Thomas Womack.

McINTOSH, HENRY   Planter.
Apr. 22, 1813; July 14, 1813.
Of Cumberland Island.
To Maria, Jane, Margaret, and Edward Bayard, chil. of my sister, wife of Dr. Nicholas S. Bayard.
Exrs: Nicholas S. Bayard, friend, Ray Sands of Camden Co.
Wit: Philip Box, Isadore Stouf, Daniel Pendleton.

MACLEAN, JOHN   Soldier.
May 3, 1814; June 6, 1814.
To friend: Malcolm Anderson.
Mentions: "money due from the U.S. for services as a private soldier, having first enlisted under David D. Twiggs, also entitled to bounty land as an enlisted soldier for five yrs., which term will expire on the 14th of June, 1817, and being a private soldier in the U.S. Infantry, 8th Regiment of foot and at present commanded by Capt. William Jones now at Savannah."
Adm: Malcolm Anderson.
Wit: John Lockhart, Thomas O. Farrell, R. W. Leach.

MILLER, ZACHARIAH
June 11, 1803; Feb. 11, 1815.
About to embark for America.
To neph. and godson: Robert, son of Rev. Dr. George Miller.
To sister: not named.
101 Exr: bro., not named.
Wit: Richard Darling, Esqr., of Dublin, William Bailie of N.Y., atty. in the U.S., William Hughes of Dublin.

MOREL, JOHN
Division of estate, Jan. 17, 1815; made on application of Thomas N. Morel, Esqr., Thomas Burks, J. Bond Read, and John P. Williamson, who were the appraisers of the slaves only, about one hundred and eighteen, one lot fell to Thomas Netherclift Morel, John Morel, and Henry Morel.
Division of estate, Feb. 19, 1817; made on application of John Morel, Esqr.
Legatees: Henry Morel, dec., Ann Rutherford, Nathaniel G. Rutherford, Thomas N. Morel, and John Morel.
Adms. appointed were J. Bond Read, John P. Williamson, Thomas Bourke.

MILLEN, JOHN   Planter.
Division of estate, Jan. 25, 1815; made on application of John H. McLeod in right of his wife, Mary McLeod, Ann Millen, Alethea M. Jones, who are the only persons entitled to the estate of John Millen.

Mentions: lands in Savannah, negroes and personal property; lands on Little Ogeechee bordering on lands of Jones, Telfair, Bellews, George Millen, and Gibbons.
Adms. appointed were George W. McAllister, George Lewis Cope, Adam Cope, Stephen S. Williams, and Robert Habersham.
Cuyler, atty-at-law.
Wit: Hon. John P. Williamson.
Divided and delivered Apr. 8, 1815.

MYERS, GEORGE   Mariner.
Apr. 16, 1813; May 6, 1816.
To wife: Lydia.
To sons: Thomas and George.
Exr: (son) George Myers.
Wit: J. Cuyler, George Atkerson, Jacob Shaffer.

102 MILLER, SUSANNAH   Widow.
Dec. 14, 1816; Mch. 3, 1817.
To gr. chil: Joseph Josiah and Sarah Ann Wilkinson, minor chil. of my dau., Susannah.
To friend: Mary Camel.
Mentions: her property in Savannah and White Bluff.
Exrs: William B. Bulloch, John Shaw, Morton Wilkinson of Beaufort District, Esqrs.
Wit: Samuel J. Bryan, Joseph Lawrence, John H. Oldershaw.

N

Will Book "A"

103 NUNGAZER, MARY APPOLONIA
May 22, 1791; Nov. 12, 1792.
Widow of Henry Nungazer.
To gr. sons: George and Henry, sons of my dec. son, Henry.
To dau: Mary, wife of Thomas Dowell.
To dau-in-law: Barbara, wife of son, George.
Exr: son, George Nungazer.
Wit: John Campbell, Mathew Salfner, Michael Densler.

NICHOLS, ISAAC   Planter.
Jan. 10, 1791. Died inestate.
Of Parish of St. Paul's, S.C.
John Wilson, Esqr., as Adm.

NORDEN, LEON
July 26, 1798; Sept. 21, 1798.
Native of Amsterdam, Holland.
To Samuel Mordecai and his son, Samuel, Jun.
To Mr. Isaac Benedix of Savannah, merchant.
To Mr. Jacob Canton of Charleston, merchant.
"None of the Sheftalls need be present at funeral."
Exr: Mr. Isaac Benedix.
Wit: John Young, Jun., Justus H. Scheuber.

Will Book "B"

NUNGAZER, HENRY, JUN.
May 16, 1786; June 12, 1786.

ABSTRACTS OF WILLS, CHATHAM COUNTY, GEORGIA

Of Christ Church Parish.
To sons: George and Henry.
To sister: Mary C. Dowell.
Exrs: wife, Mary Margaret; bro., George Nungazer; David Fisher.
Wit: Peter Thiess, Jacob Thiess, George Heisler.

NELSON, MALCOLM
Apr. 3, 1778; Nov. 18, 1782.
To mother: Jane Nelson.
To sisters: Jane Russell and Janet Nelson.
Mentions: money lying at interest in Scotland.
Exrs: William Watt, Alexander Cunningham.
Wit: James Jones, James Storie, Seaborn Jones.

Will Book "C"

NIELSON, NICHOLAS   Planter.
May 12, 1781; Mch. 9, 1790.
Of Hilton Head, S.C.
To friend: David Brydie, practitioner of physics in Savannah, who is exr.
Wit: John Barnard, Henry Talbird, Isaac Baldwin.

NUNES, MOSES   Gentleman.
Oct. 14, 1785; Mch. 28, 1791.
To bro: Daniel.
To neph: Isaac DeLeon.
To niece: Rebecca Abrahams.
To sisters: Ziperah Jacobs and Esther DeLeon.
Mentions: that funeral services to be performed by his friend, David Montaigue, Esqr.
Mentions: his lands in Burke Co.; lands on the south side of the Great Ogeechee; money due from Joseph Clay.
Wit: David Montaigue, Joseph Abrahams.
The estate was appraised by Abraham DeLeon, Isaac Abrahams, Abraham Abrahams.
Will was established by Mordecai Sheftall, foreman.

Will Book "D"

NEYLE, WILLIAM
Nov. 31, 1802; Dec. 15, 1803.
To wife: Harriett.
To daus: Harriett and Elizabeth, minors.
To bros: Gilbert N., Philip, and Sampson Neyle.
Mentions: his property on Dyals Bay in Camden District, Clarendon Co., S.C., originally granted to Sampson Neyle, Sr., dec.; property on Hutchinson Island known as "Poplar Forest"; marriage settlement in S.C. with his wife, Harriett.
Exrs: bro., Sampson Neyle, friends, William Taylor of Black Swamp, S.C., and Morris Miller.
Wit: John Wallace, Venibols Bond, John P. Williamson.

NETHERCLIFT, WILLIAM
No date; Aug. 5, 1805.
To bros: Thomas and Alexander Netherclift.
To friend: Charles Harris.
Wit: William Moore.
Attested by Nicol Turnbull, Esqr.

Will Book "E"

NEYLE, JAMES
Sept. 29, 1807; Jan. 2, 1809.
Exrs: William Davies, Richard M. Stites.
Wit: Harriot Townsend, Susan Joy.

NORTON, ELIJAH   Planter.
June 10, 1812; Sept. 7, 1812.
Of S.C.
To bro: Jonathan Norton, who is exr.
Wit: John Harbock, George Ritter, W. Lavinder.

NAZARET, NICHOLAS   Physician and Surgeon.
July 26, 1809; Mch. 4, 1811.
"Born in Versailles of Jean Nicholas Nazaret and Francoise Cheruvaux his wife, both dead, my father in Paris and my mother in Versailles. My age fifty-two yrs. and nine months, citizen of LaCroix des Bouquets of Port au Prince, St. Domingue, now an exile living in Savannah, being a citizen of the U.S."
Mentions: that Etienne Metivier is the only person authorized to use his signature or credit.
To friends: Paul Dupon, Thomas Deschevaux.
To Antoinne, the Priest, a box of gold to help in his work.
To sister: Catherine, born Nazaret, the wife of Sieur Beauvallet; after my

106   sister's death, the property to go into the hands of Sieur Louis Claude Martin, my bro-in-law, professor of mathematics, for him and my sister, Marie Jeanne Elizabet, born Nazaret, his wife and their chil.
To sister: Marie Louise, born Nazaret, widow of Dutaus, living at the house of the said Mr. Martin who is not dead.
Exrs: Paul Dupon, Thomas Deschevaux.
Wit: Charles Riffault, Louis Marchand, U. Tobler.
Appraisers of estate: Francis Roma, Thomas Deschevaux, Francis Guillemett.
Translated from the French by Miss Martha Youngblood, Savannah, Ga.

O

Will Book "A"

107   OAKMAN, WILLIAM   Innkeeper.
Oct. 13, 1794; Oct. 23, 1794.
To William Henry and Henry William, sons of Mary and George Clarke.
To cousins: John, James, and Ann Reid of London, and Charlotte, dau. of Ann Oakman.
Mentions: a bond due from the estate of Thomas Mitchell, a tavern keeper, to be given to his daus., Mary Ann and Sarah Mitchell.
Exrs: John Poullain, Stephen Britton, shopkeepers, and John Kreeger, tailor.
Wit: Theodore Gay, Stephen Britton, Jun., Joseph Welscher.

OGILVIE, CHARLES   Merchant.
Nov. 1, 1775; Oct. 10, 1788.
Of Co. of Middlesex, London.
To sons: Charles and John Alexander, when of age.
To niece: Margaret, eldest dau. of my bro., Alexander Ogilvie, Esqr., of Anchiries, North Brittain.
To nieces: Margaret, Isabella, and Rebecca, daus. of my sister, Mary.
To neph: George Ogilvie of S.C.
To friends: William Robert Cammell, Thomas Burk or Bark of Bread St., John Whitloc Edward Neufville, C. Rolleston.

ABSTRACTS OF WILLS, CHATHAM COUNTY, GEORGIA

Mentions: property in right of "my dear wife, Mary (dec.)"; most of property and debts are in America; lands and slaves in S.C. contiguous to those of my chil.
Exrs: bro., Alexander Ogilvie; neph., George Ogilvie; Alexander Garden of S.C., Esqrs; John Mitchie of London; C. Rolleston.
Codicil dated Nov. 18, 1777.
Testator revokes legacy to Neufille and Rolleston.
Will certified in London by John Fisher and William Wynne, Doctors of Law.
Robert Irvine, woolen draper, and Robert Wells of London, attest the handwriting of Charles Ogilvie of St. Clements Danes.

OATT, BARBARA   Widow.
Oct. 10, 1791; Jan. 26, 1792.
To dau: Sarah Gibson, sole heir and extx.
Wit: Slaughter Cowling, Daniel Gibson, Nich. Bauchanneau.

OSTEEN, THOMAS
Oct. 1, 1794; Jan. 2, 1795.
To sons: David and Solomon.
Exrs: wife, Sarah, and Mathew Bennet.
Wit: Edmund Bacon, Joseph Clay, Jun., Edwin L. Harris.

Will Book "B"

ORTNER, HENRY
May 11, 1785; Dec. 14, 1785.
To wife: Elizabeth.
To dau: Barbara.
Directs that his wife's son, John Weatherford, should be schooled.
Exr: Jacob McCulloch.
Wit: Joseph Ming, Elizabeth Fryer, Jacob McCulloch.
On Dec. 7, 1785, the widow petitions for adm. stating that her husband died May 12, 1785, and that the appointed exr. refused to quality.
Wit: Philip Minis.

Will Book "C"

OGDEN, SOLOMON, SR.
June 17, 1788; July 9, 1788.
To wife: Mary.
To sons: Isaac and Solomon.
To dau: Mary Wood.
Mentions: a tract of land on Lezebeth Neck; a tract of land in Hanover Co., N.C., the rights of which are in the hands of Jacob Stechelys; Isaac was left slaves by his uncle.
Exrs: Solomon Ogden; friend, George Gussat.
Wit: Thomas Woods, James West, Elizabeth West.

OATES, JOHN
--- ---; June 17, 1789.
To son: Jeremiah, now or late of Pensacola, Fla.
To Lucy, William, Peter, and Elizabeth, chil. of my dec. son, Jacob.
To daus: Tamer Waters, wife of Sinclair Waters; Mrs. Frances Mahoney, wife of Dennis Mahoney; Elizabeth Brown, wife of Thomas Brown.
To gr. sons: John Waters, minor, and Edward Brown.
Mentions: his lands on the Great Ogeechee "which was granted to me"; a small island on the Sea Coast in Chatham Co., on a branch of the Great Ogeechee River, adjoining or near the lands of one William Bird; lot in Savannah; one of his negroes now in the plantation of Lachlan McGillivray, Esqr.

Exrs: Tamer Waters, George Walton, Esqr., Jeremiah Oates.
Wit: Charles Young, Seaborn Jones, David Moses Vollaton.

Will Book "D"

OUNSEL, BARBARA   Widow.
Sept. 9, 1803; Oct. 6, 1803.
To Sally Mitchell.
To bro: John or Johanna Strobell, now in Europe.
To Mrs. Elizabeth Strohaeker, "all my liquors, and for her to live in my house until my bro. arrives, then Sally Mitchell to live with Elizabeth Strohaeker."
Exrs: John and Frederick Wul.
Wit: Rosina Hersman, Elizabeth Durr, Jeremiah Cuyler.

Will Book "E"

110   ODINGSELLS, CHARLES   Planter.
June 4, 1809; Dec. 12, 1810.
To wife: Sarah.
To dau: Mary Odingsells.
To sister: Elizabeth Lee of Mass.
To the chil. of my niece, Mary Odingsells and her husband, George Washington Allen.
To the chil. of my niece, Mary Scriven, and her husband, John Hart of S.C.
To Joseph Spencer.
To Elizabeth Wilson.
To Charles Odingsells Screven, son of my neph., Charles Odingsells Screven.
Mentions: his plantation on Skidaway Island; and the Island of Little Warsaw.
Exrs: Charles Odingsells Scriven, Joseph Spencer, John Scriven.
Wit: Joseph Frith, A. Williams, John M. Webber.

O'KEEF, PATRICK
Oct. 6, 1813; Dec. 6, 1813.
Being aged.
To dau: Margaret O'Keef.
To bros: James and Thomas.
Exr: John Dillon.
Wit: Abraham Foster.
On Apr. 8, 1817, James Hubbard and his wife, Margaret, qualified as Adms. for the estate of Patrick O'Keef.

OWENS, OWEN   Planter.
Feb. 7, 1810; Mch. 7, 1814.
Of St. Catherine's Island, Liberty Co.
To nephs: Owen Owens Fell and Owens Jones.
To Penelope Newdigate of Savannah.
Exr: Son, George W. Owens, counsellor-at-law.
Wit: John Lawson, H. C. Heenemann, Charles Dunham.

P

Will Book "A"

111   PAISLEY, JOHN
Will proved Mch. 4, 1801.   Nunc.
To wife: Jerusha.
To five chil: Rhoda, Jerusha, Eliza, Sarah Ann, Mary Caroline.

ABSTRACTS OF WILLS, CHATHAM COUNTY, GEORGIA

Child in esse.
Mentions: his lands in S.C.; lands in Savannah.
Proved by Grimball Robert.

PENDLETON, DANIEL
Feb. 26, 1800; Mch. 24, 1800.
To son: Daniel Pendleton.
Mentions: his bro., Solomon Pendleton, dec.
Exr. and Gdn: Edward White.
Wit: Mary Gilbert, Samuel Smith, Dr. George Aspinwall.
Codicil made same day with same wit.
To John Herb.

Will Book "B"

PAPOT, JAMES
Jan. 3, 1784; May 24, 1784.
To dau: Jane Judith.
To Jane Judith Bourquin, Sr., Benedict, and Judith Bourquin.
To nephs: Peter Papot, John and Isaac Weddell.
Exrs: dau., Jane, Benedict Bourquin, James Galashe.
Wit: Judith Bourquin, Thomas Taylor, Fredk. Rehm.

PALMER, GEORGE
Nov. 24, 1777; Feb. 16, 1778.
To wife: Mary Ann.
To son: William.
To dau: Elizabeth.
Exrs: Lyman Hall, John Glen, Job Pray.
Wit: William Stephens, Moses Nunes, Amedeus Chiffelle.

PRESTON, HENRY
Aug. 4, 1770; Sept. 17, 1777.
"Late wife, whose memory shall ever be held dear."
To only son: Philip Delegal Preston.
To sister: Elizabeth Preston, who resides at Appleton, near Biddo, Yorkshire, Great Britain.
To bros-in-law: Mr. David Delegal and Mr. Philip Delegal, the younger.
To niece: Elizabeth Lightenstone.
To aunt: Martha Richards.
To wife's sisters: Mrs. Eleanor Seymour, wife of James Seymour; Judith and Mary Delegal.
To Miss Ann Searles, for her care and attention to me.
To Sarah, wife of my beloved wife's bro., Philip Delegal.
Wife's wearing apparel is given to those mentioned above, consisting of: "Rich flowered brocade sack and coat full trimmed; full trimmed white satin flowered sack and coat with all the laces and ruffles belonging to it; full trimmed blue striped sack and coat; black silk sack and coat; flowered brocated silk gown; orange colored full trimmed satin sack." Also a "genteel proportion of wife's linens, caps, stockings, aprons, handkerchiefs, etc."
Exrs: Rev. James Seymour of Augusta, James Robertson, atty-at-law of Savannah.
Wit: Martha Stephens, Dr. John Irvine, Andrew Hewett.
Codicil dated Aug. 9, 1777.
To Mr. Thomas Goldsmith, a mourning ring, silver-mounted pistols, and bateau.
Wit: Eunice Hogg, Ann Searles.

PARKER, ANN   Widow.
Aug. 29, 1783; June 3, 1787.

Of Isle of Hope.
To daus: Grace, wife of Samuel Farley, Esqr.; Susannah, wife of Thomas Ross, Esqr.
To gr. chil: Ann Farley, dau. of Grace Farley; Ann, Isabella, and Thomas Ross, chil. of Susannah Ross.
Exr: son, James Parker, "now residing with me."

113 Wit: Elizabeth Parker, John Spencer, George Basil Spencer.
Codicil dated Oct. 10, 1786.
Mentions: additional property.
Wit: Elizabeth Parker, Mary Bowen.

PENDLETON, SOLOMON
Dec. 23, 1786; Feb. 3, 1787.
Now in N.Y.
To bro: Daniel, 500 lbs.; and "to care for my dear parents, as he and bro. William have large and growing families, are left balance of estate, after 150 lbs. to bro. David, who is a single man, and from his disposition not likely to be otherwise."
To neph: Edmund Pendleton.
To Miss Nancy Eaton, "for kindness in my illness."
To friends: Robert Montfort, Esqr., Richard Wylly, Esqr., William and James Bryan, Mathew McAllister, Esqr.
Mentions: his rights in mills now building in Effingham Co.; mill seat purchased from Dr. John Love on a stream called "Three Runs" near the property of George Robertson; debt of 40 lbs. due Willimpee Neefus of N.Y. State, loaned me when a prisoner on Long Island; directs that she be paid 60 lbs. for her kindness.
Exrs: bro., Daniel Pendleton of N.Y. City, Robert Montford, Mathew McAllister, Richard Wylly.
Wit: Dr. Samuel Bradhurst, William Newton, Thomas O'Hara, gentleman.

PRYCE, CHARLES, THE YOUNGER
Nov. 24, 1778; Jan. 26, 1784.
To honored father: Charles Pryce, Esqr., lately residing in Parsons Green, Parish of Fulham, Co. of Middlesex.
To William Stephens, Esqr.
To William O'Bryen, Esqr.
To aunt: Mary Jacquere.
Exrs: father, Charles Pryce, William Stephens, William O'Bryen.
Wit: Dr. James Houstoun, Patrick Houstoun, Andrew McLean.

Will Book "C"

114 PORCHER, PAUL   Planter.
May 11, 1787; Aug. 28, 1789.
Of St. Peter's Parish, S.C., residence, "Savine Grove".
To wife: Jane.
To daus: Jane Elizabeth and Rachel Ross.
To son: Josiah Dupre.
Mentions: his lands originally granted to Lewis Morgan; the Hill and settlement where Mrs. Boswood, widow, now resides; lands on Great Onslow Island in Chatham Co.; lands in S.C. originally granted to Francis Erhart near Zubly's Ferry, Purysburg Township, St. Peter's Parish, bought of Conrad Hover; marsh lands on Wrights Neck (St. Peter's Parish) originally granted to Thomas Hutchinson, bought of John Fenwick; town lot in Purysburg.
Exrs: wife, Jane, James Moore of Ga., Cornelius Dupont, William Ross, Thomas Hutson of S.C.
Wit: Peter Porcher, Sr., and Jun., William Henry Williamson.

ABSTRACTS OF WILLS, CHATHAM COUNTY, GEORGIA

PRAY, JOB
Jan. 1, 1789; June 26, 1789.
To sons: John and William Pray.
To Mrs. Mary Turpin of Charleston, S.C.
To the wardens of Christ Church Parish, for the use of the church.
Exrs: John Habersham, Samuel Strickland, Nathaniel Pendleton, Esqrs.
Wit: Mrs. Catherine Greene, Susan Pendleton, Jacob Wood.
In a codicil, 10 lbs, is given to the Grand Lodge of Savannah.
Samuel Stirk, Esqr., qualified as acting exr. as the others named in will refused to act.

PENMAN, JOHN   Merchant.
Oct. 24, 1789; Nov. 2, 1789.
Exrs: wife, Robina; friends, Andrew McCredie, John McCullough, merchants.
Wit: Ignatius Geoghegan, George Woodhouse, Joseph Welscher.

Will Book "D"

115 PARKER, ANN   Widow.
Jan. 16, 1800; Mch. 1, 1802.
Relict of Nathaniel Parker.
To niece: Sarah Louis.
To bro: William Stephens.
To Margaret McFarlin.
To Barbary Child.
To Alex M. Allen.
To Ann Hehly, my sister-in-law.
Mentions: her property in Savannah, lands leased from Furney Dickman.
Exrs: William Child, William McFarlin, also Gdns. of my niece, Sarah Louis.
Wit: Alex M. Allen, Richard Guinn, William McFarland.

Will Book "E"

PAGE, JOSEPH
Jan. 19, 1812; Feb. 2, 1813.
Of District of White Bluff.
To mother: Margaret Page.
To bros: Thomas and William.
To neph: Joseph Page Lindsey.
Exr: (bro.), William Page.
Wit: L. D. Parke, Ishan Onales, John Poullen.

PITT, THOMAS
Aug. 9, 1813; Sept. 8, 1813.
To son: Thomas.
To daus: Sarah and Ann Pitt.
Exrs: wife, Ann, and John Pettibone, Esqr.
Wit: Levi S. Delyon, Charles Lindsey, T. M. Patterson.

PAYART, CHARLES LOUIS   Confectioner.
Oct. 28, 1814; Nov. 7, 1814.
To godson: John Louis Gilleron.
To Biemame Joseph Santy.
Exr: Angelo Santy.
Wit: Paul P. Thomasson, Esqr., John B. Gaudry, John B. Berthelot.

116 PLATT, JAMES   Planter.
    Dec. 18, 1812; Dec. 5, 1815.
    Of Screven Co.
    To wife: Mary.
    To Jenet Clements her son, James Clements.
    To William, Jonathan, and Charles Clements.
    To Elizabeth Platt.
    Exrs: Jenet Clements, William Rawls, Benjamin Merrill.
    Wit: John B. Deveaux, John D. Moore, Granville Bevill.
    Codicil dated Oct. 18, 1814.
    To dau: Elizabeth Platt of N.Y.
    To son: Benjamin Clements.
    To Mrs. Hennings.
    To John Hennings.
    Exrs: James M. Wayne, atty-at-law; John Hennings.
    Wit: William Lucas, Daniel Remshart, James Hudson.

    PELOT, FRANCIS   Planter.
    June 25, 1809; July 17, 1815.
    To neph: Jacob Franklin Keall.
    Exrs: David Johnston, Nathaniel Adams.
    Wit: John Eppinger, Sr. and Jun., Joseph Stutz.

    PORTATIS, JOSEPH   Shopkeeper.
    Nov. 21, 1815; Mch. 5, 1816.
    To friend: Peter Pourid, who is exr.
    Wit: Paul P. Thomasson, --- Chevier, Gabriel L. Colmisnil.

    PORT, WILLIAM F.
    Feb. 14, 1816; Mch. 3, 1817.
    To father: James Port.
    To friend: Elizabeth Norton.
    Exr: David D. Williams.
    Wit: John Lawson, Esqr.

    PROCTOR, GEORGE V.
    Dec. 23, 1816; Mch. 25, 1817.
    To father: Richard Proctor.
    To Bryan and Richard Proctor, chil. of bro., Stephen.
    Mentions: his May River plantation.
    Exrs: wife, Harriett F., bro., Stephen R. Proctor.
    Wit: Abraham B. Fannen, Thomas Wilson, John B. Rouland.

R

Will Book "A"

117 ROSS, HUGH   Shopkeeper.
    Nov. 1, 1762; Apr. 27, 1775.
    To wife: Ann, dau. of the late Daniel Stewart, shipmaster, from Inverness, Scotland.
    To son: John.
    To my beloved chil., sons and daus., not named.
    Mentions: his lot in Savannah.
    Extx: wife, Ann.
    Wit: Peter Blythe, David Brydie, Michael Serviser?.

ABSTRACTS OF WILLS, CHATHAM COUNTY, GEORGIA

ROBINSON, JANE
Jan. 1, 1793; Sept. 30, 1793.
Widow of Israel Robinson.
To son: John Lions.
To friends: Mary and Joseph Will.
Mentions: a tract of land on the Altamaha River opposite Gov. Wright's, formerly granted to Mark Carr, Esqr., in St. John's Parish; lands in St. Patrick's Parish, including the island called "Crispinand"; a tract in St. John's Parish, which lands border on lands of William and Thomas Carr, on Medway River.
Exrs: Joseph Will, Henry Myers.
Wit: John Gromet, James Tibbets, Henry W. Williams.

READDICK, MICHAEL   Planter.
June 23, 1791; Oct. 12, 1793.
To wife: Saloma.
To sister-in-law: Catherine Readdick.
To nieces: Mary Smith, Ann Moore.
Mentions: his plantation called "Providence", some of the land "was granted to me", and some to John Young.
Exrs: wife, Saloma, and William Moore.
Wit: Joseph William Spencer, Richard Dawson, William H. Spencer.

ROSS, MOSES
July 17, 1793; Apr. 18, 1794.
Of Washington Co.
Exrs: Mr. John Hamilton, Mr. John Bunton, to dispose of property as they think best.
Wit: Thomas Spalding, Robert Harris, Justus H. Scheuber.

READ, JAMES, ESQR.
June 18, 1772; July 4, 1781.
To wife: Rebecca.
To sons: James Bond Read, Jacob, William, and George Paddon Read, minor.
To daus: Sarah Catherine Read, Susannah, and Elizabeth, minors.
To sisters: Catherine Jacques, Mary Read of Annapolis, Md., and Jane Allen of Phil.
To Thomas Savage of Charleston, Josiah Tatnall, George Houstoun, Esqrs., land on the Ogeechee, at Newport, called "Lancester", in trust for "use of my family".
Mentions: his plantation called "Chester", on Great Ogeechee; lands on Canuchee River in St. Andrew's Parish; 1000 acres on Bryan Creek; lot under the bluff; lot on the Bay; lands adjoining the lands of Benjamin Goldwire now the lands of Grey Elliott.
Exrs: wife, Rebecca; son, Jacob Read; friends, Thomas Savage, George Houstoun, Josiah Tatnall.
Wit: James Edward Powell, Grey Elliott, Capt. John Bond Randall.

RUPPERT, JOHN   Butcher.
Sept. --- 1792; Dec. 15, 1792.
Of Ewensburgh.
To dau: Mary Ruppert.
To the eldest son of my sister, Elizabeth, wife of John Cocknert, cordwainer, of N.Y. State.
To the eldest son of my sister, Hannah Fayd, widow, of Canada.
To John, son of John Eppinger, bricklayer, of Savannah.
Mentions: his lands bought from James Ross, exr. of the will of Benjamin Wall, dec.; land grant in Effingham Co. Jan. 31, 1785, bought of William Ring; and an original grant to Rodolph Strochacker in Washington Co. on the Oconee River; property in Ewensburgh; bought land from Conrad Hoover who bought the same from Serenas Mayer.

Exrs: dau., Mary; friends, William Lewden, carpenter, and John Eppinger.
Wit: James Thompson, Moses Vollotton, Jr., Joseph Welscher.

RING, JOHN   Planter.
Oct. 11, 1792; Nov. 12, 1792.
To dau: Mary Ring.
To sister: Mary, wife of John Hineman in Cassell, and to her chil.
Mentions: his lands on Great Ogeechee; and an original grant to father, Christopher Ring, dec.
Mentions: that he wishes to be buried by the side of his father.
Exrs: John Hineman, William Lawson, George Nungazer, Justus Hartman Scheuber.
Wit: Ann Margaret Ring, John Lears, David Keifer.

RAE, ROBERT   Planter.
Oct. 30, 1779; Mch. 1, 1781.
Of Augusta, Ga.
To wife: Rebecca.
To neph: James Rae of Augusta.
To bro: Mathew Rae of Kingdom of Ireland, the messuage whereon "I now live, which I possess by will of my niece, Jane Sommerville, dec."
To the chil. of friend, Samuel Elbert and his wife, Elizabeth.
To Mary Herron.
To friends: George Whitefield, Leonard Marbury, Samuel Elbert.
To dau-in-law: Elizabeth Church.
To the chil. of my bro., James, dec., of Ireland.
To the chil. of sister, Deborah Armstrong of Ireland.
To Ann Johnston, spinster, of Augusta, for kindness in painful illness.
To friends and relations: rings to Mrs. Isabelle Habersham, Mrs. Elizabeth Elbert, and others, at discretion of exrs.
Mentions: the firms of Rae, Whitefield & Co.; Rae, Elbert & Graham; slaves bought from Joshua Lockwood of Charleston; property in Ireland called "Killein"; plantation called "Rae's Hall", near Savannah; an island known as "Little Island", a tract on Hutchinson Island.
Exrs: wife, Rebecca; neph., James Rae; friends, S. Elbert, Leonard Marbury, George Whitefield.
Wit: James Gordon, Francis Bagbie, Thomas Taylor.

REHM, CATHERINE B.
Oct. 9, 1789; Feb. 18, 1794.
Wife of Dr. Frederick Rehm of S.C.
By will of Henry Bourquin, late of Little Ogeechee, dec., "I am seized and possessed of lands in my own right independent of the power and control of my husband."
To dau: Henrietta Hoskins, wife of Zachariah Hoskins.
To sons: John Bartholomew Waldburger, Jacob Henry Waldburger, who are exrs.
Wit: George Hipp, William Anderson, John Sealy Harrison.

RING, CHRISTOPHER   Planter.
Dec. --- 1787; Feb. 3, 1792.
To wife: Ann Margaret.
To sons: John and William Ring.
To dau: Mary, wife of Hessian Judge Advocate, John Hineman, now in Europe.
To sister: Agnes Parker.
Mentions: his property in Savannah.
Exrs: wife, Ann Margaret, sons, John and William Ring.
Wit: Jacob Miller, Nicholas Hainer, Jr., J. Lehr'e.

RICHARDSON, GEORGE
May 30, 1791; June 8, 1791.

ABSTRACTS OF WILLS, CHATHAM COUNTY, GEORGIA

To wife: Margaret.
To nephs: Thomas, John, Joseph, and George, chil. of my bro., Thomas Richardson, butcher, of Dewbury in Yorkshire, London.
To wife's neph: Samuel, son of Roderick Pelton of Charleston, S.C.
Mentions: his property in Savannah where he lives, adjoining the property of Mrs. Sophia Young and Noble Wimberly Jones; also a lot, the property of the Rev. John Joachim Zubly, dec.
Extx: wife, Margaret.
Wit: Simon Conner, Francis Vollotton, John Glass.

121 RUSSELL, JACOB
June 25, 1801; July 10, 1801.
To sons: Andrew, James, and Jacob.
To dau: Rebecca.
Mentions: relatives in Hassa, Franksburg.
Mentions: his lands in Effingham Co., which lands border on lands of David Lovell; bought lands from Weencoff.
Exrs: friends, John Herb, Frederick Herb, Esqrs.
Wit: W. Gardner, Joseph Rahn.

RADIGNEY, CHARLES
Oct. 22, 1798; Oct. 31, 1798.
"Born in Mortray, Province of Normandie, France, Inhabitant of Quartier D'Aquea, Island of St. Domingo, but now living in Savannah."
To wife: Mary Frances Girard, born in Paris, only heir.
Mentions: his property in France, St. Domingo, and elsewhere; and a receipt for a note to M. Francis Laincrie.
Exrs: friends, M. Lewis Micholas Allard, and M. Francis Laincrie of Savannah.
Wit: Isadore Stouf, Borden, and Thomas Decheneaux.

ROGERS, AUGUSTUS
Sept. 15, 1796; Nov. 9, 1796.
Master of Schooner Commerce.
To mother: Mary Reives of Long Island, N.Y.
To friend: Miss Elizabeth Kinder.
To friends: Messrs. Johnston, Robertson & Co., merchants in Savannah.
Wit: Jeremiah Fisher, Thomas Sadler, -- Barnard.
Testified to in Baltimore Co., by Thomas Sadler, -- Barnard, and William Buckanan, that the testator died the day after the date of the will without signing his name.

ROBERTS, JOHN H.
Feb. 10, 1798; Feb. 16, 1798.
To wife: Henrietta.
To sons: John Howell Roberts, Thomas Hilbert Roberts, left in care of Conradt Hilbert.
Exrs: wife, Henrietta, and friend, John Millen.
Wit: John Lawson, John Hamilton.

Will Book "B"

122 ROLFES, FREDERICK
Apr. 13, 1783; May 5, 1783.
All to William George Rolfes, Theresa Rolfes, Elizabeth Ann Rolfes.
Mentions: his lands in East Florida, which were sold under the British Government.
Exr: Joseph Woodruff, Esqr.
Wit: John Kell, Frederick Shick, Richard Howley.

REINSTETLER, JOHN MATHIAS   Planter.
Dec. 11, 1776; No date.
Of Vernonsburgh.
Ref. is made to deed of gift to Benjamin Goldwire, carpenter, dated Nov. 12, 1764, and recorded on the 20th., for certain property in trust for Susannah Tubear, wife of David Tubear, gunsmith, and her chil., Mary and Elizabeth Tubear. "But this (deed) may be lost, due to anarchy and confusion in this state, attending the unhappy contest between Great Britain and America."
Exr: bro-in-law, David Tubear.
Wit: Thomas Hamilton, Robert Hamilton, Thomas Morgain, Robert McDonald.

ROBE, FRANCIS
Apr. 16, 1778; Nov. 7, 1782.
To gr. son: John Milledge, the younger, gentleman.
To gr. dau: Mary Elizabeth, wife of Raymond Demere, Esqr.
Mentions: his lands on Skidaway Island; lands in Burke Co.; lands in Savannah.
Exrs: John Milledge, Jr., Raymond Demere.
Wit: Elizabeth Drummond, John B. Girardeau, Charles Milledge.

READDICK, PETER   Planter.
Aug. 21, 1778; Oct. 28, 1778.
All to wife: Catterenah.
Chil: Jacob, Gaspar, Sallome, Mary, Nancy, Sophie, Catterenah, Elizabeth.
Exrs: wife, Catterenah; bro., Michael Readdick.
Wit: James Galache, Henry Densler, Salome Readdick.
Codicil with same date and wit. as the will.
To son: Jacob, a tract of land called "Pine Island".

RUSH, JOSEPH, JR.
Sept. 19, 1784; Nov. 1, 1784.
Of Sunbury.
Everything to father, Joseph Rush, Sr., shipwright, of Phil.
Wit: John Sellington, William Brown.
A codicil gives legacy to friend, Dunworth, and appoints him "exr. of all effects in the state of Georgia, North Carolina, and all over the world."
Attested by Richard Sisk and John Sellington.

REMSHARDT, JOHN   Tanner.
Aug. 15, 1782; Nov. 20, 1782.
Of Effingham Co.
To only son: Daniel.
To daus: Catherina, Judy, ---, and Hannah.
Mentions: his lands in Effingham Co., which lands border on lands of John Flerl, John Snider, Dr. Myers, Ulrick Fetzer, Capt. Polhill; money paid to Mr. Vertsch.
Exrs: Nicholas Shubdrein, Jonathan Zipperer of Effingham Co.
Wit: Samuel Kraus, Emanuel Keiffer, Israel Reiser.
Note: The other daughter's name, not given, is believed to be Salome.

RAE, JOHN   Planter.
Apr. 12, 1777; Aug. 26, 1778.
To sister: Jane Somerville.
To Miss Ann Somerville.
To Miss Elizabeth and Miss Caty, daus. of Col. Samuel Elbert.
To Cornelis Richeson.
Mentions: his lands about twelve miles above Augusta, called "Garmency Island".
Exrs: sister, Jane Somerville, Robert Rae; Samuel Elbert.
Wit: Richard Guinn, Sarah Guinn, Mary Muere.

ABSTRACTS OF WILLS, CHATHAM COUNTY, GEORGIA

124 ROSS, WILLIAM   Gentleman.
May 30, 1783; May 2, 1786.
To bros: Hugh and Donald Ross.
To sisters: Sarah Ross, and Ann, widow, of Shadrack Wright.
Exrs: bro., Donald Ross, and James Chapman.
Wit: James Meyers, Jacob Readdick, James Whitefield.

RABENHORST, ANN BARBARA
June 30, 1779; Oct. 10, 1783.
Of St. Matthew's Parish.
To sister: Maria Rosina Krafft, in Ravensburg, Suabia.
To sisters-in-law: Mary Hoppe, in Daber, Sophy Neumann, in Berlin; and Christiana.
To the Orphan House at Halle, in Germany, and the East Indies, 40 pounds each.
To Joseph Schubtrein, negro slaves.
Mentions: that she wishes to be buried at Zion, where her husband and child are buried.
Exrs: friends, Joseph Schubtrein, Jacob Casper Waldhauer.
Wit: Israel Leimberger, Jacob Mock, John George Zitterauer.

RAYNES, JOSEPH   Planter.
No date; Nov. 29, 1784.
To wife: Sophia.
Mentions: his chil., not named.
Mentions: his lands in St. Andrew's Parish, which lands border on lands of Lewis Mattier.
Exrs: wife, Sophia; William Trenfield; Thomas Brownhill.
Wit: John McMahan, William Hill.

Will Book "C"

ROSS, HUGH   Gentleman.
Aug. 26, 1786; June 21, 1790.
To bro. and sister: Donald and Sarah Ross, rights in the estate of Hugh and William Ross, dec.
Exrs: bro., Donald Ross, gentleman, and James Chapman.
Wit: John Simpson, Francis Bigbee.

125 RUSSELL, JANE
Mch. 20, 1790; Apr. 14, 1790.
Relict of William Russell.
To neph: James Galache, son of my bro., James Galache.
To niece: Louisa Galache, dau. of bro., James.
To William Mills, son of John Mills and Anna, his wife, both dec.
To Jane Mills, dau. of John Mills and wife, Anna.
To Ann Elizabeth Mills, dau. of John Mills and Anna, his wife.
Mentions: that these three Mills chil. own property in England.
Mentions: "money due my late husband from Nicholas Haner"; land adjoining the land of Dr. Macleod and Mrs. Goldsmith; bond money due from Joseph Habersham, Esqr.
Exrs: Joseph Habersham, William Stephens.
Wit: W. Jones, Aug. Mayer, George Jones.

ROSS, SARAH   Spinster.
June 19, 1790; Dec. 27, 1790.
To Jane Ross, the dau. of Thomas Ross, Esqr., formerly of the State, property left by father and bros., William and Hugh Ross, dec.
Exr: bro., Donald Ross, merchant.
Wit: John Beatty, Andrew Johnston.

ROSS, DONALD   Gentleman.
Dec. 18, 1790; Feb. 25, 1791.
To neph. and niece: John Alexander Graham Ross and Jane Ross, the son and dau. of my sister, Jane Ross of New Providence, Chatham Co.
To neph: William Wright, son of my dec. sister, Ann Clark, formerly Ann Wright.
To neph: Mark Clark, son of William and the said Ann Clark.
To bro: William Ross.
To friend: James Chapman, the house occupied by Dr. John Beatty.
To Leonard Cecil, Esqr., money to free a negro woman, the property of James Mossman, Esqr., "as a reward for her care of me during an illness."
Mentions: lands purchased from John Walean, Esqr., called "Burnside Island".
Exrs: friends, James Mossman, Leonard Cecil, Esqrs.
Wit: Dr. John Beatty, Patrick Crookshanks, James Mirrilies.

Will Book "D"

RICE, JOHN
May 16, 1802; Mch. 8, 1803.
To my chil: Catherine, Sarah, and James Rice.
Extx: dau., Catherine.
Wit: Thomas Norton, Nathaniel Moxley, Adam Cloud.

ROBERTSON, ANDREW
Nov. 29, 1802; Oct. 6, 1803.
"Being bound for Liverpool."
To James Johnston, Jun.
To goddau: Susan B. Robertson of Charleston, S.C.
To Alexander and Daniel Robertson.
"It was my intention to have married Ann Roche, dau. of William Roche, dec., when I return, I leave her my property."
Exrs: James Johnston, James Robertson, merchants.
Wit: Matthew Johnston, Owen Jones.

ROBERTSON, JAMES
Jan. 12, 1802; June 6, 1803.
To wife: Jean Nisbitt.
To dau: Bellamy, a negro presented to her by Dr. Thomas Taylor of Jamaica, and sold to John Piles of Camden Co.
To bros: William, Alexander, Andrew, and Daniel Robertson.
Exrs: wife, Jean Nisbitt, who is also Gdn. of my chil.; bro., William Robertson of Charleston, S.C.; bros-in-law, Mathew Johnson, James Johnson, Jr., William Johnson, all of Savannah.
Wit: Sheftall Sheftall, Isaac Benedix, Douglas Anderson.

READ, GEORGE PADDON, ESQR.
May 19, 1805; Nov. 4, 1805.
To Jacob Read, Jun., eldest son of my bro., Jacob.
To neph: William George Read, son of my bro., Jacob.
To nieces: Mary Read Simons, eldest dau., and Eliza Susannah, second dau., of my sister, Elizabeth dec.
To James Read, the son of my bro., James Bond Read.
To sister-in-law: Mrs. Ann Louisa Read, wife of the said Dr. James Bond Read.
Mentions: his father, James Read, dec.
Mentions: his lands in St. Matthew's Parish, now Liberty Co., given him by Hon. Grey Elliott; a tract of land on the Canouche; a tract of land on the Altamahaw, the forfeited property of John and Hugh Poulsons.
Exrs. and Gdns: bros., Jacob Read, James Bond Read.
Wit: Andrew Johnson, S. Wagoner, Jacob Theiss.

ABSTRACTS OF WILLS, CHATHAM COUNTY, GEORGIA

Will Book "E"

RONEY, DANIEL   Shopkeeper.
Sept. 8, 1808; Nov. 14, 1808.
To Mrs. Margaret O'Conner, the wife of Peter O'Conner, shopkeeper.
Exrs: friends, Peter O'Conner, William Thompson, shopkeeper.
Wit: John Dillon, Henry Bourquin, Jun., John Grimes.

ROPER, WILLIAM
Sept. 25, 1808; Nov. 14, 1808.
To mother: Ann McLaughlin.
To orphan child: Elza.
To Margaret Corrient.
To Sarah Roper.
Mentions: his lands in Goshen; money due N. Corrient estate, papers in Gen.
Mitchell's hands, money due from I. Metzer's estate.
Exrs: Ann McLaughlin, Michael Long.
Wit: Michael Long, G. Shick, Joab H. Prosser, Alexander Fawn.

RIGGON, LEVIN
Feb. 25, 1811; Apr. 1, 1811.
To three daus: Sarah, Nancy, and Mary.
Exrs: Selby Franklin, Patrick Duffy.
Wit: Owen Hughes, John Pettibone.

RIFFAULT, CHARLES
Mch. 10, 1813; June 8, 1813.
To child: not named.
Extx. and Gdn: wife, Mary.
Wit: Ant. Carles, P. H. R. Lachicotte, Paul P. Thomassen.
Will translated by F. D. Patit de Villers.

READ, GEN. JACOB   Atty-at-law.
Nov. 19, 1801; July 25, 1816.
Of Charleston, S.C., now in New Port, R.I.
To two sons: Jacob and William George Read.
To two daus: Catherine Ann Louisa and Cornelia Annabella Read.
Mentions: his father-in-law, David Van Horne, dec., of N.Y., merchant; also his
father, the Hon. James Read, dec., of Savannah.
Mentions: debts due in Great Britain as co-partner of Messrs. Read & Mossman;
"as I have full charge of my late father's estate, I divide among my bros. and
sisters, namely, Dr. William Read, Mrs. Susannah Rose, wife of Hugh Rose, Esqr.,
George Paddon Read, Eliza Simons, wife of Thomas Simons, Esqr., and James Bond
Read."
Exrs: wife, Catherine; bros., Dr. William Read, George Paddon Read; bro-in-law
and friend, Thomas Simons.
Gdns: wife, Catherine, and William Read.
Wit: Gen. John Rutledge, James Hamilton, Chris G. Champlin.
Codicil dated Dec. 15, 1802.
Mentions: since making his will, his sister, Elizabeth Simons (Eliza in will),
wife of Thomas Simons of Charleston, S.C., has departed this life.
Child in esse.
Exrs: son, Jacob Read, friend, Thomas Winstanly.
Wit: Benjamin Hazard, Edward G. Senter, Daniel Latham, Jun.
Codicil dated June 27, 1816.
To the chil. of the late Thomas Simons, dec., the property left them by their
uncle, George Paddon Read, dec.
To friend: James Wallace.
Wit: Arabella Ann Dart, Catherine Johnson, Philip Moore.
Father proved by Dr. Richard Latham, and Jacob Read by Nathaniel Green Cleary of
Charleston, S.C.

S

Will Book "A"

129 SOMERVILLE, JANE   Widow.
Sept. 10, 1779; Feb. 28, 1781.
Of Augusta.
To neph: Robert Rae.
To niece: Ann Somerville, a lot formerly belonging to her father, Edward Somerville.
To goddau: Ann Johnston, a tract of land formerly belonging to her father, Richard Johnston of Augusta.
To Elizabeth Church, dau. of the wife of Col. Robert Rae.
To uncle: Robert Rae of Augusta.
To cousin: James Rae.
To Elizabeth Elbert, wife of Col. Samuel Elbert.
To Isabella Habersham, dau. of Col. Samuel Elbert and wife of Col. Joseph Habersham.
To Sarah, dau. of Col. Samuel Elbert and wife of Richard Guinn.
Exrs: Col. Robert Rae, Col. Samuel Elbert, and James Rae.
Wit: J. Grierson, Andrew Johnston, Robert Howe.

STIRK, SAMUEL, ESQR.
Mch. 1, 1793; Aug. --- 1793.
To son: John Williamson Stirk, under twelve yrs. of age.
To neph: Benjamin, son of my late bro., Benjamin Stirk, now living with Sir George Houstoun.
To bros: Nathan and Joseph Stirk.
To friends: Mr. John Williamson and his wife, for care of my son since his mother's death.
To friend: Charles Harris, law books.
Exrs: John Williamson, Charles Harris, Joseph Clay, the younger, William Stephens, and my neph., Benjamin Stirk.
Wit: --- Waldburger, Thomas Netherclift, Jr., John Long.

SMITH, JOHN
July 3, 1793; Feb. 11, 1794.
Of St. Peter's Parish, Purysburg, S.C.
130 To sons: Archibald and John Smith.
To daus: Elizabeth, and Sarah, wife of Sir James Wright.
Mentions: his plantation at New River, St. Peter's Parish, Purysburg, S.C.; lands on Coosawhatchie.
Exrs: wife, Elizabeth, and daus., Elizabeth Smith, Sarah Wright.
Wit: Mary Ann Cowper, John Smith, Jr., John McQueen.

SILSBY, DANIEL
Jan. 11, 1791; Dec. 16, 1791.
Native of Mass., formerly of the state of Georgia, afterwards of the state of S.C.; at present of Stamford St., in Parish of Christ Church, in Co. of Surry, Kingdom of Great Britain, gentleman.
"With God's permission to embark for America."
To sisters: Sarah and Abigail Silsby, spinsters, of Boston; Mary, widow of Ezra Curtain of Boston.
To bro: Sampson Silsby of Boston.
To nephs: Daniel Silsby Curtain, son of sister, Mary Curtain; Enoch Silsby of Boston, age about twelve yrs.
To niece: Ann Curtain, dau. of sister, Mary Curtain.
To cousin: Samuel Silsby, son of uncle, Samuel Silsby of Lynn, Mass.
To mother-in-law: Patience Silsby (sic) of Mass.

ABSTRACTS OF WILLS, CHATHAM COUNTY, GEORGIA

To friends: William Gouthit of old Fish St., London, and Paul Hamilton, late of Charleston, S.C., but now of Gibralter Row, Parish of St. George, Co. of Surry, gentleman.
Mentions: that he owns a half part in a store, wharf, and other buildings on the bluff in Savannah. "The said premises were lately in the possession of Owen Owens and William Thompson of Savannah, merchants and partners."
Mentions: lands in other parts of America in hands of John Ansley, George Bainbridge, and Thomas Gould, merchants and co-partners, lately carrying on business under the name or firm of Harrison, Ansley & Co., at 52 Bread St., London, Eng.
Mentions: his property in England.
Exrs: William Gouthit, Paul Hamilton.
Wit: Samuel Philips, John Stevens, Robert Hopper, clerks to Lincoln Inn and Middle Temple.
Enoch Silsby qualified as Adm. of the estate on Mch. 10, 1809.

131 SCRANTON, DANIEL
Apr. 5, 1793; Dec. 4, 1793.
To mother: Amy Scranton.
To bro: John Scranton.
Exr: John Coxe.
Wit: Benjamin Lloyd, Andrew Galache, William Northrop.

SEYMOUR, RICHARD   Gentleman.
June 11, 1793; Mch. 29, 1794.
To Louisa, wife of Dr. John Love, and to her chil.
Exr: Dr. John Love.
Wit: Dr. Benjamin Putman, James Nelson, Henry W. Williams.

SPIERS, ALEXANDER JOHNSTON   Merchant.
No date; Apr. 2, 1794.
To godchil: Mary Wallace, Georgia W. Owens, Samuel Spiers Ewing, James Spiers Montford, and Jean Dean in Providence.
To Samuel Dickinson.
To friends: Joseph Miller and Edward Wright of Savannah, merchants.
Mentions: that he owns property jointly with Patrick Crookshanks and Robert Montford.
Exr: Joseph Miller.
Wit: William Moore, Stephen Files, Robert F. Murdock.

SPALDING, JAMES   Planter.
Nov. 1, 1794; Feb. 5, 1795.
Of St. Simon's Island.
To son: Thomas Spalding.
To present wife: Margery.
Exrs: son, Thomas Spalding, and Thomas Gibbons, atty-at-law.
Wit: William McIntosh, John Hamilton, Charles Harris.
The exrs. refused to qualify, wit. by William Ulmer, Aug. 27, 1795.

STEBBINS, FRANCIS   Planter.
June 30, 1795; Feb. 23, 1796.
To wife: Rebecca.
To bro: Edward Stebbins.
To dau: Frances Louisa Stebbins.
Child in esse.
132 Mentions: that he wishes his sister, Diggins, living in New England, to take care of his chil. if his wife dies.
Mentions: his property in Savannah adjoining the property of Mrs. Hamilton and Mrs. Hill.

Exrs: wife, Rebecca, and bro., Edward Stebbins.
Wit: John Turner, Charles Jenkins, James Whitefield.

SALLE, VALENTINE
Aug. 2, 1797; Aug. 4, 1797.
To father and mother, not named.
To uncle: Anthony Chaix of Sevilla, Spain.
To Francis Davis of Cherokee Hill.
To Charles Maie.
To Mrs. Raimbeau.
To Mr. Joseph Porteli.
Mentions: a business connection with Paul Antoine Verriere and Valentine Casimer Pincon; the firm of Valentine Salle & Paul Anthony Verriere, purchased goods from Andrew Anthoion, living in N.Y.
Exrs: M. Bontineau Des'reviaux, John Deville.
Wit: Charles Maie, Jr., Anthony Verriere, --- Verdery, John Deville, John Anthony Aselin.

SIMPSON, JAMES   Planter.
Dec. 18, 1798; Dec. 26, 1798.
To Richard, son of Richard Shingleton of S.C., Round O.
Mentions: that he wishes Richard Keating to beat out his crop of rice at Mrs. Stebbins plantation.
Exrs: Mr. Richard Keating, Mr. Henry Woods, Col. Daniel Stewart.
Testified by Solomon Benjamin Smith, who states that Richard Keating Sr. and Jr. were present.

SMITH, CAPT. JOHN CARRAWAY
Oct. 26, 1799; May 5, 1800.
To wife: Ann.
To bro: Aaron Smith, Esqr.
To sister: Martha Deveaux, the property left by her mother, not named.
To niece: Elenor Ann Smith, dau. of bro., Aaron Smith.
Mentions: plantation called "Mount Hope", in S.C.; slaves left by gr. father of my wife, and her sister, Martha Deveaux.
133 Dr. George Aspinwall in attendance when sick.
Exrs: wife, Ann, and bro., Aaron Smith.
Wit: Dr. George Aspinwall, Richard Keating, Mrs. Keating.

SCHEUBER, JUSTUS HARTMAN
No date; Mch. 4, 1801.
To wife: Priscilla.
To John Sanscalotte Scheuber.
To stepsister: Margareth Schwalin, the house where Mr. Benedix lives.
To Mr. Michael Germain's dau., Ann.
To Mr. Balthasar Shaffer's chil.
To Polly Norton.
To the Union Society of Savannah.
Mentions: a bond and mortgage due from Mr. Abraham Bird; a note and mortgage due from Mrs. Barbara Keiffer; cattle in care of Mr. Asa Tanner; a bill of sale of Thomas Young for slaves; lands on the Great Ogeechee River; lot on the Bay; property in Savannah.
Exrs: wife, Priscilla; Balthasar Shaffer; William Henry Lange.
Wit: Isaac Benedix, postmaster.

SMITH, JOHN   Baker.
June 6, 1804; ----
To cousins: the chil. of my uncle, P. Smith of the Parish and Village of Foldishoffon, Germany.

ABSTRACTS OF WILLS, CHATHAM COUNTY, GEORGIA

To nephs., nieces, and bro., not named.
Mentions: that the property on Barnard and Duke Sts., to be sold and the money sent to Germany, to "George friederich hofman in Younholtzhousen, or in the English language, 'Younwoodhousen', and to the alter son of my alter bro.", not named.
The order of the estate entered on the minutes; he died in 1824 leaving real and personal estate in Ga., but no kin capable of inheriting. Was a citizen of the U.S. at the time of the adoption of the constitution.
Certain persons in Germany representing things and heirs of John Leonard Stephen Smith, claimed the property.
Patrick Abraham was named as an exr. in Germany.
John Smith was a lunatic, and had a Gdn. appointed by the Superior Court.
Temporary Adm: Frederick Herb, sworn the 19th of May, 1823.
Frederick Herb, Moses Cleland, Jacob Shaffer, and David Bell, adm. bond for $20,000, Aug. 5, 1822.
Samuel M. Bond testified that John Smith was not of sound mind for a long time previous to his death.
Wit: John Anderson, Abraham Becu, John Sugden.
Note: This will was forty-three pages long, written closely on both sides of the paper. Testator preached four long sermons to his relatives.

Will Book "B"

SIMMONS, JOHN   Bricklayer.
Jan. 21, 1784; June 26, 1784.
Son of Walter Simmons.
To two chil: Elizabeth and Frances.
Mentions: his houses and tenements in Stepney Parish, near St. George's Fields; two houses in Drury Lane, in the Co. of Heresfordshire; debts in Ga. for schooling chil.; lands on Little Ogeechee.
Exrs: wife, Elizabeth; David Montaigue.
Wit: Dr. John Wandin, Aaron Moore, James Wilson.

SIMPSON, WINIFRED
Nov. 15, 1786; Jan. 3, 1787.
To husband: James Simpson.
Remainder to Mr. Daniel Nunes and David Montaigue, who are exrs.
Wit: Peter Pourchet, Moses Simons, George Rolfes.

SAVAGE, THOMAS   Planter.
Feb. 22, 1786; June 10, 1786.
Of Charleston, S.C.
To wife: Mary Elliott Savage, sole legatee, and Gdn. to chil.
Exrs: wife, Mary; Thomas Heyward, Esqr.; Dr. Thomas Tuder Tucker; John Wereat; Mr. Samuel Legare; Mr. James Butler.
Wit: Simon Tufts, Samuel Stone, Benjamin Legare.

STONE, ELIZABETH
Dec. 7, 1785; Jan. 6, 1786.
Residence: Buckland Hall.
To husband: Thomas Stone.
To goddau: Elizabeth Butler Maxwell.
To Miss Ruthy Jones.
To dau-in-law: Susannah Stewart, a slave named in will of my late husband, James Stewart of Liberty Co.
Exrs: husband, Thomas Stone, friends, George Walton, William Maxwell.
Wit: Constant Maxwell, James Dunwoody, J.P., and Ruthy Jones.

STIRK, JOHN
Oct. 21, 1776; Dec. 7, 1781.
Of St. Matthew's Parish.
To son: Benjamin.
To wife: Hannah.
To bros: Benjamin, Samuel, Nathan, and Joseph, forty pounds each, when they attain the age of twenty, money now in the hands of father, Nathan Stirk.
Exrs: wife, Hannah, and bro., Samuel.
Wit: Edward Jones, Leonard Marbury, William Lambeth.

SIGFRITZ, GEORGE
Mch. 9, 1775; Nov. 19, 1777.
Exr: friend, Abraham Gable, sole heir.
Wit: Thomas Ross, Thomas Burns, James Neilson.

Will Book "C"

STILES, BENJAMIN
Nov. 7, 1789; Nov. 18, 1789.
To neph. and niece: Joseph and Jane Stiles, chil. of my bro., Samuel Stiles, Esqr.
To sister: Mrs. Frances Lightbourne of Bermuda.
To Mrs. Mary Wilkinson, dau. of Mrs. Frances Lightbourne.
To two daus: not named, of Mrs. Mary Wilkinson.
Mentions: that he wishes to be buried on Green Island.
Exrs: bro., Samuel Stiles, Esqr.; neph., Joseph Stiles; William Clark, Esqr.
Wit: James B. Sharp, Henry Montford, George Wilson.

136 SHAD, CATHERINE
Sept. 4, 1778; Aug. 12, 1790.
Of Wilmington Island.
Widow of Solomon Shad.
To son: Solomon Shad.
To daus: Margaret Shad and Ann Bessett, wife of William Bessett.
Exrs: friends, Frederick Treutlen, John Farley.
Wit: Banister Winn, John Gilbert.

SAVAGE, MARY ELLIOTT
Oct. 31, 1786; Mch. 27, 1790.
Of Charleston District, S.C.
Residence: White Point, Church St. No. 1.
To sons: William Butler Savage, Benjamin, and Thomas.
To daus: Susannah Parsons Savage, Mary Savage, and Elizabeth, the wife of Thomas Heyward, Jun., Esqr.
Mentions: "My mother, Elizabeth Butler, by her will dated Nov. 21, 1775, bequeathed to my chil. several tracts of land on the south side of the Great Ogeechee about 3,364 acres, 'Back Plantation' included."
Mentions: her lands on Harleston, formerly the "Garden"; land eight miles from Charleston, adjoining the public road leading from the City of Ashley Ferry, known as "Green Grove"; tract of land on Great Ogeechee River on the north side called "Point Plantation"; lands on the south side of the Great Ogeechee known as "Sterling Bluff"; lands on the Ogeechee adjoining Fort Argyle; lands known as "Silk Hope", on the south side of Great Ogeechee River; lands on the north side of Canoochee River called "Thorogood"; lands on Red Bird Creek called "James Point".
Gdns: cousin, William Elliott; friends, the Hon. Thomas Heyward, Jun., Esqr., Dr. Thomas Tudor Tucker, Mr. Samuel Legere of Charleston, John Wereatt, Esqr., James Butler of Ga.; and son, Thomas, when he arrives at the age of twenty-one yrs.

ABSTRACTS OF WILLS, CHATHAM COUNTY, GEORGIA

Exrs: Thomas Heyward, William Elliott, John Wereatt.
Wit: Simon Tufts, Samuel Stone, Francis Baker.
On Mch. 7, 1791, the Misses Sarah and Hester Minis wit. to the handwriting of Mrs. Mary Elliott Savage, signed Esther and Sally Minis.

137 SPENCER, GEORGE BASIL
No date; Feb. 28, 1791.
To four chil: William Joseph, Samuel, Ann, and Mary.
To wife: Elizabeth.
To Josiah Gotier.
Mentions: his wharf at end of public St. called Abercorn.
Exrs: wife, Elizabeth, bros., Joseph William and William Henry Spencer.
Attested by his two bros.
Mr. Mitchell, atty-at-law, drew up the will.

Will Book "D"

SANDRIDGE, DAVID   Merchant.
Sept. 9, 1802; Nov. 6, 1802.
Native of Spotsylvania, Va., late of Savannah, now a planter in St. Peter's Parish, Beaufort District, S.C., but at present in Savannah.
To father and mother: not named.
To bros: Austin and James Sandridge.
To four sisters: Suffier Holliday, Nancy Bronaugh, Winnifred Boxley, and Elizabeth Sandridge.
Mentions: his property in S.C.; property near Fredericksburg, Va.; property in LaFayette Co., Ky., near a village called "Mount Sterling", bought of John Childs; owes money in Europe.
Exrs: bro., Austin; Robert Bolton, George Anderson of Savannah, merchants; Samuel Fairchild of St. Luke's Parish, S.C.
Wit: Richard M. Stites, Edward Griffith, Daniel Bigbee.

STORIE, JOHN   Tailor.
July 10, 1793; Apr. 4, 1803.
To wife: Margaret.
To Archibald Clark, the son of my said wife by a former husband.
Mentions: his land in Savannah sold to William Stephens, and David Brydie Mitchell, Esqr., bearing date June 26, 1791.
Exrs: wife, Margaret; William Stephens; David Brydie Mitchell.
Wit: Joseph Welscher, Coshman Polash, Moses Cleland.

138 SCHUMAKER, PETER   Watchmaker.
Oct. 21, 1803; Dec. 5, 1803.
To friend: John Henry Dupont, thirty watches.
To Maria Susannah Toflere.
Exrs: John Henry Dupont, George Buffet.
Wit: John Williams, John Caflish, James M. Willson.

SHICK, FREDERICK
No date; Jan. 28, 1804.
To wife: Elizabeth Shick, formerly known by the name of Elizabeth Welscher.
To bro: Peter Shick.
To Solomon Nessler, now known as and called Thomas Shick.
Exrs: wife, Elizabeth, bro., Peter Shick.
Wit: John Clay, William Clarkson, James M. Willson.

SCOTT, JOSEPH JAMES   Planter.
Jan. 18, 1804; Nov. 16, 1804.

Of St. Luke's Parish, Beaufort District, S.C.
To daus: Sarah Pope, Catherine Howkins Scott, Ann Scott, and Martha Scott.
Mentions: his dau., Hannah Jenkins, dec.
To sons: Joseph Adams Scott, John Scott, and Benjamin Franklin Scott.
To bro: John Scott.
To gr. dau: Catherine Adams Jenkins.
To gr. son: Joseph Scott Pope.
Exrs: Joseph Adams Scott, William Pope, John Bolton.
Wit: Daniel W. Mongin, George H. Davidson, Thomas M. Newell.
Certified by Charles J. Jenkins.

SEAVER, PETER JOHONNAT
Dec. 1, 1802; June 3, 1805.
To infant dau: Elizabeth Grafton Woodbridge Seaver.
Gdns: sister, Mrs. Mary Woodbridge, wife of Thomas M. Woodbridge; Mrs. Dorcas Woodbridge.
Exrs: Thomas March Woodbridge, Joseph Mavhin, Thomas F. Williams.
Wit: William J. Hobby, John McIntosh, Henry Pelham.

139 SPENCER, JOHN
Dec. 19, 1805; July 8, 1806.
Of Effingham Co.
To Mary Louisa Holzendorf, dau. of John Holzendorf, Sr.
To John Russell Taylor.
To sister: Susannah Rogers.
To Ann and Mary Spencer, daus. of George Basset Spencer.
To nephs: Samuel Spencer, William Joseph Spencer.
To bro: William Henry Spencer.
Mentions: his plantation called "Fifteen Mile House", purchased from the Ebenezer congregation; and "my sword which was my companion during the American Revolution, I bequeath to William Joseph Spencer."
Exrs: bro., William Henry Spencer; nephs., William Joseph Spencer, Samuel Spencer.
Wit: Jeremiah Cuyler.

Will Book "E"

STORR, JOHN   Merchant.
June 15, 1797; Sept. 25, 1807.
Of Nassau, New Providence, Bahama Islands.
To wife: Helen.
To sons: John, Thomas, and George Kincaid Storr.
To neph: John Storr of England.
To niece: Martha Storr of England.
To John Wilson, merchant, in Hull, Yorkshire.
Mentions: his father, dec.
Mentions: the firm of Storr & Reid, merchants.
Exrs. and Gdns: wife, Helen Storr; Alexander Begbie; Walter Turnbull; James Moss; Charles McKennen; Anthony Atkinson of Hull, Yorkshire; and sons when of age.
Wit: William McLeod, Robert Thompson, John Thompson.
Codicil dated Feb. 12, 1803.
To wife: Helen.
Mentions: his plantation on Watlington Island.
Walter Turnbull's name to be obliterated from the exrs. because he has removed from the Island, and appoints Patrick Kincaid of the City of Execter, England, in his place.
Same wit. as in will.

ABSTRACTS OF WILLS, CHATHAM COUNTY, GEORGIA

140 SHEFTALL, LEVI
July 4, 1808; Mch. 7, 1809.
To wife: Sarah.
To sons: Solomon, Abraham, Emanuel, Mordecai, Benjamin.
Mentions: his son, Levi, dec., a minor, died in Charleston, S.C. On his death bed requested his uncle, Mr. Emanuel D. L'Motte to remember he left his property to godson and bro., Abraham Sheftall.
To daus: Hannah, Judith, Abigail Minis Sheftall, Pearla, the wife of Isaac Russell, and Sarah Delyon, the wife of Abraham Delyon.
Exrs: wife, Sarah; daus., Hannah and Judith Sheftall; Benjamin Mordecai Emanuel.
Wit: Josiah Penfield, Joseph McBride, U. Tobler.

STEBBINS, REBECCA   Widow.
Dec. 5, 1807; May 10, 1808.
To daus: Frances L. and Rebecca L. Stebbins.
To two gr. chil: Edward A. and John Davies, sons of my late son, Edward L. Davies, dec.
To son: William Davies, atty-at-law.
Mentions: her property on the Bay and Drayton St.
Exrs: son, William Davies; bro., Edward Lloyd, and Charles Harris.
Wit: Sarah Murray, Eliza Wood, Thomas Edward Lloyd.

SILSBY, SARAH   Single Woman.
Aug. 26, 1808; Oct. 27, 1808.
Of Boston.
To sister: Abigail Silsby.
To bro: Samson Silsby.
Exrs: David Shillaber of Boston, trader, Charles Harris of Savannah.
Wit: Sarah Pike, Charles Cunningham, R. Chamberlain.

SIMMONS, PAUL   Merchant.
May 22, 1806; Dec. 5, 1809.
To bros: Sampson, Montague, Somerville, and Moses.
To cousins: Luckey (Hester) Harris, "who is now married to a gentleman in London whose name I do not know"; Sally Marks, widow, of Charleston, S.C.
To Lazarus Harris of London.
141 To friend: Andrew Harris of Jacksonborough, S.C.
To neph: Moses Simons, who is now in College at New Haven.
To housekeeper: Hannah Leion, and to her chil., David and Ritta Leion.
Mentions: his house and lot in Beresfort St., Charleston, S.C., lot in Savannah, adjoining the property of Green R. Duke and the estate of Joseph Roberts, dec.
Exrs: bros., Sampson and Montague Simons.
Wit: John Pooler, Thomas Robertson, F. T. Flyming.

SIMS, JAMES
Nov. 24, 1807; Mch. 5, 1810.
To sons: James and William Richard Sims.
To daus: Mary, Rachel, and Esther.
To wife: Sarah.
To gr. dau: Sarah Elizabeth Graves.
Exrs: wife, Sarah; son, James Sims; John Waters.
Wit: Daniel Roney, William Riggs, Henry W. Williams.

SAVERY, JOHN
Mch. 9, 1810; June 6, 1810.
To son: George Sanders Savery, now in the West Indies.
To dau-in-law: Margaret Jane Savery.
Exrs: son, George Sanders Savery; dau-in-law, Margaret Jane Savery; John Pooler.
Wit: Ann Pooler, Ellen S. Ledger, John Fraser.

SMITH, ELIZABETH
Mch. 15, 1809; Mch. 5, 1810.
Widow of John Smith of S.C.
To daus: Jane Bourke, widow; Elizabeth Smith; Mary Cowper, widow; Anne McQueen; Sarah Wright, wife of Sir James Wright.
To son: Archibald.
To gr. daus: Elizabeth and Catherine Bourke; Elizabeth T., Helen T., Jane Wallace Smith; Mary Ann and Margaret Cowper; Eliza Mackey; Sarah Williamson.
To gr. sons: William McQueen, Thomas Bourke, Archibald Smith.
To dau-in-law: Helen Smith.
To Eliza Tubley, now Mrs. M'Agill.
To Isabella and Elizabeth Hunter.

142 Mentions: her lot in Beaufort; Islands of Oatlands; lot near the Filature in Savannah; lot on the Bay now occupied by Mr. Steinert; lands in Camden Co., which lands were sold to John H. McIntosh, Esqr.; lands called "Red Bluff" in S.C.; lot called "Hawthorne Lot" in Savannah.
Extxs: daus: Mary Cowper, Jane Bourke, Elizabeth Smith, Sarah Wright.
Wit: Isabella and Betsey Hunter.

STUTZ, JOSEPH
No date; Apr. 1, 1811.
To mother: Jane Griggs.
To dau: Jane Ann Stutz.
To nieces: Margaret and Eliza Adams, daus. of Edmund Adams, dec.
To half-bro: Samuel Griggs.
To sister: Elizabeth Parker, wife of Ebenezer Parker, and to her chil., not named.
To George Stutz Parker.
Exrs: John Eppinger, Capt. George Herb, Robert S. Gibson.
Wit: James Eppinger, Edmund Roberts, John Eppinger, Jun.

SCOTT, GAVIN   Hairdresser.
No date; Feb. 3, 1812.
To sister: Jane Scott of Glasgow, Scotland.
To bro: not named.
Mentions: his property in Savannah near Mr. Fell's lot.
Exrs: friend, Robert Fair, shoemaker, and Thomas Williams, mariner.
Wit: G. Campbell, James Madden.

SHAFFER, BALTHASAR, ESQR.
June 14, 1810; June 3, 1811.
To wife: Mary Ann Gertrude.
To dau: Hannah.
To sons: John William, eldest, Simon Peter, George, James, Frederick, and Jacob.
To gr. chil: Joseph Lawrence and Sarah Shaffer, chil. of my son, John, dec.; Elizabeth Margaret and Harriot Shaffer, chil. of my son, James, dec.; John Martin Gugle; chil. of my son., Frederick, not named.
Mentions: his wife's dower, the lands formerly of John P. Langs, under lease to
143 John Glass; two houses in Carpenter's Row in Savannah; lot in Ewensbergh; lot in New Leids; lands in the upper part of Oglethorpe Ward, formerly the village of St. Gall; money due to Mr. John Smith.
Gdns: George and Jacob Shaffer, for the chil. of Hannah and Simon Peter Shaffer.
Exrs: George and Jacob Shaffer, Ulrick Tobler, Jeremiah Cuyler.
Wit: Joseph S. Pelot, Caleb Harryson, Philip Jones.
Codicil dated Jan. 5, 1811.
Appoints his son, Frederick, one of the exrs. of his will.
Wit: George Myers, Jun., Randsom Stone, George Penny.

STUART, ANN   Spinster.
Apr. 18, 1812; Dec. 8, 1812.

ABSTRACTS OF WILLS, CHATHAM COUNTY, GEORGIA

To Mrs. Ann Maxwell, widow of Simon Maxwell.
To John Houstoun McIntosh.
To Catherine Ann McIntosh, dau. of John A. McIntosh.
To Mrs. Eunice Hogg.
To Mrs. Sarah Johnston, widow of the printer.
To Mrs. Elizabeth Box.
To Mrs. Martha Stevens, sister of Mrs. Hogg.
To Philip Box.
To Mr. John Lawson.
Mentions: her lot on Broughton St.
Exrs: John H. McIntosh, John Lawson.
Wit: Philipen Box, E. Fort, Charles Dunham.

SCULL, ANN   Widow.
Jan. 11, 1816; May 6, 1816.
To dau-in-law: Mary Scull.
To nieces: not named.
To friend: Mary Hinley.
Exrs: John Helvinstein, Willian Sims.
Wit: John Lillibridge, William King, John Dawson.

STITES, RICHARD MONTGOMERY   Atty-at-law.
Feb. 26, 1811; Jan. 26, 1813.
To three chil: Richard Wayne Stites, Eliza Clifford Stites, Sarah Anderson Stites.
To mother: Sarah C. Noel.
Mentions: his wife, not named, dec., buried in Savannah.
To sister: Mrs. Anderson.
To friend: Mrs. Eliza Anderson.
To Eliza Dennis, dau. of Richard Dennis.
To James M. Wayne.
To the chil. of George Anderson, Esqr.
To the chil. of Richard Wayne, that is, Mary and Eliza C. Wayne.
To cousins: Abraham Stites of Ky., and John Stites Mitchell.
To Sampson Mordecai.
To the Chatham Academy.
Mentions: his daus, Eliza and Sarah, to be in the care of my friend, Mrs. Eliza Anderson, and son, Richard, now in the West.
Mentions: his circuit business to be taken care of by my friends, Cuyler & Davies; plantation called "Oryza" and "Wayne Ham" on the Little Satilla; house on Reynolds Square and other property in Savannah; property from the estate of Richard Wayne, Esqr.; a small plantation in Elbert Co.
Exrs: George Anderson, James M. Wayne, Thomas Young, William B. Bulloch.
Wit: John Eppinger, S. Mordecai, William Nichol.
Codicil not dated.
To mother: Sarah C. Noel.
To Mrs. Eliza Clifford Anderson, wife of George Anderson.
Wit: S. Mordecai, Eliza Arnold, John C. Nicoll.

SPENCER, WILLIAM HENRY
Feb. 25, 1817; Apr. 8, 1817.
Of Little Ogeechee Dist.
To wife: Lucretia.
To sons: James John Whittendel Spencer and William Spencer.
To dau: Elizabeth Spencer.
Mentions: his lands in McIntosh Co., on the Altamaha River; property in Savannah; lands on Little Ogeechee.
Exrs: wife, Lucretia, and son, James John Whittendel Spencer, when he is twenty-one yrs.
Wit: William Davies, George W. Owens, John Drysdale.

145 SMITH, JANE
July 1809.
Mentions: slaves to be the right of my chil. if it meets with the approbation of Eliza Postell and J. B. Porcher.
"It is my wish that my servant Binah be given to Rachel, Black Binah be given to Josie, Eliza to be given to Maria. My husband has mentioned his intention of giving Lydia to Jane A. Postell. I wish Violet to be given to Mary J. Sweet."
Wit: Uel Merrill.

T

Will Book "A"

146 THOMPSON, WILLIAM
Dec. 2, 1782; May 10, 1794.
Extx: wife, Sarah, sole heir.
Wit: Isaac Raaily, Thomas Croitey, John Joyner, Capt. of the S.C. ---, and Thomas White, Lieut.

TREUTLEN, FREDERICK   Planter.
Feb. 17, 1798; Nov. 15, 1798.
Of Wilmington Island.
To wife: Margaret.
To daus: Catherine; and Ann, wife of Peter Provost.
Exrs: John Tebeau, William Lewden.
Wit: John Dillon, Henry Addington, Ann Mary Dillon.

TERRIEN, JOHN
June 24, 1797; July 2, 1797.
Exrs: wife, not named, and Louis Huguenet.
Wit: Pierre Michel Joseph Minant, Pierre Guenin, Gabriel Ivonet, Charles Harris, atty-at-law, Dr. Martin, surgeon.

THOMPSON, WILLIAM   Merchant.
Mch. 12, 1794; Mch. 18, 1794.
To friend and partner: Owen Owens.
To Mrs. Rebecca Judah.
To Miss Jean, eldest dau. of Mr. James Johnston, printer.
To friend: James Dickson.
To Mathew Johnston, merchant.
Mentions: his stores and wharf under the Bluff, and other property in Savannah.
Exrs: Owen Owens, Mathew Johnston.
Wit: Thomas Gibbons, Edmund Bacon, Robert Dillon.

TRANDFIELD, MARY   Widow.
May 26, 1797; June 17, 1797.
To daus: Elizabeth Doyle, Polly Trandfield, Sarah Trandfield.
147 To godson: John Davis, son of Frank Davis.
Mentions: her property on Broughton St., where she lives.
Exr: Frank Davis, who is Gdn. for dau., Sarah.
Wit: Thomas Norton, Thomas Palmer, John Gable.

THOISON, DE LA ST. MARE
Aug. 18, 1798; Jan. 19, 1801.
To Bergrand Gagel, who is to look after the affairs.
To Mr. Caradue, the eldest.
To goddau: De La toison dee Jour, dau. of my uncle, De la Toison Roche blanche.

ABSTRACTS OF WILLS, CHATHAM COUNTY, GEORGIA

To the three sons of Mr. Caradue, that is, Hercule, Agathe, and Archille of St. Domingo, now living in Carolina about eleven miles from Charleston.
Wit: Charles Harris, Sheftall Sheftall, Charles Manns.

Will Book "B"

THOMPSON, WILLIAM   Merchant.
Mch. 23, 1786; Nov. 22, 1786.
"If bro. John be still alive, twenty pounds."
All to friend, Thomas Anderson, carpenter, "for the love I bear him."
Mentions: debts due to himself and dec. bro., James Thompson, in Ga. and S.C.; lands in Ga. and S.C.
Exrs: Thomas Anderson, John Foulis.
Wit: John Thompson, Edward Griffith, James Hogg.

THREADCRAFT, GEORGE
Apr. 29, 1742; May 4, 1785.
To bro: Thomas Threadcraft.
To son: George, and "my chil."
Mentions: his property on Wanaman River.
Exrs: wife, Esther, and bro., James Lesesne.
Wit: William Cripps, William Poole, Abraham Warnock, Henry Warner.
Note: Copy of will attested in Charleston by John Vanderhorst, Sec. of State.
Sarah, a dau. of the above George Threadcraft, was the wife of Gen. Lachlan McIntosh.
James Lesesne, was wife's bro. C.P.W.

TURNER, LEWIS   Planter.
July 22, 1784; Mch. 9, 1786.
To wife: Jesten.
To sons: Richard, John, and Lewis.
To daus: Sarah Jenkins, Lucy Barnard, Ann Barnard, and Elizabeth Turner.
Mentions: his estate on Whitemarsh Island, where he lives; land in St. Mary's Parish, which lands border on lands of James Simmons.
Exrs: sons, Richard and John.
Wit: William Barnard, Nicholas Bouchonneau, William Gilbert.

TONDEE, PETER   Carpenter.
Oct. 21, 1775; Aug. 29, 1776.
Died Oct. 22, 1775.
Extx: wife, Lucy.
"My own chil."
Wit: intended, Peter Gandy, gentleman; William Pickering, tailor; Hon. William Young, Esqr., now dec.; Jacob Oates, now dec.
In re. the above will: Record Room, Savannah Court House, Book "H", pp. 61-62-63.
"Heirs at law" of Peter Tondee: son, Charles Tondee; daus., Mary, wife of Benjamin Jones; Elizabeth, wife of Nicholas Champagn or Champi; Ann, wife of Elisha Elon; Lucy, wife of John Hero. Nov. 7, 1789. C.P.W.

Will Book "C"

TEISSIER, STEPHEN   Merchant.
June 2, 1789; June 26, 1789.
To friend: John Frederick Kachler, who is exr.
Wit: John Hamilton, James Simpson, Abraham Becu.

149 TUFT, SYNISTON
Jan. 16, 1790; Jan. 27, 1790.
To bro: John Tuft.
To sister-in-law: Elizabeth Trenchard.
To sister: Elizabeth Clark.
To bro-in-law: Edward Trenchard.
Mentions: his plantation in N.J. township called "Piles Grove."
Exrs: friend, John Fisher, Joseph Stiles.
Wit: John Hale, William Pinder, J. G. Taylor.

Will Book "D"

THOMPSON, JANE   Widow.
Nov. 9, 1786; July 10, 1800.
To son: Samuel Shelly.
To Burke Pooler, son of John Pooler, Esqr.
Exr. and Gdn: John Pooler.
Wit: Simon Conner, Joseph Welscher.

THIRD, JOHN
Mch. 1, 1801; Jan. 3, 1803.
In trust to John Gardiner, shoemaker and tanner.
"I have a dau. married to Thomas Stiff, hair-dresser and perfumer in Phil."
Mentions: ground rent to be paid to L. H. Holsendorf.
Exr: John Hoseberry.
Proved by John Gardiner.

THOMPSON, WILLIAM   Mariner.
Feb. 26, 1803; Mch. 3, 1803.
"I do hereby declare to leave to my bro., Joseph Thompson of Warren Co., all my property whatever."
Wit: Christopher Gunn, Thomas French, Le Mercier, priest, rector of St. John's Church.

150 TATTNALL, JOSIAH, JUN.
Feb. 13, 1803; Dec. 5, 1803.
"About to sail to Europe with his family".
Mentions: his wife, dec. Does not name wife or chil.
To the chil. of my dec. bro., John M. Tattnall, not named.
To the chil. of the late Macartin Campbell, Esqr., vis. Maria Kollock, Sarah, Martha, Harriett, and Edward Campbell.
Mentions: his plantation called "Bonaventure".
Exrs: neph., Josiah M. Tattnall; George Jones; Nichol Turnbull; William Stephens; Ebenezer Jackson.
Wit: Joseph Habersham, Barach Gibbons, James Hunter.

TEW, PARACLETE   Physician.
Jan. 6, 1802; May 3, 1802.
Of Bryan Co.
To niece: Henrietta Allen.
To friends: Edward Harden, James Benjamin Maxwell, Obadiah Jones.
Exrs: Edward Harden, James Benjamin Maxwell.
Wit: B. B. Bellinger.

TURNER, LEWIS   Planter.
July 11, 1800; July 28, 1803.
To sister: Elizabeth Whiting.
To Lewis T. Whiting, son of Elizabeth Whiting.

ABSTRACTS OF WILLS, CHATHAM COUNTY, GEORGIA

To bro: John Turner.
To Ann Lucy and Lewis Turner Whiting.
To the chil. of my bro., Richard Turner.
To Lewis Turner, son of Richard Turner.
Mentions: his plantation on Wilmington Island.
Exrs: bros., Richard and John Turner; Solomon Shad.
Wit: Charles Harris, James Bullock, M. Sheftall.

Will Book "E"

TEBEAU, JOHN   Planter.
Apr. 30, 1807; Dec. 7, 1807.
To wife: Catherine.
To sons: Frederick Edmond Tebeau. Charles Watson Tebeau.
Exrs: wife and sons.
Wit: W. B. Bulloch, Thomas Whitefield, William B. Maxwell.

TELFAIR, EDWARD
Nov. 6, 1799; Jan. 4, 1808.
To wife: Sarah.
To sons: Josiah, Thomas, and Alexander.
To daus: Mary, Sarah, and Margaret.
Exrs: William Gibbons, Jun., Barrach Gibbons.
Wit: William Scott, John P. Williamson, James T. Coit.
Codicil dated July 19, 1802.
Mentions: his sons, to be exrs. when they reach the age of twenty-one yrs.
He wishes his exrs. to see that he be placed in a rough wooden coffin with common nails in it, and black crape only for such as may incline to mourn.
Wit: N. W. Jones, Ralph Clay, Ann Clay.

TIOTT, CHARLES   Gentleman.
July 6, 1799; Jan. 2, 1809.
To wife: Sarah.
To dau: Charlotte, age about six yrs.
To son: Charles, Jun., about thirteen yrs. old, born of my first wife, Ann Macquinear.
Mentions: his two lots in Savannah; lot in Ewensburgh; the estate worth about $14,000.
Exr. and Gdn: Robert Bolton, Esqr.
Wit: Samuel Smith, Archibald Wilkins, Richard H. Leake.

TIOTT, CHARLES, SR.
Division of estate, Feb. 25, 1813; made on application of John Waters, William A. Moore, Seth G. Threadcraft.
Dr. Moses Sheftall to take charge of the property, rents, etc., the property being in various locations in the City, that is, Mr. Howes' Vandue Store, Michael's Store.
Mentions: Mr. Kopman and Mr. William Starr, the hatter.
Mrs. Eliza Swain can furnish information.
Legatees: Sarah and Charles Tiott, exrs.
Wit: Joseph Abendanone.
William Starr testifies that Joseph Abendanone, dec., signed his name Jan. 4, 1816.

TRUSHET, CHARLES
Oct. 12, 1810; Dec. 3, 1810.
To mother: Elizabeth Trushet.
To Levan Newman Mitchell. "After my mother's death the child, Levan Newman Mitchell, to be taken from his mother and raised by my friend, Henry Tucker."

Mentions: his lot in Yamacraw.
Exrs: friends, Henry Tucker, Jacob Strobart.
Wit: Nathaniel Wade, Elias Woodruff, G. R. Duke.

TAYLOR, MRS. ANNE
Oct. 21, 1812; Dec. 2, 1812.
To Mrs. Mary Deveaux, wife of Peter Deveaux, Esqr.
Exrs: Peter Deveaux, William Stephens, Esqr.
Wit: Charles Stephens, Eliza Box, William A. Moore.

TURNER, JOSEPH
Feb. 26, 1813; Apr. 14, 1813.
Late collector of St. Simon's Island, Glynn Co.
To four chil: Joseph, William, Emeline, and Albert G.
Exrs: son, Joseph Turner, at present of St. Simons; John Couper; William Page of St. Simons, Esqr.; James White, Esqr., of Savannah.
Wit: John G. White, S. White, J. G. Almy.

THREADCRAFT, ELIZABETH   Widow.
May 13, 1815; July 20, 1815.
To gr. daus: Esther Caroline, Julia Maria, Mary Catherine, and Elizabeth Margaret Threadcraft.
To gr. son: George Threadcraft.
Exrs: son, Seth G. Threadcraft, and Charles Harris.
Wit: Charles Ulmer, Keziah Ulmer, William J. Spencer.

153 TUFTS, JANE JUDITH
Apr. 13, 1816; Apr. 26, 1816.
To husband: Francis Tufts.
To bro-in-law: Gardner Tufts.
Mentions: lands originally granted to John Hanner, which were conveyed on Apr. 7, 1795, "by my father, Benedict Bourquin to John Jacob Bourquin for my separate use".
No exrs. mentioned.
Wit: James Willey, George F. Wing, Mary Ann Werage.

THOMPSON, LEWIS B.   Shopkeeper.
No date; June 6, 1816.
To Maj. Thomas Bourke in trust, who is exr.
Wit: Thomas F. Williams, Christian D. Labey, John Anderson.

TATNALL, JOSIAH, JUN.
Division of estate, Jan. 14, 1816; made on application of James Hunter, Noble W. Jones, Alexander Telfair, John Glen, and William Barnard.
Legatees: Harriett, Edward F., and Josiah Tatnall, now a minor.

<u>U</u>

Will Book "D"

154 ULMER, PHILIP, SR.   Planter.
Mch. 11, 1806; July 9, 1806.
Of Laurel Hill.
To wife: Ann.
To eldest son: William, and to his son, Philip.
To my two younger sons: Charles and Philip.
To John Fitzpatrick and to his wife, my dau., Eliza, and to their chil., Ann, Philip, and Eliza Fitzpatrick.
To Anne, Eliza, and Mary, chil. of my son, Charles.

ABSTRACTS OF WILLS, CHATHAM COUNTY, GEORGIA

Mentions: his property known as "Ritter's land".
Exrs: sons, Charles and Philip Ulmer of Effingham Co., and Christopher Frederick Triebner of Savannah.
Wit: Samuel Howard, Peter Deveaux, John Y. White.

Will Book "E"

ULLAM, JOHN
Oct. 24, 1807; Dec. 7, 1807.
Belonging to the Guard of Savannah Town.
To Henry Haugens, mariner and Adm., belonging to the Guard of the same Port.
Mentions: money due from Thomas Dowell and Capt. Knaric.
Wit: Charles Frederickson, Caleb Brainard, Joseph Gockler.

ULMER, WILLIAM
Sept. 22, 1808; Nov. 14, 1808.
To wife: not named.
To my only child and son, Philip.
Exr: bro., Philip Ulmer, who is to rear his son.
Wit: Elias Robert, Eliza Fitzpatrick.

V

Will Book "A"

155 VALLOTON, DAVID MOSES   Cordwainer.
Apr. 12, 1794; Jan. 25, 1795.
To wife: Mary.
To sons: Moses, Jeremiah Oliver, Paul Jonathan, and Benjamin Volloton.
To dau: Mary Glass.
Mentions: lands in Burke Co., originally granted to Richard Capers, and bought in the name of Moses Valloton, the younger, son of the said David Moses Vollotton; lands originally the lands of James Papott; property in Ewensburgh.
Exrs: wife, Mary, and son, Moses.
Wit: John Eppinger, Christopher Gugel, Peter Miller or Millen.
Codicil dated Apr. 13, 1794.
To dau: Mary Glass.
Mentions: his lands in Liberty Co.
Same wit. as will.

VESSEY, ABRAHAM   Mariner.
July 12, 1800; Mch. 3, 1801.
Of Bryan Co.
To wife: Joanna.
To mother: Elizabeth Vessey.
To three nieces: Sarah, Nancy, and Fanny Crawford.
Mentions: his property on Island of Bermuda, known as the "Cross Lane House" and the "Salt Kittle House".
Exrs: Robert Bolton, William Belcher.
Wit: John Lawson, William Brown, George Throops.

Will Book "E"

156 VILLEPONTOUX, JANE
May 22, 1812; June 15, 1813.
Widow of the late Benjamin Villepontoux, factor, of Charleston, S.C.

To daus: Maria Williamson Villepontoux, Frances Susannah Villepontoux, who are extxs.
Wit: Slaughter Cowling, M. W. Cowling, N. W. Jones.

VALLOTTON, ELIZABETH   Widow.
Aug. 9, 1809; Oct. 18, 1813.
To son: Jeremiah.
To daus: Elizabeth Fenden, Elizabeth Martin, Elizabeth Johnson, Elizabeth Stevens, now Elizabeth Guinn; Ann Vallotton Patterson; Harriott Vallotton Tubbs.
Mentions: an action was entered in the Court of Equity in S.C. for land by James Vallotton and Elizabeth Vallotton, whose maiden name was Knott, as heir of Jeremiah Knott, against Humphrey Somers, half the land to William Patterson and the other half to me, Elizabeth Vallotton.
Bondsmen: William Lewden, Paul Vallotton.
Wit: William McFarland, John Pettibone, John Y. White.

W

Will Book "A"

157 WILLIAMS, STEPHEN   Planter.
--- 1790; July 20, 1792.
Of Little Ogeechee.
To dau: Polly, and "all my chil."
Exrs: James Cochran, Esqr., Col. John Elliott, Mr. Richard Milton, Thomas Francis Williams.
Wit: S. Russell, Ann Russell, Alexander Keith.

WALLACE, WILLIAM   Schoolmaster.
Oct. 4, 1792; Oct. 5, 1792.
To friend: Mrs. Ann Thiess, widow of Peter Thiess, who is sole heir and extx.
Wit: John Carson, Andrew Lebey, Baker Solomon.

WAY, MARTHA   Spinster.
May 4, 1794; Mch. 25, 1795.
Of Liberty Co., now of Savannah.
To sisters: Susannah Fielder and Rebecca Way.
To bro: Moses Way.
Exrs: Richard Fielder, merchant, of Savannah, and John Way, planter, of Liberty Co.
Wit: Joseph Miller, George Throop, John Cunningham.

WALDBURGER, JOHN BARTHOLOMEW
Nov. 29, 1797; Apr. 6, 1801.
To wife: Sarah.
To dau: Anne.
To son: John Alexander Waldburger, minor.
To Jacob Waldburger.
To Thomas, son of John Morel.
To the chil. of Henrietta, wife of Zachariah Hoskins.
158 Mentions: his lands in Glynn Co., granted to Bartholomew Zouberbuler; lands in St. Peter's Parish, S.C.; lands in Effingham Co.; lands in Camden Co.; lands in Savannah.
Exrs: John G. Williamson, John Morel, Donald McLean, Mathew McAllister, Zachariah Hoskins.
Wit: Stephen S. Williams, Benedict Bourquin, Margaret Bourquin.

ABSTRACTS OF WILLS, CHATHAM COUNTY, GEORGIA

WATTS, JOSEPH   Planter.
Feb. 28, 1795; July 14, 1796.
Of Burke Co.
To bros: James, John, and William Watts, of Liverpool, Eng.
To Sally, dau. of Ebenezer Hills.
To daus. of Balthasar Shaffer.
To Harford and William Watts, sons of Harford Montgomery.
To George Lord of Augusta.
Rings to John H. Montgomery, Stratford Brown, John McIver, Ebenezer Hills, Sally Hills, David Reid, Patrick Hays of Augusta, George Lord, Balthasar Shaffer.
Mentions: his friends, Balthasar Shaffer of Savannah, and Patrick Hays of Augusta, as "friends valuable and truly honest"; he wishes to be buried near his friend, John Hall in Burke Co., where his (John Hall's) parents also lie.
Mentions: his property in Liberty Co.; property in Wilkes Co.
Exrs: Patrick Hays, Balthasar Shaffer, Stratford Brown, John Harford Montgomery, Ebenezer Hills.
Wit: George J. Hull, Robert Mein, Mathew Eppinger.

WALDBURGE, JACOB
Dec. 17, 1796; Apr. 1, 1797.
To wife: not named.
To sons: Jacob and George, minors.
To nephs: David and George Keall.
To bro: Bartholomew Waldburge.
To sister: Henrietta Hoskins.
To Mrs. Henrietta B. Jones.
To George Millens, a ring.
To the Union Society of Savannah.
Refers to marriage settlement with present wife.
Mentions: that Georgia is the only state which now admits the importation of slaves.
Mentions: his property in Savannah.
Exrs: John Morel, John Milledge, Donald McLeod, James Jones.
Wit: William Lamb, Sarah Evans, Sarah Jane Lamb.

WHITFIELD, ELIZABETH   Widow.
July 9, 1796; Sept. 4, 1798.
To gr. dau: Ann, dau. of my son, Dr. John Love and his wife, Louisa.
To gr. dau: Elizabeth, dau. of my dau., Elizabeth Mary Evans Johnston and Mathew Johnston, merchant.
To son: Dr. John Love.
To dau: Elizabeth Mary Evans Johnston.
To dau-in-law: Louisa.
Mentions: a grant to her gr. father, John Teasdale, in 1767 and to her uncle, John Teasdale, Jr., who was never in this country, both of whom died before the war, but which property was confiscated as British property; property in Savannah on Broughton St., and on the Bay now in the possession of Mathew Johnston, and other property occupied by Hillsmay, Woodbridge, and Thomas Smith.
Exr: son, Dr. John Love.
Wit: Ann Hamilton, D. B. Mitchell, James Box.

WILKINS, ANN   Widow.
Dec. 15, 1798; Feb. 27, 1799.
Of Exuma, one of the Bahama Islands, but now of Savannah.
To son: Samuel.
To daus: Martha and Elizabeth J.
To gr. son: Archibald O. Wilkins, son of Samuel.
Mentions: her property in the Bahamas; property in Savannah; property in Ga., on "Pipe Makers Swamp".
Extx: daus, Martha and Elizabeth J. Wilkins.

Wit: David Bettison, Seth G. Threadcraft, William Hobbs.

WILLSON, GOODWYN   Physician.
July 15, 1799; Apr. 9, 1800.
To ğoddau: Caroline Pooler, young dau. of T. S. Young.
To godson: Gilbert Naylor.
To Henry Jackson, "now living with me".
To James Box Young.
To Capt. William Smith, "my sword and musket".
To William Neal.
To G. R. Nale.
Exrs: James Box Young and William Smith.
Mathew McAllister and Josiah Tatnall attest to the handwriting.

WOODHOUSE, ROBERT   Merchant.
Mch. 19, 1800; July 10, 1800.
To bros: William, Archibald, and George.
To father and mother: Thomas and Elizabeth Woodhouse.
To the chil. of Agnes Shaw, late wife of James Shaw, blacksmith, of the village of Dalbeath, Co. of Galloway, Scotland.
To Mary, dau. of Sarah, widow of John Cusack, tailor.
Mentions: his property in Savannah.
Mentions: that he wishes the exrs. to buy slaves from James Mossman, Esqr.
Exrs: friend, Daniel Johnston of White Bluff, gentleman, and his neph., Daniel Johnston; Ulrick Tobler, merchant; Cunningham Newall, merchant.
Wit: John Lawson, Patrick Houstoun, George Glen.

WEREAT, JOHN   Planter.
Apr. 8, 1798; Feb. 1, 1799.
At present of Bryan Co.
To Gr. dau: Elizabeth Fishbourne.
To neph: Thomas Collier of Louisville, his mother, dec.
To Dr. Michael Burke.
Mentions: his dau. Ann Burke, dec.; and that he has no other relations by blood.
To Joseph Clay, Jun., and Thomas Savage, Esqrs., in trust for dau. Ann Burke, dec.
Mentions: that Dr. Michael Burke should occupy his house on Broughton and Whitaker Sts., and also the use of my lands on the Great Ogeechee River until Elizabeth should marry or need the property; lands adjoining the property on the Great Satilla River, purchased from the confiscated estates as formerly the property of Jonathan Belton; grant from the Province, now the State of S.C.; two tracts of land in Burke Co., originally granted to William Handley, late of Savannah, merchant; tract of land near the Augusta Creek, originally granted to James Muter, and by him sold to William Smith, and by the said William Smith to me; plantation in Columbia Co. called "Deverill", in three tracts granted to --- Anderson, --- Lewis, and Thomas Grierson, and by me purchased from the confiscated estates, adjoining a small grant to me on St. James Square; plantation in Columbia Co. called "Mount Hope"; lot in Hardwicke.
Exrs: Edward Telfair, James Jackson, Joseph Clay, Jun., Thomas Savage, Esqr., and Dr. Michael Burke.
Wit: John B. Wilkinson, A. Abrahams, Isaac Abrahams.

WATER, PETER   Shopkeeper.
July 26, 1801; Aug. 3, 1801.
To Elizabeth Colder, sole heir, wife of the late Thomas Colder.
Money to Thomas Dallaghan.
Money to Montmollin & Heron.
Extx: Elizabeth Colder.
Wit: Barnard Clissis; Jean Baptiste Audebert; J. S. De Montmollen.

ABSTRACTS OF WILLS, CHATHAM COUNTY, GEORGIA

WITZEN, NICHOLAS   Retailer.
Jan. 4, 1794; Jan. 6, 1794.
To parents: George Henrich Witzen and wife, Sophia, of Wovflet, Co. of Agen, Electorate of Hanover.
To my bro. and two sisters, not named.
To James Momford.
To David Lebey.
To John Haupt, Jun.
Exrs: John Gromet, John Haupt, Justus Hartman Scheuber.
Wit: Justus H. Scheuber, John Gromet, John Haupt, Claud Simon, Judith Lebey, widow.

WHITEFIELD, MARTHA   Widow.
June 6, 1796; Aug. 9, 1796.
Mentions: that she appoints Gen. James Jackson and James B. Young to take charge of all property of herself and chil., and directs that in the event of her death all her wearing apparel be given to Mrs. Sarah M. Day, in token of gratitude for her kindness.
Recommends that the relations take care of her step-mother, Mrs. Wright.
Wit: Eliza Box, Thomas R. Box.

WHITEFIELD, JAMES   Atty-at-law.
Sept. 2, 1795; Feb. 19, 1796.
To wife: Martha.
To sons: Thomas, James, George, and William.
To William Stephens, in trust for son, Thomas.
Mentions: his property in Savannah.
Exrs: wife, Martha, and sons, at age of seventeen.
Wit: John Berrien, Charles Jenkins, Peter Deveaux.

WADE, HEZEKIAH
Dec. 14, 1800; Apr. 6, 1801.
To wife: Mary Wade.
To chil: John M., Ann, Hezekiah, Nathaniel, Nehemiah, Elizabeth.
Mentions: that some of his slaves now in the possession of Alexander Gardner, Gen. John Barnwell, late of the Island of Portrogal, in S.C., dec.
Exrs: wife, Mary, and son, John M. Wade.
Wit: Elias Robert, William Possey.

Will Book "B"

WELLS, ANDREW ELTON
Jan. 7, 1776; Mch. 30, 1778.
To wife: Jane.
To chil: not named.
Exrs: wife, Jane; bro-in-law, John Sandiford; James Maxwell.
Wit: Anthony Norroway, Thomas Hamilton, Thomas Burns.

WYLLY, WILLIAM, ESQR.
May 25, 1774; No date.
To dau: Ann or Nancy.
To son: Thomas Wylly when he is sixteen.
Mentions: his lands on the Ogeechee; plantation on Cherokee Hill, "where I now live".
Mentions: that if no heirs, the estate to be placed in the hands of my bro., Richard, who is my exr., in trust for his son, Alexander, who receives the entire estate at the age of twenty-one.
Exrs: bro., Richard Wylly, James Habersham, Jun.

Wit: Israel Young, John Bowles, Philip Bowles.
Codicil dated May 26, 1774.
Gives freedom to slave, Ben.
Allots tract on Ogeechee to dau. Ann, and son, Thomas.
Same wit. as will.
Thomas Wylly gives bond for $1,200 for estate of William Wylly, dec., with Thomas R. C. Hamilton, William Alexander, and William C. Wylly, the 6th day of Jan. 1802.

164 WALKER, CHARLES   Planter.
Dec. 26, 1779; Oct. 21, 1783.
Of West Fla., Dist. of Mobile, Charlotte Co.
To bro: Joel Walker.
To neph: Joel Walker.
Mentions: his lands on Tombigby River known as "Horse Shoe Neck".
Exrs: neph., Joel Walker, Mr. Peter Swanson.
Wit: Robert McGillivray, Abraham Littell.
Thomas Brackett attests to handwriting of Robert McGillivray.

WHELOCK, THOMAS   Tavern-keeper.
Apr. 24, 1780; May 1, 1780.
To Frederick Bollinger.
Remainder to Elizabeth Hopt (Haupt) and Mary Bollinger.
Exrs: Benjamin Wright, Frederick Fahm.
Wit: William King, Charles Boyd, John Poullis, shopkeeper.
John Poullis says, "The said Thomas was an elderly man, tall, and not very fat."
Note: Elizabeth Bollinger, the dau. of Frederick, married first, John Haupt, and second, Charles Boyd.
Ref: Haupt, Gene. by M. F. La Far.

Will Book "C"

WARREN, JEREMIAH
Feb. 18, 1788; Mch. 31, 1788.
To bros: Goodloe and John Warren.
To William Downs of Wilkes Co.
Mentions: his property and slaves.
Exrs: William Downs and his son, Jonathan Downs.
Wit: Simons Maxwell, Alex Stephens.

165 WIGGINS, EDMUND
Apr. 21, 1789; Feb. 10, 1790.
To bro: John Wiggins.
To father and sister: not named.
Mentions: his lands bought of Thomas Norton.
Extx: wife, Mary Wiggins.
Wit: James Port, Thomas Palmer, Mary Palmer.

Will Book "D"

WEYMESS, WALTER Y.   Merchant.
Sept. 17, 1804; Nov. 5, 1804.
Of Savannah, late of Scotland.
To wife: Mary, sole heir.
Exrs: George Buckanan & Co.; William Dixon, James Dixon.
Wit: William Cocke, Matthew Shearer, James McConky.

ABSTRACTS OF WILLS, CHATHAM COUNTY, GEORGIA

WILLIAMS, JOSHUA   Overseer.
May 13, 1805; Aug. 5, 1805.
To "all my chil."
Exr: John G. Williamson.
Wit: Young Beckham, Patrick H. Brown.

WAYNE, ELIZABETH
Oct. 10, 1801; Nov. 4, 1805.
All to my husband, Richard Wayne, merchant, who is exr.
Wit: John Fry, John Wilds, Dimas Ponce.

WINN, BARNARD
Dec. --- 1805; Jan. 6, 1806.
To my beloved mother: not named.
To sister: Jane Williams.
Wit: John Pearson, Thomas Stewart, D. D. Williams.

Will Book "E"

166 WILSON, WILLIAM   Merchant.
Sept. 8, 1807; Dec. 7, 1807.
To wife: Ann Abigail.
To son: William.
To dau: Ann Maria.
To father: Thomas Wilson.
To mother: Hannah Wilson.
To bros: John and Thomas.
To sister: Mary Webster.
To neph: Thomas Wilson, son of bro., Thomas.
To James G. Greenhow.
To my wife's aunt, Mrs. Elizabeth Goldwire.
To James King.
To my wife's niece, Mary C. Lucas.
To Eliza Rudolph.
To Ebenezer Stark.
To Rev. Henry Holcombe.
To Rev. John Goldwire.
To the poor of the Parish of Branham, in Yorkshire, Eng.
Exrs: wife, Ann Abigail, and Ebenezer Stark.
Agent: Joel Bridge.
Wit: Benjamin Brooks, Joel Bridge, William Joyner, Thomas F. Williams.
Codicil dated Sept. 24, 1807.
Appoints Joel Bridge as an exr.
Same wit. as will.

WAYNE, MAJ. GEN. ANTHONY
July 14, 1794; Feb. 15, 1797.
Commander in chief of the Legion of the U. S. of America.
To only son: Isaac Wayne, student-at-law.
To only dau: Margaretta Atlee, wife of William R. Atlee, Esqr.
167 Mentions: his landed estate called "Waynesborough", in the township of East Town and Willis Town, in the Co. of Chester, Penn.; lot and three story brick house in Phil.; lot in Harrisburgh, in the Co. of Dauphin; "lands granted me by Congress for my services"; inland rice swamp on the waters of the Little Satilla in Co. of Camden, Ga., known as "Hazzard's Cowpen", mentioned in a deed of conveyance made to me by William Hazzard, Esqr., of S.C., in the year 1785; landed estates in Nova Scotia; lands granted me by the Legislature of Penn. for services as a Brig. Gen. during the late war.

Exrs: son, Isaac Wayne, friend, Sharp Delany, Esqr.; William Lewis, Esqr., of
Phil.
Wit: James O'Hara, Thomas Lewis, --- De Butts.
George Campbell, Esqr., registrar for probate of wills in Phil.

WAYNE, RICHARD   Merchant.
Oct. 21, 1808; July 13, 1809.
To sons: James Moore and William Clifford Wayne.
To daus: Elizabeth Clifford Wayne, wife of George Anderson, Esqr., and Mary
Stites, wife of R. M. Stites, Esqr.
To gr. sons: George Wayne Anderson, John Wayne Anderson, James William Anderson,
the sons of my dau., Elizabeth Clifford Anderson; Richard Wayne Stites.
To gr. daus: Elizabeth Mary Anderson; Elizabeth Clifford Stites, Sarah Anderson
Stites.
Trustees: for the four chil. of my son, Richard Wayne, viz. George Anderson,
R. M. Stites, and son, James Moore Wayne.
Mentions: his lands in Augusta; lands in Savannah.
Exrs: son, James Moore Wayne; George Anderson, R. M. Stites, Esqr.
Wit: Ephraim Cooper, Samuel S. Lightbourn, Henry Tucker.

168 WINECOFF, ANN ROSANNAH   Widow.
Oct. 4, 1810; May 12, 1812.
To dau: Catherine Winecoff, who is extx.
Wit: C. H. Dasher, John Wisenbaker, John Keebler.

WILLSON, WILLIAM
Feb. 15, 1813; Apr. 8, 1813.
Formerly of New Port, now residing in Ga.
To father: Jonathan Willson, Sr.
To sister: Sarah Tew.
To Jonathan Willson, Jun.
To Caleb Willson.
To niece: Mary Burdick, all of New Port, R. I.
Exrs: friends, John Lillibridge, Benjamin Raynes.
Wit: G. Shick, B. McKinne, Josiah Lawrence.

WELLS, ELIJAH
Sept. 16, 1814; Sept. 22, 1814.
To son: not named, now in N.H.
Mentions: notes due from Joseway Idlot.
Exrs: Isaac Minis, Robert Bleakly.
Wit: Isadore Stouf, Moses Herbert, merchant.

WHITE, MAJ. EDWARD
Aug. 23, 1806; Feb. 20, 1812.
To wife: Milcey S. White.
To sons: Benjamin Aspinwall White and Thomas White.
To dau: Maria Susannah White, not yet eight yrs. old.
To nephs: Edward Seaver and Benjamin Franklin Seaver.
To niece: Sucky White Seaver.
The Seaver chil. are chil. of my sister, Susannah Gore, wife of Samuel Gore, of
Boston; Susannah Gore was formerly the wife of Nathaniel Seaver of Boston,
merchant, dec.
Mentions: that should my wife marry again, my friend, Mrs. Mary Woodbridge or
her dau., Maria M. Woodbridge to be Gdn. of my dau., Maria Susannah White.
Mentions: his property in Savannah; the yellow house now occupied by Mrs.
Susannah Jenkins; "by deed of gift of land to my son, Benjamin, by my father-in-
169 law, James Stubbs, though in part I paid the money to Philip Milledge, I have
since bought about five acres adjoining my son's property at Sheriff's sale and

ABSTRACTS OF WILLS, CHATHAM COUNTY, GEORGIA

sold as the property of Richard Wylly"; sold negro girl to Mr. John Bigar; lot in Yamacraw; property in Glynn Co.
Mentions: land bought at Marshall's sale as estate of Hobkirk; military lands in Wabash Co., patent signed by John Adams, President of the U.S.; half of the purchase of rum with T. M. Woodbridge, Adventure to Bremin consigned to William Woodbridge; a demand against the estate of James Carter, dec., for amount of judgment costs, etc.; paid Edward Swarbrick exclusive of interest demands against Solomon Ellis, Esqr.; a cow given to my son Thomas, by Mrs. Robinson; $70.00 due by Mrs. Jane Adams for Parson Beck; $14.00 due by David Adams for a saddle and two chances in the land lottery of John Poullen; sold lot in Yamacraw to William Posey and was wit. by Thomas W. Rodman, alderman, Aug. 23, 1806; bond and mortgage against Charles Gachet.
Charles Harris or John M. Berrien to be the atty.
Exrs: bro., Oliver White; neph., Benjamin Franklin Seaver; friends, Charles Gachet, Thomas March Woodbridge; sons, Benjamin Aspinwall White and Thomas White, at the age of seventeen yrs.
Wit: Randsom Stone, John Love, John N. Brailsford.

WHITEFIELD, GEORGE   Merchant.
Nov. 12, 1812; Aug. 5, 1813.
To bros: William and Thomas.
To Miss Bellamy Crawford Robertson, "to whom I am bound by an ardent affection".
Mentions: lands bequeathed to bro., Thomas, by Gen. James Jackson; the firm of Johnston & Whitefield; lands in Savannah.
Exrs: father, Col. James Johnston, and his niece, Miss Bellamy C. Robertson.
Wit: James Morrison, Eliza Morrison, Eben S. Rees.

WILLIAMSON, JOHN G.   Planter.
July 2, 1812; May 2, 1814.
To son: John P.
To dau: Mary Ann Houstoun, the wife of Col. James Houstoun, late Mary Ann Williamson.
Mentions: his lands in Savannah, purchased from John D. Dickinson, and other property in Savannah; lands in the village of St. Gall, purchased from Ambrose Gordon, Esqr., dec.; "Brampton plantation", purchased from the heirs of Jonathan Bryan, dec.; plantation called "Retreat", purchased from Robert Mackey, Esqr., and Andrew Cooper McLean, the plantations adjoining.
Exrs: son, John P. Williamson; bro., William Henry Williamson; friend, William B. Bulloch, atty-at-law.
Wit: Robert Mackay, William A. Moore, John Kell.

WILLIAMS, JORDAN   Mariner.
Sept. 26, 1814; Oct. 12, 1814.
To friends: Henry Piper, Jack Scott, William Gilbert, James Dixon, Charles Jamieson, James W. Stewart, Thomas Carlton.
Mentions: "money due me as a seaman on board the U.S. Ship _Essex_, Capt. Porter, for services performed."
Exr: friend, Simon Jackson.
Wit: Levi D'Lyon, John Nolan.

WOOLF, JOHN   Planter.
Apr. 16, 1815; Sept. 4, 1815.
To wife: Penelope.
To sons: George, Charles, and Stephen.
To dau: Levina Bandy.
To gr. son: Josiah Hawthorn.
Mentions: two plantations; lands in Wayne Co.; money in hands of John Elkins.
Exrs: wife, Penelope; son, Stephen Woolf; John Vanbrackel.
Wit: Benjamin Varn, James King, Cader Vining.

171 WRIGHT, SARAH
Aug. 26, 1813; Apr. 26, 1816.
Wife of Sir James Wright, Bart. of Little Eating, Co. of Middlesex.
To nephs: John McQueen of Ga., William McQueen, James Wright.
To nieces: Margaret McQueen, Mary Ann Cowper, Eliza Mackay, Sarah Williamson, Catherine and Elizabeth Bourke.
To great-niece: Mary Ann Mackay.
To friend: Mrs. Heron.
"Everything left to me by my mother, so I have not mentioned my husband."
Mentions: her lands in Savannah; lands on Red Bluff, "bequeathed to me by my mother's will".
Atty: John McQueen.
Exr: John McQueen of Ga.
Wit: Archibald Smith of Savannah, merchant.

WILSON, MARY M.   Widow.
Oct. 10, 1816; Nov. 13, 1816.
To gr. dau: Ann Reynolds.
To bros. and sisters: not named.
Exrs. and Gdns: bro., Alexander Travis; William T. Williams; Isaac R. Douglas.
Wit: Anthony Porter, William R. Waring, A. B. Fannin.

WILLIAMS, THOMAS F.   Merchant.
Sept. 25, 1816; Dec. 12, 1816.
To wife: Sarah.
To dau: Hannah Lorke Williams.
To son: Ebenezer Hills Williams.
To Miss Hannah Hills.
To Mrs. Mary Stackhouse.
To Capt. Ebenezer Hills, his father, dec.
To Jane E. Clancy, the dau. of my mother's bro.
To Mary Ann Clancy, James' sister.
To bro: Stephen S. Williams.

172 To friend: George D. Sweet, "the care of all my manuscripts."
Mentions: that he acquits Mr. Thomas Hills of a balance due him on account; the property of S. S. Williams may be secured to him, at his death the same to go to his chil., Margaret C. and Stephen B. Williams; negroes in the possession of Capt. Marbury, and after the death of Mr. and Mrs. Marbury, belongs to the estate of our dec. father; the property awarded Richard Dennis by the Judge in Federal Court in suit against Stephen S. Williams has become mine by settlement with Richard Dennis.
Mentions: cattle purchased from the estate of William Butler and now in the care of Edward Bourquin; a house on the Filature lot; land on Crooked River; plantation called "Woodville".
Exrs: bro., Richard F. Williams, who owns a brick-yard; son, Ebenezer Hills Williams, who will be eighteen yrs. old on Feb. 15, 1831.
Wit: Stephen S. Williams, Hannah Hills, Jane E. Clancy.

WOOD, JAMES
July 17, 1811; Mch. 3, 1817.
To wife: Catherine Wood.
To dau: Mary Wood.
To stepdau: Elizabeth Prescott.
Mentions: his property in Savannah; lands in Wilkinson Co.
Exrs: wife, Catherine; Thomas J. Prescott; William Sawyer.
Wit: John Pettibone, James McAnnully, John Jones.

ABSTRACTS OF WILLS, CHATHAM COUNTY, GEORGIA

Y

Will Book "B"

173 YOUNG, ISAAC
Oct. 11, 1766; No date.
To wife: Martha.
To sons: William, Isaac, and Thomas.
To daus: Mary, when of age; Elizabeth Weddell.
Mentions: negroes now in the possession of Benjamin Weddell.
Extx: wife, Martha.
Wit: John Patton, John Benson, Frederick Churchill.

YOUNG, WILLIAM   Gentleman.
May 4, 1786; Mch. 10, 1787.
Of Charleston, S.C.
To friend: John Stewart of Savannah, sole heir and exr.
Wit: James McNeal, W. Hardy, John Low.

Will Book "D"

YOUNG, ELIZABETH
Mch. 29, 1804; May 18, 1804.
To Robert Dillon and wife, Christiana.
To Gen. James Jackson, in trust for his chil.
To nephs: John and Alfred Cuthbert.
To Miss Elizabeth Brabant.
To niece: Ann Wallace.
To bro: Joseph.
To bro: Ralph, in trust for his chil.
To father: in trust for my mother, neither named.
174 To William Wallace, in trust for my sister, Sarah, and her chil.
The context shows that her husband was the son of William Young and wife, Sophia.
Mentions: her property in Savannah; lands at White Bluff; lot in Yamacraw.
Mentions: that it is her desire that her slaves should be owned by such masters and mistresses as they may choose; my husband owes money to Francis Levett, the money in part sustained him while he was studying medicine.
Mention is also made in will of the firm of Willson & Young.
Exrs: Robert Dillon, Rev. Joseph Clay, Jun.
Wit: William Wallace, Mary Clay, Mary Gould.

Will Book "E"

YOUNG, THOMAS, ESQR.
Sept. 3, 1804; Nov. 14, 1808.
To the poor of the Parish of Dalmeny near the Queen's Ferry, Scotland.
To the Union Society of Savannah.
To Ann Nasmith and Sarah Patton, the two daus. of my uncle, the Rev. James Nasmith, dec.
To --- Parlene and Margaret Parlene, the two daus. of Margaret Parlene, dec.
To my old friend: Mr. James Kettle, writer, in Edinborough.
To Helen Fleming of Savannah.
To nephs: Thomas Young, the eldest son of Thomas Kettle and Sarah, his wife; Alexander Kettle.
To sister: Sarah Kettle.
Mention is made of a marriage settlement with his wife in Liberty Co.
Mentions: his house in Savannah; plantation called "Ham plantation".

175 Exrs: wife, Elizabeth; friends, James Benjamin Maxwell, Esqr., of Bryan Co.; the Rev. Thomas Kettle of Leuchars; James Kettle, writer, of Edinborough; nephs., Thomas Young, Alexander Kettle, when he is twenty-one yrs. old.
Wit: Thomas Palmer, Wansford Court; G. Tomlinson, London.
Subscribers: G. Woodruff, M. Houstoun, R. J. Houstoun.
Codicil dated August 7, 1806.
To Robert Mackay, Joseph Clay, Richard Stites, David B. Mitchell, William Bulloch, Andrew Turnbull, John Pray, all of Ga., property left in trust with the exrs. for my neph., Alexander Kettle.
Wit: Thomas Palmer, --- Tomlinson, G. Kenda, Copthall Court, London.

YOUNG, MARGARET
Aug. 4, 1793; Jan. 2, 1809.
To neph: John Miller.
To niece: Margaret Miller, chil. of Susannah and Philip Miller.
Exrs: friends, Philip Miller, William Lewden.
Wit: James Bulloch, David and Michael Miller.

YOUNG, ELIZABETH   Widow.
June 15, 1814; July 5, 1814.
To gr. nieces: Mary C. Maxwell, dau. of my neph., the late Thomas B. Maxwell and Mary Habersham Maxwell, his wife; Jane Eliza Pelot, dau. of James B. Maxwell; Esther or Hetty Maxwell, dau. of James B. Maxwell; Susan Jefferson Maxwell, dau. of James B. and Mary Habersham Maxwell.
To gr. nephs: John Maxwell, son of neph., John Butler Maxwell; John Stephens Maxwell, son of my late neph., Moultrie Maxwell; Richard, Henry, William, and Edward Footman, sons of my late niece, Elizabeth Caldwell Footman.
176 To James Habersham Maxwell, son of James B. Maxwell and Maria Schley Maxwell, his wife.
To the chil. of my dec. neph., Simon Maxwell, viz, Hannah G. Maxwell, James Alexander Maxwell, and Mary Maxwell.
To Maria McIntosh, dau. of Mrs. Mary McIntosh, late Mary Maxwell of Sunbury.
To Mrs. Mary Maxwell, widow of my late neph., Dr. John Maxwell, and her three chil., not named.
To the chil. of my late neph., Stephen Maxwell, not named.
To niece: Ellen or Nelly Flemming.
To sister: Constant Maxwell of Belfast.
Mentions: money left in trust to Thomas Young and John Jackson Maxwell, Esqrs., to be paid to Joseph S. Pelot for the support of Susan Jefferson Maxwell; the balance to the chil. of John Jackson, Simon, Dr. John, Stephen, and Moultrie Maxwell.
Exrs: Thomas Young, John Jackson Maxwell.
Wit: Jane Montgomery, Dr. James Bond Read.

Z

Will Book "A"

177 ZETTLER, NATHANIEL, SR.
June 16, 1800; Sept. 16, 1800.
Of St. Peter's Parish, S.C.
To three chil: Mary, Catherine, and Nathaniel Zettler, minors.
Mentions: lands in Effingham Co.; land in Savannah, now in the possession of Joseph Rahn.
Exrs: neph., Gideon Zettler of Ga.; Joseph Rahn.
Wit: Seth Stafford, Thomas Grimball, James Dupuis.

ABSTRACTS OF WILLS, CHATHAM COUNTY, GEORGIA

INDEX OF NAMES

Abendanone, Joseph	3
Abrahams, A.	161
A. D.	95
Abraham	104
Isaac	161
Joseph	104
Rebecca	104
Achord, Ann	3
Jane	(2)3
John S.	3
Lewis	3
Lewis D.	(2)3
Achors, Stephen	76
Adams, Ann	2,3,11
David	169
Edmund	142
Eliza	142
Jane	3,169
John	169
Margaret	3,142
N.	93
Nathaniel	2
	(2)3, 11, 12, 93,116
Samuel	11
Susan	3
Susannah M.	93
Thomas	(3)3
Addington, Henry	12,146
Aikin, Fleming	32
Alexander, Charles	1
William	163
Alger, James	3
Preserved	(2)3
Sarah	(2)3
Allard,	
M. Lewis Nicholas	121
Allen, Alex M.	(2)115
Garrett	29
George	31,67,96
George W.	22,96
George Washington	110
Henrietta	150
Jane	118
Mary E.	96
Mary Odensells	110
Robert	2
Robert H.	2
Allison, George	(2)25
Allman, Ann	2
Jane	1
Philip	(2)1
Almy	72
J. G.	152
Alter, Peter	12
Amy	66
Anciaux, Eliza	46,53
Lydia	46
Mrs.	46
Anciaux, Nicholas	46
Anderson	161
Douglas	126
Eliza	(2)144
Eliza Clifford	144
Elizabeth	1,2,(2)93
Elizabeth Clifford Wayne	166
Elizabeth Mary	166
George	63,68,93,137
	(3)143,(3)166
George Wayne	166
James	30
James William	166
John	2,87,134,153
John Edmund	87
John Wayne	166
Malcolm	(2)100
Mary	28,63
Mrs.	144
Susannah	93
Thomas	(2)147
William	120
Andrews, Israel	36
Anna	93
Ansley	130
(see also Harrison)	
John	130
Anthoion, Andrew	132
Antoinne	105
Archer, Margaret	7
Ardis, Abraham	1
Christian	1
Daniel	1
David	1
Elizabeth	1
Isaac	1
Jacob	1
John	1
Mary	1
Mathias	(2)1
Sarah	1
Armaignac, Claire Adelaide	34
Armbrister, James	7
Armour, John	(2)35
Armstrong, Deborah	119
James	6,58,87,99
John	65
Arnets, Jonathan	21
Arnold, Eliza	144
Artrobus, J.	2
Aselin, John Anthony	132
Ash, Hannah	49
John H.	69
Matthew	75
Richard Russel	44
Ashbrook, Mary	72
Aspinwall, George	111,(2)133
Atkerson, George	(2)52,101

Atkerson, Joseph Lee	54	Barnwell, John Bernis	(3)4
Margaret	54	Martha	4
Mary Susannah	54	Mary	(2)4
Susannah	54	Phebe Sarah	(2)4
William John	54	Barrington, John	83
Atkins, Charles	32	Barron, Joseph	23
Atkinson, Anthony	139	Barton, Elizabeth	22
Atlee, Margaretta	165	Theodocius	15
William R.	165	William Cornelius	22
Audebert, Jean Baptiste	160	Bauchanneau, Nich.	108
Austin, Josiah William	97	Bayard, Edward	100
		Jane	100
Bacon, Edmund	98,108,146	Margaret	100
Jonathan B.	54	Maria	100
Joseph	8	Nicholas S.	(3)100
Sarah	8	Beal, Helena	11
Backett, Thomas	163	Bealer, Charles	25
Bagbie, Francis	120	Beatty, Eleanor	(3)5,14
Bagwith, Mary	64	John	5,91,125,126
Bailie, George	89	John Patrick	5
Harriet Louisa	57	Beauvallet	106
Robert	88	Catherine Nazaret	105
William	101	Beck, John	6
Baillie, Elizabeth	70	Parson	169
Thomas	70	Sophia	6
Baillou, James	8,55	Becket, John	28
Mary Elizabeth	8	Beckham, Young	165
Baillow	41	Becroft	79
Bainbridge, George	130	Becu, Abraham	16,134,148
Baisden, Solomon	83	Mary	16
Baker, Francis	136	Bedenfield, John	1
Joseph	25	Beecroft,	18
Stephen	19	Elizabeth Ann	(3)11,16
Baldwin, Isaac	104	Robert	11
Ball, Elias	96	Samuel	11,16
John	6	Begbie, Alexander	139
Joseph	3	Belcher, James	19
Ballow, Elizabeth	8	William	8,93
Bandy, Levina	170	Belin, Peter	47
Bannatyne, William		Bell, David	
Macleod	94		(2)5,(2)55,134
Bannon, Cynthia O.	33	Jane	5
Barbarroux, Jean Andre	34	John	5
Barber, Penny	21	Robert	5
Bard, Ann	9	William	5,84
Peter	9	Belleneas, Marie Madeline	
Susannah	9	Henrietta Rossignol de	54
Bard & Thompson,		Bellemy, Esther	13
firm of	9	Bellews	101
Barnard	(2)121	Bellinger, B. B.	150
Ann	148	Belscher, William	93,98,155
Edward	55	Belton, Jonathan	161
James	55	Benedix	133
John	104	Isaac	
Lucy	148		(2)103,126,133
Mary	16	Bennet, Mathew	108
William	55,148,153	Bennett, Thomas	84
Barnes, George	63	Benson, John	173
Barnwell, John		Berge, Elizabeth	33
	(2)4,99,163	Berger, Mary Ann	72

ABSTRACTS OF WILLS, CHATHAM COUNTY, GEORGIA

Berger, Peter	72
Bergmann	60
Catherine	60
Barrien, John	162
John M.	169
Berthelot, John B.	115
Berthelos, S. B.	15
Bessett, Ann	136
William	136
Bettison, David	160
Beverly, James	20
Bevill, Granville	116
Beynard	18
Bigar, John	168
Bigbee, Daniel	137
Francis	124
Binah	(2)145
Bintham, James	6
Bird, Abraham	133
Andrew	42,(2)61
Isabella	61
Samuel	82
William	109
Bissett, Robert	76
Blake, Daniel	4
Blakeway	4
Blanchard, Reuben	81
blanche, De la Toison	
Roche	147
Blane, John	26
Blanks, James	70
John	70
Bleakly, Robert	168
Blount, Charlotte	13
Elizabeth Ann	12
Jane	12
Stephen	12
Stephen William	12
Blythe, Peter	117
Boifeuillet, Charles	
Peter Caesar Picot De	
Charlotte Angelique	7
Sersanne	7
Mary Anna De Larmandie	7
Joseph Balthazer	7
Michael	7
Boisfeillet, Charles	
Pierre Cesar Picot De	8
Jean Marie	8
Joseph Balthazar Charles	8
Michael	8
Sersanne	8
Servanne	8
Boisfeuville	17
Bolding, William	66
Bolinger, Elizabeth	164
(see also Bollinger)	
Bolinger, George	78
(see also Bollinger)	
Bolinger, Mary	164
Bollinger, Frederick	(2)164
(see also Bolinger)	
Bolles, Job T.	96
Bolton, Ann	93
Curtis	12,26,31,93
Edwin	12
Francis Lewis	12
J.	82
James	12
James McLeah	12
John	(2)12,13,26,31 55,58,68,84,138
Nancy	12
Rebecca Newell	12
Robert	(3)11,(3)12,(2)26 (2)30,58,64,71,(3)93 137,151,155
(see also Newell)	
Robert & John, concern of	12
Sally	12
Sarah	(2)12
Bond, Samuel M.	63,134
Samuel Miller	24
Venibolds	105
Bonett, Elizabeth	49
Bonnell, John	67
Winefred	67
Bonner, Catherine	62
Eliza	62
Peter	62
Boone, Thomas	(3)88
Boquet, Peter	50
Borden	121
Bosomworth, Thomas	47
Boswood, James	12
Mrs.	114
Bottomley, Michael	6
Bouchonneau, Nicholas	148
Bourk, Hugh	59
Bourke, Ann	77
Catherine	141,171
Elizabeth	141,171
Jane	23,141,142
Thomas	23,141,153
Bourn, Benjamin	13
Bourquin	33
Ann Sophia	7
Benedict	(2)7,39,(2)111 152,158
Benjamin	97
David Francis	(2)7 12,24,41,61
Edward	172
Harriet	(2)9
Henry	8,9,11,16 39,62,63,64,(3)72,91 97,120,127

Bourquin, Henry Lewis	9,72
Jane Dollar McCaw	97
Jane Judith	7,72,111
John	72
John Jacob	152
John Lewis	72
Judith	(2)111
Margaret	46,158
Mary Ann	7
S. G.	31,67
Sophia	97
William Henry	72
Bowen, Elizabeth Ann	11
Jabez	13
James Flint	(2)11
Jane	8
Jane Elizabeth	(2)11
Mary	11,113
Mary D.	16
Oliver	13
Samuel	8,88
Bowles, John	8,163
Philip	163
Philippa	8
Bowman, Robert	31
Box, Eliza	152,162
Elizabeth	26,99,143
James	158
Philip	100,143
Philipen	143
Thomas R.	162
William G.	70
Boxley, Winnifred	137
Boyd, Ann	39
Barbara	14
Charles	(3)14,(3)39 (2)67,(2)164
Eston	39
James	14,39
Mary	39
Brabant, Elizabeth	31,172
William	48
Bradhurst, Samuel	113
Brailsford, Elizabeth	(2)14
John N.	99,169
Samuel	14
Brainard, Caleb	154
Brant, Samuel	66
Brent, Will Lee	96
Brickell, James	14
John	9,14,49
Brickerstuff, Johnson	85
Bridge, Joel	(3)165
Bridges, Joseph L.	22
Briere, Jean	15
Jean Francois	15
Jeanne Margueritte Cazeaux	15
Julien	15
Brisbane, Adam	7,13
James	6
John	13
John Stanyarne	7
Margaret	6
Robert	6,13
William	6
Briton, John	13
Stephen	(2)13
Britton, Stephen	(2)107
Bronaugh, Nancy	137
Brooks, Benjamin	12,13 16,53,166
Charles	(2)16
F.	19
Robert	16
Broughton, Elijah	16
Lydia	16
Brown, Ann	30
Archibald	20
Edward	109
Elizabeth	109
Frances	9
James	21,(2)30
James DeNeaux	30
John	9
Obadiah	13
Patrick	7
Patrick H.	165
Stratford	(2)158
Thomas	(2)9,109
William	21,123,155
Brownhill	(2)5,41,124
Brownson, James D.	13
Samuel	49
Bruston, David	71
Bryan, Elizabeth Mary Judith	16
Hugh	10
James	(2)10,113
Jonathan	10,64,170
Joseph	10,15,61
Josiah	10
Samuel	16
Samuel J.	102
William	10,113
Brydie, David	20,81,104 117
Bubia, Elizabeth	5
Buchenau, Margaret	5
Nicholas	5
Buckanan	121
George & Co.	165
Buckhalter, Catherine	15
Jacob	15
Joshua	15,80
Buckholter, Elizabeth	57
Buckley, Philip	6
Buffett, George	14,138
Mary Ann	14

ABSTRACTS OF WILLS, CHATHAM COUNTY, GEORGIA

Bugg, Nich. H.	9
Bull, Absalom	6
John	40
Thomas	(2)6
Bullinger	3
Bulloch	18
Ann	(2)70
Archibald	9,28.29
	(2)36,74
Archibald Stobo	51
James	52,70,89
	150,175
Mary	9,(2)29,70
Sarah	(2)51,77
W. B.	151
William	175
William B.	(2)70
	95,98,102,144,170
Bunton, John	117
Burdick, Mary	168
Burk or Bark, Thomas	107
Burke, Ann	(2)161
Michael	95,(3)161
Thomas	(2)101
Burnet, Charles	64
Burns, Thomas	135,163
Burrington, Thomas	64
Burton, S.	41
Butler	41
Ann	
Anthony	67
Benjamin	9
Edith	10
Elizabeth	(3)10,40,42,136
James	10,134,136
Jane	10
John	10,11,(2)59
Joseph	(2)10
Shem	(2)10
Thomas	10
William	172
Buys, Edward	71
Byrn, Martin	82
Burns, James	82
Bysam, William T.	60
Cable, Denbo	29
Caflisch, John	138
Caig, John	60
Caig & Mitchell	97
Cale, William	(2)96
Calhoun, J. Ewing	10
Camel, Mary	102
Cammell, William Robert	107
Camp, Mary	14
Thomas	14
Campbell	32
A.	20
Arthur	21

Campbell, Cartan	52
Edward	150
G.	142
George	167
Harriet	23,150
John	78,103
Macartin	150
Martha	150
Martha Gadsden	23
McCartan	(2)76
Sarah	158
Camphor, Jeremiah	48
Priscilla	48
Canton, Jacob	103
Capers, Richard	155
Caradue	(2)147
Agathe	147
Archille	147
Hercule	147
Cardoza, David	48
Carey, Alexander	14
Jessey	14
Carles, Ant.	54,86,128
Carlton, Theodore	13
Thomas	32,170
Carr, Joseph K.	16
Mark	89,90,117
Thomas	117
William	117
Carson, John	156
Carter, James	169
Thomas	40
Cartledge, Edmund	81
Casey, John A.	16,33
Cater, John	(2)19
Stephen	(2)19
Susannah	19
Thomas	25
Cattel, Aunt	92
Claudia	92
Cattelle	92
Cattels, Aunt	92
Caven, James	43
Caves, Lucy	33
Cazeaux, Briere	15
Cecil, Leonard	125,126
(see also Ciecel)	
Chairs, Thomas P.	16
Chaix, Anthony	132
Chamberlain, R.	140
Chambers, Langston & Co.	65
Champagn, Elizabeth	148
(see also Tondee)	
Nicholas	148
(see also Champi)	
Champi, Nicholas	148
(see also Champagn)	
Champlin, Chris G.	128
Chapman, James	18,20,29,(2)124,125

Chappedelaine, John Baptiste Mark Michael de	17	Clark, Margaret	(2)20
Julien Joseph Hyacinthe de	17	Mark	125
Rene' Ann Mary Caeser de	17	Mary	20,97
Chapus	26	Matt	2
Charlton, Thomas U. P.	96,99	Moses	60
Charon, Marie Joseph Emile De	(2)7	Samuel	41
(see also De Charon)		Susannah	53
Charrier, Joseph	70,86	Thomas	45
Chauvin, William	12	Weston	20
Chavenet, Senior	18	William	2,19,20,89 (2)90,125,135
Cheruvaux, Francoise	105	Clarke, George	107
Chessa, Jacques De	7	Henry William	107
(see also Dechessa, Jacques Aubert)		Mary	107
Chestnut, Mary	14	William Henry	107
Chevalier, Charles F.	87	Clarkson, William	52,138
Chevier	116	Clay, Ann	37,64,151
Chew, Benjamin	(2)22	Catherine	58
Caleb	22	James	58,64
Obedience	22	Jeanne Mary	7
Chiffell, Anna Alecea	31	John	138
Philothews	31	Joseph	9,12,(4)37,41,46 (2)58,60,61,(4)64,79,94 98,104,108,129,(2)161 171,175
Thomas	31		
Chiffelle, Amedius	83,112		
Child, Barbary	115	Mary	37,174
William	115	Ralph	7,151
Childs, John	137	Susan E.	37
Christ, Ann Elizabeth	33	Thomas S.	37
Christiana	124	Cleary, Nathaniel Green	128
Christie, Robert	53,96	Cleaver, Sarah	23
William	96	Cleland, Moses	134,137
Christopher, George	20	Clements, Benjamin	116
Jacob	20	Charles	116
Church Elizabeth	119,129	James	116
Churchill, Frederick	173	Jenet	(2)116
Ciecel, Leonard	89	Jonathan	116
(see also Cecil)		William	116
Clancy, James	171	Cleran, Arch. M.	33
Jane E.	171,172	Cline, John	13
Mary Ann	171	Clissis, Barnard	161
Clanton, Catherine Eliza	55	Cloriviere, Picot de	17,54
Clark, Ann	(2)125	Cloud, Adam	126
Archibald	20,137	Clyatt, Dianna	21
Barbara	90	Clyatte, Ann	21
Elizabeth	91,149	David	21
George	13	James	(2)21
Henry	20	Rebecca	21
Herodias	(2)19	Samuel	21
James	5,20,34,91 (3)97	Saragh	(2)21
		Coales, William	50
Jane	20	Cochran, James	24,49,157
John	5	Jane	24
Jonathan	19	Cocke, William	165
Joseph William	97	Cocknert, Elizabeth	118
Lemuel	19	John	118
		Cohen, Philip	32
		Philip Jacob	21
		Coit, James T.	151

ABSTRACTS OF WILLS, CHATHAM COUNTY, GEORGIA

Colder, Elizabeth	(2)161
Thomas	161
Coleman, Alice	61
Thomas H.	61
Collier, Benjamin	21
Thomas	160
Collings, Kethea	58
Colmesnil, Gabriel L.	15,86
(see also Colmisnil)	
Colmisnil, Gabriel L.	116
Colon, a slave	26
Conner, Simon	120,149
Connolly, John	5
Cook, John	61
Martha	61,89
Mary Ann F.	61
Samuel D.	61
Shem	88
Cooper, Charles	96
Ephraim	167
Thomas	40
Cope, Adam	13,68,101
Charles	14,42
George Lewis	101
Copp, John	21
Coppat, Aime	26
Corker, Charles	21
Leah	21
Mary	21
Susannah	21
William	21
Cormick, S. M.	(2)94
Cornelius, Elizabeth	63
Corrient, Margaret	127
N.	127
Couper, John	24,152
Course,	
Charlotte Rebecca	18
Daniel	18,91
Elizabeth	18,19
Isaac	18
John	18,91
Courtney, Ann	76
Courvoisie, Charlotte	23
Francis	(2)54,84
John Francis	22
John Francis William	22
Louisa	23
Mary	22, 23
Mary Fox	22
Cowling, M. W.	156
Slaughter	108,156
Slaughter W.	6
Cowper, Andrew	89
Basil	23
Margaret	141
Mary	23,141,142
Mary Ann	130,141,171
Cox, James	47
Coxe, John	131
Crafts, Stephen	55
Craig, William	23
Crane, James	23
John	23
Mathew	17
Patrick	17
Cravellier, William	22
Crawford, Barbara	24
D. John	24
Fanny	155
Nancy	155
Sarah	155
William	24
Crighton, Alexander	41,64
Elizabeth	41
Cripps, William	147
Croitey, Thomas	146
Crookshanks, Patrick	18
	126,131
Cropp, Benjamin	22
John	21
Sarah	21,22
Croswaite, William	18
Crow, John	2
Culberson, Penelope	51
Cummings, Eli	29
Cummins, Esther	76
Cunes	96
Cunningham, Alexander	104
John	6,18,(2)45
	82,157
Currie, Alexander	18
Catherine	18
Elizabeth	18
Jane	18
John	(2)18,63
Joseph	18
Curtain, Ann	130
Daniel Silsby	130
Ezra	130
Mary	(3)130
Curtis, John	72
Mary	9
Polly	9
Cusack, John	160
Mary	160
Sarah	160
Cuthbert, Alexander D.	61
Alfred	173
Annie	23
George	18,(3)20
	23
James	(2)20,(2)23
John	173
Joseph	(2)20
Lewis	23
Lewis G.	22
Mary	20
Cuyler	83,101
Davies	144

Cuyler, J.	13,77,101
Jeremiah	14,(2)32,33, 53,60,(2)61,(2)68,76,96, 109,139,143
William Henry	61
Dallaghan, Thomas	161
Daniel, Adam	4
Daniell, William C.	44
Dansler, Barbara	31
(see also Densler)	
Darling, Richard	101
Darnell, Henry	26
Dart, Arabella Ann	128
Darthiangue, Clarissa	27
Jean Marie Galat	27
John	27
Dasher, C. H.	168
Christian	30
Joshua	63
Davant, Elizabeth	30
James	30,31
John	(2)31
Rebecca	31
David, Berenin Isaac	32
(see also Davis)	
Hannah Isaac	32
Joseph	32
Samuel Isaac	32
Davidson	18,45
Crawford	45
George H.	138
William	73
Davies, Dinah	14
Edward	27
Edward A.	140
Edward L.	140
Edward Thomas Lloyd	27
Francis	27
(see also Davis)	
John	14,15,27,140
Mary	27
Peter	(2)27
Sarah	26,27
Thomas	27
Thomas W.	69
W. John	26
William	14,15,21,27,56, (2)67,80,105,(2)140,143
Davis, Berenin Isaac	32
(see also David)	
Edward	27
Elizabeth	33
Francis	27,132
(see also Davies)	
Frank	(2)147
Hannah Isaac	32
(see also David)	
John	46,48,87,147
Davis, Joseph	13,54
Joseph	32
(see also David)	
Reason	54
(see also Rezin)	
Rebecca	27
Rebeckah	73
Rezin	33
(see also Reason)	
Richard	29,30
Samuel Isaac	32
(see also David)	
William	29,35
Dawson, James	33
John	25,(2)33,143
Joseph	25,33,65
Mary	25,27
Mary Hatcher	27
Richard	27,33,117
Thomas	25,33
Day, Elizabeth	25
Joseph	25,26
Sarah M.	162
Sarah Mary	26
Thomas	25
William	(2)25,91
Deakins, Francis	(2)34
Jane	34
Leonard Marbury	34
William	34
Dean, Jean	131
DeButts	167
DeChappedelaine	17
(see also Chappedelaine)	
DeCharon, Marie Joseph Emile	(2)7
Mrs.	7
Decheneaux, Thomas	17,18, 26,27,43,(2)66,86, 92,121
Dechessa, Jacques Aubert	
(see also Chessa, Jacques De)	
Dechisse, J. A.	92
DeCloriviere, Picot	54
(see also Cloriviere, Picot de)	
D'Erbage, George	78
D'Espinose, Caroline	
Victoire Adelaide	34
Jean Jaques	34
Jerome Francois	34
Jerome Jules Joseph Jean Genevieve	34
Dehl, David	21
DelaCroixe	46
DelaMater, Benj. W.	16
Delany, Sharp	167
Delberghe, John	70
DeLarmandie, Armand	7
(see also Larmandie)	

ABSTRACTS OF WILLS, CHATHAM COUNTY, GEORGIA

DeLavardie, Henrietta	7
Delegal, David	112
George	28
Jane	24,(2)28
Judith	112
Mary	112
Philip	64,(2)112
Sarah	112
DeLeon, Abraham	104
Esther	104
Isaac	104
Deleval, Joseph	8,46
Delony, Robert	18
Delyon, Abraham	54,140
Levi S.	115
(see also D'Lyon)	
Sarah	140
Demere	92
Frances	26
Mary	25
Mary Elizabeth	25,26,122
Raymond	(2)25,(2)122
Demetre, Daniel	(2)64
DeNeaux or Deneaux	66
Ann or Anne	29,30
James	29
John Bermers	29
Mary Olivia	30
Peter	30
Sarah Martha	30
William	29
William Fairchild	29
Dennis, Eliza	144
Richard	63,144
	(2)172
Dennison, Ezra	19
Densler, Ann	31
Ann Margaret	31
Catherine Barbary	30
(see also Dansler)	
David	(2)31
Frederick	31,67,69
(see also Dansler)	
Henry	30,31,122
(see also Dansler)	
John	31
Michael	(2)3,30,(2)31,103
Sophia	31
Susannah	30,31
(see also Dansler)	
Derkson, Wuckpt	
Margaretta	62
Deschevaux, Thomas	105
	(2)106
Desmouliens, Julien	70
Des'reviaux, M. Bontineau	132
Dessaussure, D.	(2)4
Daniel	4
Deubell, Ann	33
John H.	33
Deubell, John Henry	79
Deveaux, Andres	(2)4,28
Ann	(3)4
Catherine	(2)4
Elizabeth	(2)4,64
Hannah	4
James	4,28
DeVeaux, James	9
Deveaux, John B.	116
Margaret	28,29
Martha	4,(2)132
Mary	3,152
Peter	24,(2)28,29
	85,100,(2)152,154,162
Sophia	28
William	4,28,29
Deville, Henrietta	26
John	26,(2)132
John Anthony Mary	26
Mion	26
Devine, James	97
Dews	18
Dickinson, John D.	170
Samuel	131
Dickman, Furney	115
Dickson, James	146
Diggins	131
Dillon, Ann Mary	146
Christiana	31,172
Edmund	35
John	17,31,62,86
	110,127,146
(see also Fry)	
Mrs.	75
Robert	(2)31,75,145
	172,173
Dimon, R. M.	99
Dixon, James	76,165
Joseph	32,170
Thomas	13,67
William	165
Dixsee, Isabella	28
James	(2)28
William	(2)28
D'Lyon, Levi	170
Levi S.	32,68
(see also Delyon)	
Doder, Emanuel	26
Maria	26
Dodere, Martha Gamelle	26
(see also Doder)	
Dollaghan, Thomas	6
Donaldson, Arthur	20,21
Isaac	20
Margaret	20
William J.	20
William P.	20
Doon, Ann	32
John	(2)32
Mary Ann	32

Dotson, Ann	31
Celia	31
Douglas, Douglass,	
Benjamin	96
Davice	58
David	89
Isaac R.	171
K.	89
Doumoussay	17
(see also Dumousay)	
Dowdy, Nath.	39
Dowell, Mary	103
Mary C.	103
Thomas	103,154
Dowl, Peter	40
Thomas	30
Downs, Jonathan	163
William	(2)163
Doyle, Elizabeth	146
Drayton, Charles	76
Dorothy	10
Eliza	36
Glen	36
Dresler, Dressler,	
Elizabeth	28
George	8,28
Mary	28
Driscoll, Margaret	32
Thomas	32
Timothy	33
Dronico	93
Drummond, Elizabeth	122
Drysdale, Eliza J.	44
John	44,(2)77,144
Sarah	44
Duclos	92
Dufara, Antoine Jacques	34
Dufaure, A.J.M.J.	34
Duff, David	45
Duffield, George	20
Duffy, Mary	84
Patrick	(2)66,67,99,127
Duhigg, O.	18
Duke, Ann	15,67
G. R.	152
Green R.	15,33,67,141
Dumont	7
Dumousay, Francis Maria	
Loys De Lavaure	27
Duncan, David	79
Dunham, Charles	85,110,143
Dunlap, Joseph	24,26
Dunn, George	49
Dunwoody, James	135
Dunworth	123
Dupon, Paul	22,105,106
Dupont, Cornelius	114
John Henry	(2)138
Peter	66
Dupuis, James	177
Durr, Elizabeth	109
Dutaus	106
Marie Louise Nazaret	106
Dyer, Henry M.	65
Henry Moreton	65
Ealy, Mary	97
Eaton, Ann	83
Nancy	113
Edwards, Ann	94
Elizabeth	91
George	97
Eirick, Catherine	(2)35
Isabella	35
John Adam	35
Ruth	35
Elbert	3,79,120
(see also Rae, Graham)	
Caty	123
Elizabeth	(2)37,(2)119 123,129
Hugh Rae	37
Matthew	37
S.	119
Samuel	37,79,89 (2)119,(2)123,(4)129
Samuel Emanuel De Lafayette	37
Sarah	37
Elfe, Thomas	89
Eliza	93
Eliza (servant)	145
Elkins, John	170
Elliott, Benjamin	(2)36
Eliza Ann	36
Elizabeth	36
Grey	8,20,73,(2)118 127
(see also Gray)	
John	70,157
Ralph	10,37
Ralph E.	37
Robert	2
Samuel	36
Stephen	10,(2)37,94
Thomas	36
William	(2)10,(3)37,94 (2)136
Ellis, Henry	64,88
Solomon	169
Elon, Ann	148
Elon (see also Tondee)	
Elisha	148
Elza	127
Emanuel, Asa	59
Benjamin Mordecai	140
Enoe, George	37,62,63
William	37

ABSTRACTS OF WILLS, CHATHAM COUNTY, GEORGIA

Eppinger	75
Barbara	(2)36
(see also Barbarah)	
George	37
James	36,55,142
John	(2)36,55,68,69,71 (2)116,(2)118,119,(2)142 144,155
Margaret	37
Mathew	158
Mathias	37
Sarah	37
Winifred	37
Erhart, Francis	114
Espinose	34
(see also D'Espinose)	
Eustace, John Shey	(2)92
Margaret	(2)92
Evans, Jonathan	20,35
Martha	35
Sarah	(2)35,159
Sophia	70
William	(2)35,70
William M.	3,35,69,(2)93
Ewen, Margaret	35,36
Richard	(2)35
William	35,36
Ewing, Samuel Spiers	131
William	19
Exley, John	93
Experience	66
Fahm, Frederick	39,72,164
Jacob	(2)39
Fair, Robert	63,142
Fairchild, Samuel	137
Faning, Joachim Noel	84
Fannen, Abraham N.	116
Fannin, A. B.	171
Farley, Ann	(2)41,42,112
Benjamin	41
Elizabeth	42
Grace	43,(2)112
John	(2)42,47,136
Joseph	19,42
Samuel	8,112
Sarah	(2)42,44
Farrar, George Y.	85
Farrell, Thomas O.	100
Fawn, Alexander	127
Fayd, Hannah	118
Feather, John	66
Feaveaux, Rebecca	11
Feay, Esther	44
L. H.	33
Launcelot H.	44
Obadiah M.	44
William	(2)44
Fee, Amelia	73
Fell	141
Fell, Frederick S.	38
Owen Owens	110
Fenden, Elizabeth	156
Fenwick, John	114
Ferguson, James	40
John	7,40
Joshua	40
Mary	44
William	59
Ferrier, James	72
Fetzer, Ulrick	123
Fecklen, Elizabeth	31
Samuel	31
Fidd, Benjamin	43
Fielder, Richard	157
Susannah	157
Files, Stephen	131
Finden, Mary	41
William	41
Fips, Daniel Goffe	(2)50
Elizabeth	50
Fishbourne, Elizabeth	160
	161
Fisher	95
David	103
Hendk.	85
Jeremiah	121
John	82,108,149
Thomas	80
Fitzpatrick, Ann	154
Eliza	(3)154
John	154
Philip	154
Fleming, Helen	174
Flemming, Ellen or Nelly	176
Flerl, John	123
Flowers	62
(see also Gamble)	
Floyd, Margaret	39
Richard	39
Flyming	12
F. T.	11,14,76,141
Thomas	48
Flyn, Mary	33
Footman, Edward	175
Elizabeth Caldwell	175
Henry	175
Richard	175
William	175
Forbes, Thomas	7,(2)65
Fordham, John N.	60
Foreman, Thomas M.	15
Forsyth, Benjamin	42
Margaret	42
William	42
Forsythe, Mary	26
Fort, E.	143
Foster, Abraham	110
Foulis, John	147

Fox, Ann	40,41,61
Benjamin	40,(2)41
Catherine Elizabeth	46
Charles	40,(2)46
David	(2)40,(3)41
Elijah	40,42
Eliza	61
Elizabeth	(2)40,(2)41,42 61
Frances	(2)9,40,72
Francis	24
George	(3)40,(2)41
Jacob	41
James	23,40,(3)41
James D. Courvoisie	23
John	9,24,39,(5)40 (3)41,64,72
Jonathan	(2)40,(2)41
Joseph	(2)40
Joseph William	46
Josiah	(2)40,41,42
Martha	45
Mary	61
Mary Ann	23,(2)41
Nicholas	16
Rebecca	46
Richard	(3)41,64
Susannah	40,42,61
William	(5)40,(4)41,83
William B.	(3)23
Franklin, Selby	127
Fraser, Alexander	44
Alexander G.	43
Caroline	(2)44
Caroline Ann	(2)43
George	43,44
Harriett Maria	(2)43
John	141
John L.	44
John S.	43
Mary	43
William	44
Frazer, Alexander	84
Caroline	84
George	84
Harriett	84
John	84
Mary	84
Richard Ash	84
William	84
Frederickson, Charles	154
French, Thomas	149
Fretot, Charles Eutake Charles John Baptiste Nicholas	43
Mary Margaretta	43
Michael Thomas August	43
Frith, Joseph	110
Fry, John	165
Fry, John Newton	17
Fry & Dillon	17
Fryer, Elizabeth	108
Fulerton, Eleanor (see also Fullerton)	21
Fulford, James Haviland	39
Fuller, Thomas	99
William	98,99
Fullerton, Arthur	20
Furches, John	16
Furse, James	42
Gable, Abraham	50,78,135
Elizabeth	78
Elizabeth Susannah	50
John	50,78,147
Gachet, Charles	(2)167
Gaddy, James	54
Gagel, Bertrand	147
Galache, Andrew	131
Ann	50
Ann Elizabeth	50
James	(2)50,88,111 122,(4)125
Gale, Washington	24
William	(3)6
Galphin, Thomas	26
Gamble & Flowers (see also Flowers)	62
Gandy, Peter	148
Garbet, George	60
Garbett, W.	84
Garden, Alexander	107,163
Gardiner, John	(2)149
Gardner, James	51
W.	121
Garey, John	65
Garrett, John	21
Garvin, Elizabeth	22
Gaudry, John B.	86,115
Gay, Abraham	78
Theodore	107
Goeghegan, Ignatius	114
Germain, Ann	48,133
Ann Amelia	53
Michael	45,48,53,133
Priscilla	48
Gibball, Sarah Powell	58
Gibbon, Ann	40
Esther	40
Gibbons	101
Ann	45,(2)46,47,52
Ann B.	52
Barach, Barack, Barrack	(4)46,48,(2)50,(2)52,53 55,77,99,149,151
Charlotte S.	54
Hannah	8,46,47
James Martin	48

ABSTRACTS OF WILLS, CHATHAM COUNTY, GEORGIA

Gibbons, John	48,(2)52,53,55
John Barton	46,53
Joseph	41,(5)46,(3)47 (3)48,(2)50
Josiah	(2)48
Mary	48
Mrs.	46
Rebecca	52
Sarah	46,(3)48,50,52
Thomas	40,41,(2)46,47 48,51,60,100 131,146
Valaria	(2)46,47,52
William	31,(5)46,(5)47 (4)48,(2)50,(2)52,55,64 151
Gibson, Ann	12,93
Daniel	(2)49,108
Joseph Robert	(2)55
Louisa Catherine	55
Richard Turner	55
Robert	49
Robert S.	55,142
Robert Stewart	49,55
Sarah	55,108
William	49
Gigant, F.	43
Gilbert, Ann	45
Elizabeth	45
Hezekiah	82
Jean B.	86
John	45,136
Martin	32
Mary	111
Mary Ann	45
William	30,45,148,170
Gildchrist, Thomas	76
Gilleron, John Louis	115
Gillivary	80
Gilzean, John	45
Ginovely, Mary	54
Gionioley, Benjamin	48
David	48
Hannah	48
Helena	48
John	(2)48
Jonathan	48
Joseph	48
Nicholas	48
Samuel	48
Gionovle, John	48
Giovansle	48
Girard, Mary Frances	121
Girardeau, Elizabeth	49
Hannah	49
John B.	49,122
John Bohun	(2)49
Mary Ann	49
Peter	49
Gisnovoly, John	64
Glass, John	53,57,120,142
Mary	(2)53,(2)155
Glasgow, Michael	32
Patrick	32
Glen, Ann M.	51
Catherine	51
Catherine Jones	74
Charlotte	51,77
George	21,(3)51,52,77 160
James	21,(3)51,52,73,74
John	21,(2)47,50,51,57 (2)73,87,112,153
Margaret	73
Mary J.	51
N. W.	100
Noble Wimberly	51
Sarah	47,50,(3)51,(2)73 77
Thomas	(2)51,68
Gnann, David	80
Gobert, Benjamin	28
Gockler, Joseph	154
Goffe, Benjamin	50
Francis	36
Jane	50
John	50
Mary	50
Susannah	51
Goldsmith	64
Mrs.	125
Thomas	112
Goldwire, Benjamin	118,122
Elizabeth	166
John	91,166
Joseph	83
Goodall, Jane	27
Gordon, Ambrose	51,170
Ann	45
Catherine	60
Elizabeth	(2)51,68
Esther	68
James	120
John	4
Julia	51
Lloyd	68
Margaret	51
Mary	45
Mississippi	51
Nancy	51
Tombigby	51
William Washington	51
Gore, Samuel	168
Susannah	(2)168
Gorham, John	52,88
Gostling, George	42
Gotear, Josiah	53
Gotier, Josiah	137

Gould, Mary	174	Gugel, Daniel	49
Thomas	130	David	49
Goupy, J. B.	26	John	49
Gouthit, William	(2)130	John Martin	142
Graham	119	Joshua	49
(see also Rae, Elbert)		Mary Ann	49
Grandmont, J. P. Rossignol de	34	Samuel	(2)49
		Sophia	39
(see also Rossignol)		Guidon, Etienne Mavis	1
Jacques Philipe Rossignol de	54	Guillemett, Francis	106
		Guinan, Pr.	7
Grant, Alexander	18	Guinn, Elizabeth	(2)49,156
Ann	18	George	49
Lewis	18	John	49
Peter	84	Richard	49,115,123
Grantell, Elizabeth	27		129
Mrs.	27	Sarah	49,123,129
Graves, Sarah Elizabeth	141	Gunn, Christopher	54,149
Gray, David	36	Christopher S.	54
James	11	James	53
John J.	74	John C. C.	54
Mary	11	Sarah	53
Green, Charles	88	Gussat, George	109
John	39,(2)88	Guy, Benjamin	53
Margaret	88	Benjamin R.	53
William	14	Elizabeth	53
Greene, Catherine	114	George William	53
Greenhow, James G.	166	Mary	53
Mrs.	91	Richard	53
Greenwood, William	60	Gwin, James	25
Greer, John	82	Margaret	25
Richard	51	Gwinett, Gwinnett, Ann	47
Robert	27,61	Button	47
Greethead, Catherine	42	Elizabeth	47
J.	42		
Gribben, Thomas	(2)100	Habersham	29,52
Grierson, J.	129	Alexander	23,64
Thomas	161	Ann	92
Griffin, John	17	Hester	64
Mathew	47	Isabella	119,129
Griffith, Edmund	5	James	21,40,42,48,52
Edward	6,(2)51,137,147		(10)64,163
Mary	5,6	John	12,25,37,58,(3)64
Griggs, Jane	6,142		(5)92,(2)93,114
Samuel	142	John Bolton	52
Grimball, Thomas	177	Joseph	24,25,37,58,(3)64
Grimes, Catherine Jones	(2)77		87,94,(2)125,129,150
James	74	Joseph Clay	52
John	127	Richard W.	14
Sarah Jones	77	Robert	37,101
Gromet, John	117,(2)162	William	16
Groves, John	23	Hadrick, Alexander	58
Guenin, Pierre	146	Haig, George	67
Guerard, Bridget	(2)4	Maham	(2)67
Martha	(2)4	Hainer, Nicholas	120
Peter	64	Haist, Elizabeth	60
Richard	4	George	(2)60,72
Gugel, Christian	49	Hale, John	149
Christopher	(2)49,81,155	Hall	75

ABSTRACTS OF WILLS, CHATHAM COUNTY, GEORGIA

Hall, Ann	46,47,65
Hall, see also Inglis	
Christopher	17
George Webb	65
Henry	(2)99
John	(2)158
Joseph	65
Lyman	47,82,112
Nathaniel	47,65
Samuel	65
Sarah	99
T.	67
Thomas Wm. Burley	7
William Lister	60
Hamilton	92
Ann	159
James	25,128
John	11,39,118,121,131,148
Mrs.	132
Paul	84,(2)130
Robert	122
Thomas	9,122,163
Thomas R. C.	163
Hammerer, John Daniel	72
Hammond, Charles	8
Rebecca	49
Handley, George	90
William	161
Haner, Nicholas	125
Hanikswell, Jas.	42
Hanner, Elizabeth	(2)57
John	153
Nicholas	(2)57
Harbeck, Henry	39
Mary	39
Harbock, John	67,105
Harden, Charles	25,(2)59
Edmund	59
Edward	11,(2)59,71,82,(2)150
Edwin	(2)60
Jane	60
Mary	59,60
Sarah	59
Thomas Huston	60
William	(2)59
Hardie, James	90
Harding, Hezekiah	82
Hardy, W.	173
Harn, Henry	(2)59
Henry H.	61
Henry Hunter	59
James	(2)59
John	59,61
Martha	61
(see also Heron)	
Mary Elizabeth	61
Samuel	11,59
Harn, Thomas	59
William	10,11
Harper, Ann	63
Thomas	63
Harriet (negro)	67
Harris	29
Andrew	141
Catherine McCauley	97
Charles	3,(2)15,(2)23,67,95,97,98,99,105,(2)129,131,(2)140,146,147,150,152,169
Edwin L.	108
Elizabeth	58
Ezekiel	82
Francis	64,73
Francis H.	94
Francis Henry	58
James Mordica	59
John H.	80
Lazarus	140
Luckey (Hester)	140
Mary	59
Mordica	59
Robert	118
Thomas	64
William	30
Harrison, Ansley & Co.	130
(see also Ansley)	
Cynthia	66
Edward	66
Edward Lawson	66
John	(2) 5
John Sealy	120
William	31,66
Harryson, Caleb	143
John	63
Hart, John	110
Hart, Levy & Co.	32
(see also Levy)	
Mary Scriven	110
Hartee, Elijah	25
Harstene, Hartstene,	
Ann M.	63
Anna	62
Benjamin	38,(2)62,(3)63
Catherine	38,(2)62, 63
Jacob	38,(2)62,(3)63,82
Joachim	62
Harvey, Henry	36
William	71
Haugens, Henry	154
Haupt	164
Elizabeth	164
(see also Hopt)	
John	1,27,28,(3)161,164
Hauthwat, Francis	35
Haven, Stephen	9
Hawthorne, Josiah	170

Hays, Patrick	(3)158	Higgins, Ichabod	58
Hazard, Benjamin	128	John	(2)58
Hazzard, William	167	Martha	58
Hearn	79	Hightower, John P.	85
Hebel, Joseph	79	Hilbert, Conradt	121
Hebere, Peter	66	Hill, Ebenezer	19
Heenemann, H. C.	110	Joseph	68
Hehly, Ann	115	Maria	68
Heisler, George	22,103	Mathew	26
John	61	Mrs.	132
John George	(2)80	Sarah	30
Mary	61	Thomas	24
Helbert, Mary Magdelen	61	William	124
Helvinstein, John	143	Hills, Ebenezer	(3)158,171
Hemingway, Samuel	11	Hannah	170,171
Hemphill, James	42,58,73	Sally	(2) 158
Hendlen, James	65	Thomas	172
John M.	65	Hillsmay	159
Hennings, John	(2)116	Hineman, John	(2)119,120
Mrs.	116	Mary	(2)119,120
Herb, Catherine	(3)69	Hines, James	21
Fredk., Frederic, Frederick	30,33,(3)60 121,133,134	Hinley, Mary	143
		Hipp, George	120
		Hobbs, John	61
George	55,60,142	Rebecca	61
Hannah	69	William	160
John	(2)60,62,69 111,121	Hobby, William J.	138
		Hobkirk	169
John F.	69	hofman, George friederich	133
Mary	60,(2)69	Hogg, Ann	63
Rebecca	60	Ann Rebecca	63
Ursuala	(2)60	Hog, Hogg, Eunice	13,67 112,143
Herbert, Moses	16,168		
Herbock, Henry	58	James	147
Jacob	58	John	63
John	58	Maria	63
Mary	58	Maria Frances	63
Michael	(2)58	Mrs.	142
Hero, John	148	Thomas	39,63
Lucy	148	Hoggatt, John	40
(see also Tondee)		Holcombe, F.	13
Heron, see also Harn		Henry	(2)13,53,166
Heron	161	Holliday, Suffier	137
(see also Montmollin)		Hollinger, Martha	(2)54
Mrs.	171	Murriah	54
Herron, Mary	119	Sally	54
Herson, Herman	11,35,39 49,(2)62	Sinia	54
		William	54
Johannah Christianna	(2)62	Holman, John	36
Hersman, Rosina	109	Priscilla	36
Hewett, Andrew	112	Holmes, Bee	14
Hews, Owen	96	David G.	(2)69
Heyward, Heywood	51	Elizabeth	68
Eliza	37	Joseph B.	68
Elizabeth	136	Mary M.	68
James	37	Thomas Golphin	19
Mrs.	62	Holsendorf, Holzendorf, Holzondorf, John	139
Thomas	(2)37,134,(3)136		
Hickman, Furney	17	L. H.	149

ABSTRACTS OF WILLS, CHATHAM COUNTY, GEORGIA

Holsendorf, Holzendorf, Holzondorf, Mary Louisa	139
William	62
Hoover, Conrad	119
(see also Hover)	
Hopkins, Elisha B.	17
Francis	84
John L.	84
Hoppe, Mary	124
Hopper, Robert	130
Hopt, Elizabeth	164
(see also Haupt)	
Hornby, William	47
Horskins, Hoskins, Henrietta	(2)72,120,157 159
Henrietta Catherine	61
John	61
John Henry	94
William	58
Zachariah	36,61,72,120 157,158
Hoseberry, John	149
Houstoun	30
Ann	74
Ann Priscilla	57
Dolly	68
G.	29
George	57,(3)59,(2)88 (2)118,129
Hannah	10
Harriet Thompson	57
James	57,59,113,170
James Edmund	57,58
Joanna	57
John	(2)10,52,(2)57 59,79
M.	175
Mary Ann	170
Mossman	57,95
Mrs.	18
Nancy	68
Patrick	18,58,59,88 113,158
R. J.	175
Richard D.	68
Robert J.	76
Sarah	68
William	57,59
Hovenden, Thomas	47
Hover, Conrad	114
(see also Hoover)	
Howard, Francis	53
Samuel	154
Howe & Dimon	32
Howe, Robert	129
Sarah	79
Howell, John	51
Howes'	152

Howley, Catherine Ann	58
Richard	58,122
Sarah	59
Hoye, Paul	34
Hubbard, James	110
Margaret	110
Hudson, James	116
Hues, Patrick	25
Hugenet, Louis	146
Hugenin, Daniel	65
Hughes, Edward	67
Eliza Maria	67
Michael W.	(2)67
Middleton	81
Owen	67,95,129
Thomas	(2)4
William	101
Huginnin, David	8
Susannah Maria	8
Hull	72
George J.	158
Sophia	72
Hulse, Amey	66
Hultz	66
Hulse, Daniel	66
George	66
Hannah	66
Justus	(2)66
Humbert, Esther	33
Joseph	33
William	33
Hume, James	57
Hunt, Littleton	94
Mrs.	36
Rebecca	25
Hunter, Betsey	142
(see also Elizabeth)	
Dalziel	82
Elizabeth	99,141
(see also Betsey)	
Isabella	52,63,99,141 142
James	52,63,150,153
John	99
Lydia Elizabeth	63
Margaret	(2)51,(2)63,77
William	51,63
Hutchison, Eliza	66
James	66
Thomas	114
Hutson, Thomas	114
Hylton, Thomas	87
Hyrne, Henry	49
Idlot, Joseway	168
Ihly, Samuel	(2)93
Susannah	93
Imfeld, Anthony	70
Inglis, Alexander	120

Inglis & Hall	75
Irvine, Alexander	(2)70
Ann Elizabeth	70
Charles	52,70
Eliza	44
Isabella	70
James	70
John	29,59,70,75,89,112
Kenneth	(2)70
Margaret	(2)3, 70
Robert	108
Sarah	70
William	29
Isabella	107
Ivonet, Gabriel	146
Jackson, Abm.	5
Abraham	30,75
E.	23
Ebenezer	51,63,76,150
Henry	(2)75,160
Jabez	75
James	47,(2)74, 89, 90 161,162,169,173
John	12
Joseph	75
Mary Charlotte	74
Simon	(2)32,170
Simon (negro)	
William Henry	74
Jacobs, Claus	62
Ziperah	104
Jacols, Benj.	38
Jacquere, Mary	113
Jacques, Catherine	118
Jaffray, Alexander	76
Jamieson, Jamieson,	
Charles	32,170
Emelia	73
John	64,73
May	73
Jane	98
Jansac, James	72
Jarvis, Edmund	55,71
John	(2)71
Jauvin	92
Jenckes, John	13
Jenkins, Catherine	
Adams	138
Charles	132,162
Charles J.	138
Hannah	138
Joseph	4
Sarah	148
Susannah	148
Jepson, Anna	82
John	7,49
Johnson, Andrew	(2)74,127
Catherine	128
Elizabeth	156

Johnson,, James	87,126
Marion Ann	74
Mathew, Matthew	74,126
Nathaniel	97
Nisbit	74
Thomas de Mattos	(2)75
William	126
Johnston, Alexander	43
Andrew	2,58,125,129
Andrew William	(2)73
Ann	14,16,(2)43,119,129
Ann Farley	43
Bellemy	77
Daniel	(2)160
David	60,(3)76,116
Elizabeth	73,159
Elizabeth Mary Evans	73
	159
Henry	21
James	50,58,63,71,73,75 (4)76,77,83,(2)126, 146
	169
James Thompson	73
Jane	50
Jane E.	14
Jean	146
John	76
John Jamieson	89
Lewis	77
M. A.	67
Mathew, Matthew	73,83,126 (2)146,(2)159
Rachel	44,77
Richard	129
Sarah	43,67,75,76,77, 143
Thomas	(2)14,89
Wilhelmina	76
Johnston, Robertson & Co.	121
Johnston & Whitefield	169
Joiner, Daniel	31,63
Jones	101
Alethia M.	71,101
Benjamin	148
Catherine	73
Edward	73,76,135
George	23,(2)46, 47, 50 51,(2)52,(2)55,63,73,74 (3)76,(2)77,95, 125,150
Harriett	76
Henrietta B.	72,159
Inigo	73
J. P.	135
James	37,46,71,82,104,159
John	20,73,172
John B.	22
Lewis	71
Maria	76
Martha	76
Mary	36,46,50,(3)73, 148
(see also Tondee)	

ABSTRACTS OF WILLS, CHATHAM COUNTY, GEORGIA

Jones, Mrs. 39,72
  N. W. 77,151,156
  Noble 36,48,51,(2)73
  Noble W. 153
  Noble Wimberly 50 51
    (2)52,55,64,(2)73,(3)74,120
  Obadiah 150
  Owen 71,73,110,126
  Philip 143
  Priscilla 35
  Rebecca Martin 50
  Ruthy (2)135
  Sarah 23,46,(2)73,74(2)76,(2)77
  Sarah Fenwick 23
  Sarah Gibbons 50,52,55,74
  Seaborn 104,109
  (sister) 52
  W. 50,125
  William 48,54,57,(5)72,81,100
  Wimberly 47
Jordan, Willian 71
Jordine, Ann 2
Joseph 173
  (see also Young, Elizabeth)
Joseph, Israel 21
Jour, De La toison dee 147
Joy, Susan 105
Joyner, John 146
  William 43,166
Judah, Rebecca 50,146

Kachler, John Frederick 148
Kane, John 94
Kay, M. 80
Kayor, James M. 80
Keal, Keale, Keall,
  David 9,79,158
  David Washington 79
  George 158
  Henry 9,79
  J. 31
  Jacob Franklin 116
  John (2)9,72,(2)79
  Lewis 9,72
  Lewis Bourquin (2)79
Keating, John 59
  Mrs. 132
  Richard (5)132
  Richard T. (2)15
Keebler, Joshua 168
Keiffer, Kieffer,
  Barbara 133
  David 78,(2)80,119
  Elizabeth Catherine 80
  Emanuel 123
  Frederick 78,80

Keiffer, Kieffer,
  Susannah 78,80
Keith, Alexander 78,157
Kell, John (2)20,122,170
Keller, George Adam 78
  George Paul 78
  John 22
  John Adam 78
  Mary 78
  Paul 55
Kelley, W. M. 69
Kelsall, 29
  Ann 80,90
  Hodge 80
  John 80,90
  Lucretia 80
  Roger (2)80,90
Kenda, G. 175
Kennedy, 16
Kenty, John M. 63
  Patrick W. 63
Kerblay, Lequinio 80
Kern, John Peter 79
  Sophie 79
Kerr, Elizabeth 78
  James 65
  Peter 35,78,90
Kettle, Alexander 174
  (2)175
  James 174,175
  Sarah 174,175
  Thomas 174,175
  Thomas Young 174,175
Key, Elizabeth 54
Kicklighter, Mary 30
Killpatrick, William 67
Kincaid, Patrick 139
Kinder, Elizabeth 121
King, Benjamin 62
  Elizabeth 62
  James 166,170
  John 50
  Joseph 62
  Mary 62
  Thomas 62
  William 62,143,164
Kinley, Sarah M. 90
Kinsey, William 70
Kinsley, Samuel 5
Kirkland 76
Knarik 152
Knott, Elizabeth 156
  Jeremiah 156
Knox, Andrew 33,55
  William 21
Kollock, Lemuel 46,63
  Maria 150
Kopman 3,152
Kozsburg, John 5
Krafft, Maria Rosina 124

Kraus, Samuel	123
Kreeger, John	107
Krutman, Edward	79
Labey, Lebey, Andrew	157
Christian D.	153
David	162
Judith	162
Lachicotte, P. H. R.	128
Lachoux, La Mettrie	17
Ladson, Abram	92
John	25
Lafalloise, Antoinette	17
LaFar, M. F.	164
Lafitte, Laffitte,	
Peter S.	2,39,59
Peter Samuel	39
Lafond, John	7
Laincrie, M. Francis	(2)121
Lamardie, Marie De	8
Lamb, George	93
Sarah Jane	159
William	159
Lambertoz, Desire	22
Lambeth, William	135
Lamkin, Griffin L.	99
Lange, William Henry	133
Langley, Benj.	22
Langs, John P.	142
Langston	65
(see also Chambers)	
Lanier, Lemuel	90
(see also Lenier)	
Lewis	62
Sally Ann	3
Lapey, Jean B.	85
Lapeyere, John B.	86
Larking, Edward	82
LaRoche, Elizabeth	39
Larogue	66
Latham, Daniel	128
Richard	128
Latour, Alexander	
Grasset	86
Peter (Pierre)	
Grasset	86
Lawrence, Joseph	102
Josiah	168
William	17
Lawrey, John	42
Lawson, John	55,(2)65,110
	116,121,(2)143,155,160
Thomas	17
William	119
Lawton, Robert	19
Laval, John De	7
Lavaure, De	27
(see also Dumousay)	
Lavinder, W.	105
Leach, R. W.	100
Leake, Richard	14
Richard H.	151
Lears, John	119
Leaver, Gabriel	78,79,89
Ledbetter, Jain	49
Thomas	49
Ledger, Ellen S.	141
Lee, Ann	83
Elizabeth	110
Mary Ann	(2)83
Rebecca	(2)83
Thomas	73,83
William	83
Lefils, Bernard	27
Legare, Legere,	
Benjamin	134
Samuel	134,136
Leggett, Abraham	(2)19
Lehr'e, J.	120
Leimberger, Israel	124
Leion, Anna	85
David	(2)32,85,141
Hannah	141
Ritta	141
LeMercier	149
Lemoyne, John	27
Lenier, Clement	(2)3
(see also Lanier)	
Leonard, Catherine	
Maria	11
Lesesne, James	147,148
Leslie, Alexander	81,82
Alexander A.	82
Ann	82
Charlotte	82
Elizabeth	81,82
James	82
John	80
Lucy	81
Robert	82
Levett, Charlotte	83
Charlotte Julia	83
Francis	83,92,174
John	83,84
Levis, de	80
Levy	32
(see also Hart)	
Lewden, John	85
Mary	86
Rebecca	85
Selina	85
William	11,35,39,85,119
	146,156,175
Lewis	161
Ann	83
Christiana	83,84
Francis	83
Nathaniel	16

ABSTRACTS OF WILLS, CHATHAM COUNTY, GEORGIA

Lewis, Oliver	82
Selah	82
Seth	(2)82
Thomas	167
William	82,167
Lightbourne, Francis	(2)135
Samuel S.	167
Lightenstone, Elizabeth	112
Lilibridge, Lillibridge,	
Ann	82
Hampton	71,(2)82
Henrietta	82
John	82,99,143,168
Oliver M.	99
Oliver Martin	82
Lindsay, Lindsey	
Benj., Benjamin	5,15
Charles	115
John	15,88
Joseph Page	115
Lions, John	117
Littell, Abraham	164
Livingston, John Cattle	84
Lloyd,	
Ben, Benjamin	1,10,27,83 85,131
Edward	20,27,83,85,140
Elizabeth	81
Francis	81
James	81
Jane	81
John	81
Mary	85
Patience	(2)81
Rebecca	(2)83
Rebecca Frances	85
Samuel	81
Sarah A.	(2)85
Thomas	(2)81
Thomas Edward	23,85,140
L'Motte, Emanuel D.	140
Lockhart, John	100
Lockwood, Joshua	119
LoCroix, Andrew	65
Loehier, Herodia	(2)42
James	42
Loemaride, Mrs. de	17
London, John	90
Long, Catherine	39
John	129
Michael	(2)127
Longworthy, Edmund	36
Lord, George	(2)158
Louis, Sarah	(2)115
Love, Ann	159
John	113,(2)131,(3)159 169
John N.	51
Louisa	131,(2)159
Lovell, David	121
Low, Alexander	22
George L.	53
Lowrey, Ann	88
Elizabeth	81
Hugh	88
Jane	81
John	47,81,90,173
Rachel	81
Loyer, Adrian	8,81
Christiana	(2)81
Edward	81
Isabella	81
Luben, Jean	85
Lucas, Mary C.	166
William	44, 116
Lucena, Hannah	85
Isabella	85
Jane	85
John	85
Lucas	85
Lucinda	85
Suckey	85
Thomas	(2)85
Lunier, James	64
Lydia	46
Lydia (servant)	144
Lyon, John	45,68,83
Mabry, Pharo	68
Machin, Joseph	60
Mackay, Mackey	52
Adam	95
Archibald	75
Eliza	141,171
James	89,90
Mary Ann	171
Michael	87
Robert	23,(2)170,175
Maclean, John	100
(see also McClane, McLean)	
William	94
Macleod	125
(see also McLeod)	
Ann	94
Catherine	(2)94
D.	37
Donald	(2)94
Elizabeth	(2)94
Francis H.	(3)94
John	94
Mary Eliza	94
Norman (Mrs.)	94
Norman	94
Rodonick	94
Maconchy, William	58
Macquinear, Ann	151
Madden, James	142
M'Agill, Mrs.	141

Mahoney, Dennis	8,109
Elizabeth	32
Frances	109
Lawrence	32
Maie, Charles	(2)132
Mall, Margaret	97
Mann, John	90
Luke	83,(4)90
T.	68
Thomas	90
Manns, Charles	147
Manus, Lemle	61
Marbury	(2)172
Elizabeth	71
James Jones	71
Leonard	(2)71,119,120,135
Mrs.	172
Nancy or Ann	71
William	71
Marchand, Lewis	66
Louis	106
Margaret	107
Marks, Sally	140
Marmion, Agnus	1
Marshall, J.	55
Margaret	1
Martin	106,146
Elizabeth	156
John	28,(2)48,89
Joseph	52
Louis Claude	106
Marie Jeanne Elizabet Nazaret	106
Mary Debora	89
Mary	66,107
Mason, John Thompson	34
Mathews, William	91
Matthew, David	43
Matthews, Ann	42
Mattier, Lewis	124
Maurel, Francis	66
Mavhin, Joseph	138
Maxwell, Ann	(3)90,143
Barbara	90
Constant	135,176
Elizabeth Butler	135
Hannah G.	176
Hetty or Esther	175
J. Benjamin	98
James	89,90,163
James Alexander	176
James B.	(3)175,176
James Benjamin	(2)150,175
James Habersham	175
John	90,175,(2)176
John Butler	90,175
John Jackson	(3)176
John Stephens	175
Joseph	14,43,68,84
Maxwell, Maria Schley	176
Mary	90,(3)176
Mary C.	175
Mary Habersham	(2)175
Moultrie	175,176
Simon	143,(2)176
Simonds	90
Simons	164
Stephen	90,(2)176
Susan Jefferson	175,176
Thomas B.	175
Walter	30
William	(2)90,135
William B.	98,151
Maybank, Andrew	49
Mayer, Aug.	125
Augustus	50
Serena	119
McAllister, Amelia Mary	94
Archibald	(2)94
George W.	101
George Washington	94
Hannah	47,52,(2)65
Harriot Hannah	65
Louisa	(2)94
Mathew, Matthew	47,(2)52 61,(2)65,74,94,(2)113 158,160
Mathew Hall	(2)65
Matilda Maria	94
Richard	94
McAlpin, Henry	33,44
McAnnully, James	172
McBride, Joseph	140
McCann, Barnard	95,96
McCartney, John	65
McCarty, Daniel	100
McClane, William	52
(see also Maclean, McLean)	
McCleran, Archibald	44
McConkey, Andrew	(2)6
James	165
Jane	5
McCormick, David	15
Dorothy	96
Robert	96
Samuel	95
McCredie, Andrew	18,98,114
David	(2)98
James	98
McCulloch, Jacob	(2)108
John	114
McDermott, John	85
McDonald, Charles	24
Robert	122
McDowall, John	71
McFarlain, McFarland, McFarlane, Mcfarlen, McFarlin, John	59,89,90

ABSTRACTS OF WILLS, CHATHAM COUNTY, GEORGIA

McFarlain, McFarland, McFarlane, Mcfarlen, McFarlin,		McLeod, Donald (see also Macleod)	159
Margaret	115	John H.	101
Susannah	89	Mary	101
William	68,97,(2)115 156	Norman	75
		William	139
McGarvan, Daniel	96	McLuer, John	(2)83
Dorcas	96	Mary	83
McGee, Mary	97	McMahon, John	8,26,40,124
Rebecca	97	McMillan, Duncan	44
McGillen, Ann	18	McNatt, William	54
Elizabeth	18	McNaughton, John	7
McGillivray, Lachlan	64,109	McNeal, James	173
Robert	(2)164	McNish	9
W.	19	John	72
McGowen, James	5	Mary	9,72
McIntosh, Catherine Ann	142	McQueen, Alexander	95,98
Clarissa	96	Ann, Anne	23,99,141
George	(2)88,96,97,98	Eliza	98,99
Georgiana	88	Elizabeth	98
Hampden	97,98	Harriet	98
Henry	97,98,100	John	(2)23,80,95,(2)99 130,(3)171
John	57,58,59,88,138		
John A.	143	Margaret	171
John H.	142,143	Maria	98
John Houstoun	143	Sarah	99
Lachlan	97,148	Thomas	99
Maria	176	William	99,141,171
Mary	176	Mead, J.	51
Sarah	97	Meed, John	85
William	59,131	Nancy	85
McIver, John	158	Meers, Samuel	17
McKain, Mary Ann	14	Megarven, Daniel	12
McKay, Daniel	64	Mein	33,52
McKennen, Charles	139	Robert	158
McKensie, George	89	William	23,65,(2)98
McKenty, Catherine	100	Mellisimo, Anthony	86
Patrick	100	Mendelhall, John	(2)99
McKey, John	87	Thomas	(3)99
McKinley, Sarah	7	Mercier, John	(2)25
McKinne, B.	168	Le	149
Barna	68	Merrill, Benjamin	116
McKinnen, Charles William	29	Uel	145
McKnight, Mary Ann	96	Metivier, Etienne	85,105
McLaren, Archibald	(2)65	Metzer, I.	127
James	65	Meyers	79
McLaughlin, Ann	(2)127	Adrien	62
McLean, Andrew	46,89,113	Caspar	62
(see also Maclean, McClane)		James	2,124
Andrew Cooper	170	Middleton, Henry	97
Catherine	89	Midy, H.	43
Donald	158	Miles, James	25
Josiah	(2)24	John	25
Margaret W.	46	Millan, John	96
Mary	89	Millar, Joseph	(2)18
Sophia	24	Thomas	18
William	89	Milledge, Charles	27,122
McLeod, D. (see also Macleod)	99	John	3,29,(3)71,92 95,(2)122,159

Milledge, Mrs.	88
Philip	169
Millen, Ann	101
Elizabeth	96
George	101
John	(2)101,121
Martha	96,97
Martha Bane	96
Peter	49,155
Salome	49
Millens, George	159
Miller, Christiana	97
Daniel	87,(2)91
David	(2)86,175
Dorcas	85
Elizabeth	85
F. S.	5
George	2,100
Hariet	91
Isabella	85
Jack	53
Jacob	120
James	64,91
John	175
John Stephen	46,55
Joseph	96,98,(2)131,157
Judith	91
Magdalena	91
Margaret	175
Martha	91
Mary	91
Michael	175
Morris	25,105
Nicholas	28
Peter	45,155
Pheneas	51
Philip	28,38,(2)175
Robert	91,100
Samuel	25,(2)91
Sarah	85
Susannah	28,85,102,175
Tom	53
Thomas G.	46
Thomas Glen	55
William	86
Zachariah	100
Mills, Ann	(3)13
Ann Elizabeth	125
Anna	(3)125
Jane	125
John	(3)125
Sarah	(3)91
Thomas	8,28,(2)47,49 (3)91
William	45,125
Milnor, Mary	77
Milton, John	(2)89
Lucius Quintius Cincinnatus	89
Milton, Richard	157
Minant, Pierre Michel Joseph	146
Ming, Joseph	108
Mingledorph	6
Minis, Abigail	(2)87,98
Abraham	87
Esther	(3)87,136
Francis	87
Hannah	87,93
Hester	136
Isaac	(2)16,87,168
Judith	85,87,93
Leah	(2)87,93
Philip	16,87,108
Philipa	87
Sally	136
Sarah	87,93,136
Mion, Congnaey	92
Elizabeth	92
Mirante	17
Millilies, James	126
Mitchie, John	107
Mitchel	152
Mitchell	97,127,137
(see also Caig)	
D. B.	84,159
David B.	175
David Brady	13
David Brydie	75,92,98 (2)137
John	24
John Stites	144
Levan Newman	(2)152
Mary Ann	107
Sally	(2)109
Sapho	79
Sarah	107
Thomas	107
Mock, Jacob	124
Moies, Christian	33
Momford, James	162
Mondonville, Francis	54
Mongin, Daniel W.	138
Montaigut, David	19,20 28,52,81,87,(2)104 (2)134
Montford, Henry	135
James Spiers	131
Montford, Montfort, Robert	(2)113,131
Montgomery, Harford	(2)158
Jane	176
John	2
John H.	158
John Harford	158
William Watts	158
Montmollen, J. S. De	161
Montmollin, Heron	161

ABSTRACTS OF WILLS, CHATHAM COUNTY, GEORGIA

Moodie, John	59
Moore, Aaron	91,134
Ann	(2)93,117
Catherine	88,92
Elizabeth	(3)91
James	(3)91,114
John	91
John D.	116
John M.	93
Philip	128
Susannah	93
William	(2)91,105,117 131
William A.	96,151 152,170
Mordecai, Abram	83
S.	24,32,63,(2)144
Sampson	32,144
Samuel	95,(2)103
Morel, Ann	44
Benjamin	44
Bryan	10,99
Henry	(2)101
John	(2)9,39,95,(4)101 157,158,159
John H.	95
Mary	9,(2)10
Peter Henry	9,30,50,95
(see also Sawyer)	
Richard	(2)44
Thomas	157
Thomas N.	(2)101
Thomas Netherclift	101
Morgain, Thomas	122
Morgan, Ann	57,88
Elizabeth	88
Lewis	114
Mrs.	57
Thomas	(2)88
William	57,88
Morrice, I. A.	22
Morrison, Eliza	66,169
James	67,68,77,169
Mortimer, William	87
Moss, James	139
John	65
Thomas	65
Mossman	128
(see also Read)	
Isabel	18
James	(2)18,29,30,47 57,80,90,91,95,125 126,160
Moullin, Thomas	91
Moultree, Moultrie,	
Clarissa	2,87
Lueza	2
Thomas	2
Moxley, Nathaniel	126
Muere, Mary	123
Muires, Elizabeth	93
Frances	93
Sarah	93
Mulcaster, George	99
Mullryne, Mulryne,	
Claudia	88
John	8,88
Murdock, David	5,90
Robert F.	131
Murray, John	(2)87
Sarah	140
Muter, James	161
Robert	99
Myers	123
Amealy	78
Elizabeth	78
George	82,(3)101,143
Henry	117
James	(3)78
Lewis	16
Lydia	101
Mary	78
Thomas	101
Nale, G. R.	160
Nasmith, Ann	174
James	174
Naylor, Gilbert	160
Nazaret & Co.	60
Jean Nicholas	106
N.	92
Nicholas	105
Neal, William	160
Neasman, Mary	61
Neefus, Willimpee	113
Neil, Maturin	53
Neilson, James	135
Nelson, James	5,131
Jane	104
Janet	104
Malcolm	104
Nessler, Solomon	138
Netherclift, Alexander	105
J.	57
T.	2,57
Thomas	99,105,129
William	105
Neufville, Edward	107,108
Neumann, Sophy	124
Nevill, John	11
Robert	11
Thomas	11
Newall, Cunningham	160
Newdigate, Penelope	110
Newell	12
Bolton	12
Newell & Bolton, firm of	12
Cunningham	18

Newell, Rebecca	12,26,93
Robert	3,(2)12,26,93
Samuel	93
Thomas	(3)12,26,(2)93
Thomas M.	138
Newton, William	113
Neyle, Elizabeth	104
Gilbert N.	104
Harriett	(2)104,105
James	105
Philip	104
Sampson	104,(2)105
William	104
Nichol, William	144
Nichols, Isaac	103
Nicol, Betty Crawford	24
M.	24
Nicoll, John C.	144
Nielson, Nicholas	104
Nixon, John	29
Noble	58
Mrs.	88
Robert	45
Winenwood	88
Noel, John Y.	76,95
John Young	72
Sarah C.	95,143,144
Nolan, John	32,170
Norden, Leon	103
Nornent, William	21,81,93
Norris, Alexander	6
John B.	33
Norroway, Anthony	163
Northrop, William	131
Norton, Ann Stephens	67
Elijah	105
Elizabeth	116
Jonathan	105
Joseph	26
Kinnaway	4
Polly	133
Thomas	126,147,165
Thomas D.	53
Nowlan, George Galphin	60
Nunes, Daniel	104,134
Moses	104,112
Nungazer, Barbara	103
Elizabeth	15
George	30,31,57 (5)103,119
Henry	15,31,(5)103
Mary Apolonia	78,103
Mary Margaret	103
Nunigate	31
Oakman, Ann	107
Charlotte	107
William	13,107
Oates, Elizabeth	109
Jacob	109,148
Jeremiah	(2)109
John	109
Lucy	109
Peter	9,109
William	109
Oatt, Barbara	108
O'Brien, William	36
O'Brion, Henry	71
O'Bryen	36,(2)113
O'Conner, Margaret	127
O'Connor, Peter	31,(2)127
Odensells, Odingsells, Charles	22,60,71 82,84,96,110
Mary	110
Sarah	110
Offutt, Ann	82
Lettuce	82
Ogden, Isaac	(2)109
Mary	108
Solomon	108,(2)109
Ogg, George	52
Ogilvie, Alexander	(2)107
Charles	(2)107,108
George	(2)107
John Alexander	107
Margaret	107
Mary	107
Peter	19
Oglesby, Betsy	39
O'Hara, James	167
Thomas	113
O'Keef, James	110
Margaret	110
Patrick	(2)110
Thomas	110
Oldershaw, John H.	102
Oliver, Christopher	(3)95
James	(2)95
Jane	95
John	95
Margaret	(3)95
Ralph	95
Onales, Isham	84,115
O'Neal, Ferd, Ferdinand	(2)18,63,71
James Gunn	53
Joseph	18
Orme, John	94
Sarah	94
Ortner, Barbara	108
Elizabeth	108
Henry	108
Osgood, John	48
Osteen, David	108
Sarah	108

ABSTRACTS OF WILLS, CHATHAM COUNTY, GEORGIA

Osteen, Solomon	108
Thomas	108
Ounsel, Ounsell,	
Barbara	109
Daniel	81
Elizabeth	81
Owens, George W.	110,144
Georgia W.	131
Owen	50,76,110,130 (2)146
Padden, Thomas	90
Page, Joseph	115
Margaret	115
Thomas	115
William	(3)152
Paisley, Eliza	111
Jerusha	(2)111
John	111
Mary Caroline	111
Rhoda	111
Sarah Ann	111
Palmer, Elizabeth	111
George	111
Mary	(2)93,165
Mary Ann	111
Richard	29
Thomas	27,91,(2)93,147 165,(2)175
William	29,111
Papot, Papott, James	111 155
Jane	111
Jane Judith	111
Peter	5,8,58,111
Paris, Francis	58
Parke, L. D.	115
Parker, Agnes	120
Ann	112,115
Ebenezer	6,142
Elizabeth	6,(2)113,142
George	18,60
George Stutz	142
Henry	51
James	112
John	17
Joseph	48,99
Lidia	53
Mary	53
Nathaniel	115
William	43,44,85
Parlene	174
Margaret	(2)174
Parsons, George	10
James	10
Pastorius, Hannah	99
Sarah Ann	99
Patterson, Ann Vallotton	156
Henry	25
Patterson, John	26
T. M.	115
William	156
Patton, Eleanor	5
John	173
Ruth	5,39
Sarah	174
Payart, Charles Louis	115
Pazaret	66
Pean, Julienne	15
Pearis, Richard	80
Pearson, John	165
Peat, Jonathan	48
Pelham, Henry	138
Pelot, Francis	116
Jane Eliza	175
Joseph S.	143,176
Richard	22
Pelton, Roderick	120
Samuel	120
Pendleton	92
Daniel	100,(2)111,(2)113
David	113
Edmund	113
Nathaniel	5,9,114
Solomon	111,113
Susan	114
William	113
Penfield, Josiah	140
Penman, John	114
Robina	114
Penny, George	143
Peper, James	12
Perry, John	23
Nancy	82
Peter	58
Peters, George	48
Petigru, Robert H.	44
Petrie, Ninian	1
Pettibone, John	33,67,115 129,156,172
Philips, Samuel	130
Pickering, William	148
Pickles, Desdemona	(2)33
Picot	7
Pierce, William	9
Pierce, William & Co.	9
Pike, Sarah	140
Piles, John	126
Pinckney, Charles Cotesworth	76
Pincon, Valentine Casimer	132
Pinder, William	149
Piper, Henry	170
Pitt, Ann	(2)115
Sarah	115
Thomas	13,(2)115
Platt, Elizabeth	(2)116
James	22,116
Mary	116

Plumer, Ezra	6
Mary	6
Polash, Coshman	137
Polhill	123
Thos.	91
Poloch, Isaac	21
Pomeroy, Eliza S.	37
Mary H.	77
Ponce, Dimas	165
Ponyat, John Francis	54
Poole, William	147
Pooler, Ann	141
Burke	149
John	32,33,(2)141,(2)149
Rebecca M.	44
Robert W.	32
Pope, Joseph Scott	138
Sarah	138
William	96,138
Porcher, J. B.	145
Jane	(2)114
Jane Elizabeth	114
Josiah Dupre	114
Paul	114
Peter	(2)114
Port, George A.	99
James	10,116,165
William F.	43,116
Portatis, Joseph	116
Porteli, Joseph	132
Porter	32,170
Anthony	171
Joseph	43
Posey, William	169
Possey, William	163
Postel, Postell	51
Eliza	145
James	89,90
Jane A.	145
Poulen, Poullain, Poullen, Poullin	27
John	1,2,20,27,28,50,57,84,107,115,169
Poullis, John	26,(2)164
Poulsons, Hugh	127
John	127
Pounia	85
Pourchet, Peter	134
Pourid, Peter	116
Powell, Elizabeth	52
James	83
James Edward	118
Joseph	41
Josiah	91
Sarah	65
Pray, Job	112,114
John	60,114,175
William	114
Prescott, Elizabeth	172
Thomas J.	172
Preston, Elizabeth	112
Henry	73,112
Philip Delegal	112
Price, Charles	88
Prignet, J. P.	7
Prince (negro)	13
Proctor, Bryan	116
George V.	116
Harriett F.	116
Margaret	81
Richard	(2)116
Stephen	116
Stephen R.	116
Prosser, Joab H.	127
Provost, Ann	146
Peter	146
Pryce, Charles	(3)113
Purcell, John	42
Pury, Rudolph	64
Putman, Benjamin	131
Quarterman, Mrs.	40
William	40
Raaily, Isaac	146
Rabenhorst, Ann Barbara	124
Radigney, Charles	121
Mary Francis Girard	121
Rae, Catherine	37
Rae, Elbert & Graham, firm of (see also Elbert, Graham)	119
James	(2)119,120,(2)129
John	123
Mathew	119
Rebecca	119,120
Robert	119,123,(4)129
Rae, Whitefield & Co. firm of (see also Whitefield)	119
Rahn, Joseph	121,(2)177
Raimbeau, Mrs.	132
Rainsford	80
Ralph (see Elizabeth Young)	173
Randall, John Bond	118
Randolph, George	48
Rasberry, Esther	64
Rawls, William	116
Raynes, Ben., Benjamin	7,168
Joseph	40,124
Mary S.	7
Mary Screven	97
Sophia	(2)124
Read, Ann Louisa	127
Catherine	(2)128
Catherine Ann Louisa	128
Cornelia Annabella	128

ABSTRACTS OF WILLS, CHATHAM COUNTY, GEORGIA

Read, Elizabeth	118
George Paddon	118,126
	(3)128
J. Bond	(2)101
Jacob	(2)118,(3)126,127
	(4)128
James	29,36,118,(2)127
	128
James Bond	118,(3)127
	128,176
Mary	118
Read & Mossman	128
(see also Mossman)	
Rebecca	118
Sarah Catherine	118
Susannah	118
William	118,(3)128
William George	126,128
Readdick, Readick,	
Catherine	117
Catterenah	(3)122
Elizabeth	122
Gaspar	122
Jacob	122,123,124
Mary	122
Michael	28,(2)117,122
Nancy	122
Peter	122
Sallome	(2)122
Saloma	(2)117
Sophie	122
Rebecca	107
Redd, Charles A.	85
Reddy, Catherine	58
Reed, Robert	60
Rees, Eben S.	169
Rehm, Catherine	72
Catherine B.	120
Fredk., Frederick	111
	120
Reid	139
Alex	73
Ann	107
David	159
James	107
John	107
Thomas	81
Reims, Rheims,	
Frederick	9
Katherine	(2)9
Reingeard, Mathurin	66
Reinstetler, John Mathias	122
Reiser, Israel	123
Reives, Lewis	4
Mary	121
Remshardt, Remshart,	
Catherina	123
Catherine	100
Daniel	100,116,123
Remshardt, Remshart,	
Hannah	123
John	123
Judy	123
Peggy	100
Rensselvai, John Van	48
Rents, John	59
Resser, Dorothea	49
Rester, Frederick	35
Reynolds, Ann	171
Frederick	99
John N.	78
Rhem, Frederick	79
Rhodes, John	4
Thomas	61
Rice, Catherine	(2)126
James	126
John	126
Sarah	126
Richards, John	11,50
Martha	112
Richardson, George	(2)120
H.	96
Henry	84
James B.	96
John	43,84,96,120
Joseph	120
Margaret	(2)120
R.	16
Thomas	(2)120
Richeson, Cornelis	123
Riffault	66
Charles	106,127
Mary	128
Riggon, Levin	127
Mary	127
Nancy	127
Sarah	127
Riggs, William	141
Riley, Ann	(2)93
John	97
Ring, Ann Margaret	119
	(2)120
Christopher	119,120
John	119,(2)120
Mary	119
Susannah	47
William	118,(2)120
Ritter, George	39,105
Ritton, Michael	49
Rivers, L.	4
Robe, Francis	122
Robert, Edwin	14
Elias	(2)13,154,163
Grimball	111
J. H.	61
John Henry	61
Thomas Elbert	61
Roberts, Charles	23

Roberts, Edmund	142	Rosques, John De La	81
Henrietta	(2)121	Ross, Abner	44
James	33	Ann	112,(2)117
John H.	121	David	29,(4)124,(2)125
John Howell	121	Hugh	117,(3)124,125
Joseph	37,141	Isabella	112
Thomas Hilbert	121	James	62,118
Robertson	121	Jane	(3)125
(see also Johnston)		John	117
Alexander	(2)126	John Alexander Graham	125
Andrew	(2)126	Moses	118
Bellamy	126	Rachel	114
Bellemy C.	77,169	Sarah	(2)124,125
Bellemy Crawford	169	Susannah	(2)112
Daniel	(2)126	Thomas	9,58,(2)112
David	13		125,135
George	113	William	2,81,114
James	9,(2)73,74,112		(2)124,(2)125
	(2)126	Rosser, James	53
Jean Nisbit	(2)126	Rossignol	54
John	92	(see also Grandmont)	
Robert	2	Roth, Peter	45
Susan B.	126	Rouland, John B.	116
Thomas	95,97,141	Royston, William	42
William	(2)126	Rudolph, Eliza	166
Robeson, Sylvanua	90	Ruppert, John	35,59,118
Robilliard	66	Mary	(2)118
Katy	66	Rush, Joseph	(2)123
Robinson, Elizabeth	96	Russell, Andrew	121
Israel	117	Ann	157
James	74	Isaac	140
Jane	117	Jacob	(2)121
Mrs.	169	James	121
Thomas	13,96	Jane	50,104,125
Roche	147	Pearla	140
Ann	126	Rebecca	121
Matthis	29	S.	157
William	126	William	125
Rodman, Thomas W.	76,77,169	Rutherford, Ann	101
Rodott, E.	15	Nathaniel G.	101
Rogers	75	Rutledge, John	128
Augustus	121		
Susannah	139	Sackman, Ann	33
William	26	Sadler, Thomas	(2)121
Rolfes, Elizabeth Ann	122	Sague	66
Frederick	122	Salfner, Mathew	103
George	47,134	Salle, Valentine	(2)132
Theresa	122	Salome	123
William George	122	Sanders, Mary	38
Rolleston, C.	(2)107,108	Sandiford, John	163
Roma, Eliza	43	Sandridge, Austin	(2)137
Eugena	43	David	137
Francis	43,86,106	Elizabeth	137
Roney, Daniel	127,141	James	137
Roper, Sarah	127	Sands, Ray	100
William	127	Santy, Angelo	115
Rosco, Elizabeth	97	Biemama Joseph	115
Rose, Hugh	128	Sapp, Mary	90
Susannah	128	Sarah	173

ABSTRACTS OF WILLS, CHATHAM COUNTY, GEORGIA

Sarah	73
(see also Young, Elizabeth)	
Sass, Jacob	71
Saul	32
(see also Solomon)	
Sauls, Mary	53
Saunders, Margaret	45
Mary	35
William	36
Saussey, Catherine	(2)62
(see also Sorcy, Surcy)	
David	(3)62
Gabriel	62
Joachim	62
Savage, Benjamin	37,136
Jeremiah	(2)10
Mary	134,136
Mary Elliott	10,134
	(2)136
Sarah H.	14
Susannah Parsons	136
Thomas	10,(2)37,47,(2)118
	134,(2)136,(2)161
William	(2)37
William Butler	136
Savery, George Sanders	(2)141
John	141
Margaret Jane	(2)141
Sawyer & Morel, firm of	50
(see also Morel)	
William	172
Saxe, Daniel	15
Scales, Frances	73
William	73
Scarborough, Thomas	73
Scherer, George	53
Scheuber,	
John Sanscalotte	133
Justus	39
Justus H.	27,50,60,79
	103,118,162
Justus Hartman	119,133
	162
Priscilla	53,(2)133
Schewbart, Fredk.	13
Schick, John	60
(see also Shick)	
Schmit, John	60
Hannah	60
Schmuber, James	26
Schubtrein, Joseph	(2)124
(see also Shubdrein)	
Schumaker, Peter	138
Schwalin, Margareth	133
Schweicoffer, Mary	38
Scoffield, Eliza H.	98
Scott, Ann	138
Benjamin Franklin	138
Catherine Howkins	138
Scott, Gavin	142
Hugh	(2)37,50
Jack	170
Jane	142
John	32,(2)138
Joseph A.	63,82
Joseph Adams	(2)138
Joseph James	138
Martha	138
Robert	23
William	151
Scranton, Amy	71,131
Daniel	131
John	131
Screven, Scriven,	
Charles	82
Charles O.	69
Charles Odensells	(3)110
John	15,110
Scull, Ann	143
Mary	143
Seabury, Esther	21
Searles, Ann	(2)112
Sears, Susannah T.	19
Willard	19
Seaver, Benjamin Franklin	(2)168
Edward	168
Elizabeth Grafton Woodbridge	138
Nathaniel	168
Peter Johonnat	138
Sucky White	168
Susannah	168
Sefetre, John T.	67
Sellington, John	(2)123
Senoile, James	20
Senter, Edward G.	128
Serviser, Michael	117
Seymour, Eleanor	112
Gordon Isaac	19
James	(2)112
Richard	131
Shack, John	35
Shad, Catherine	136
Margaret	136
Solomon	2,45,55
	(2)136,150
Shaffer, Balthazer	37,50
	60,78,(2)79,(2)133
	142,(4)158
Elizabeth Margaret	142
Fredk., Frederick	31
	53,(2)142,143
George	142,(2)143
Hannah	142,143
Harriot	142
Jacob	101,133,142,143
James	(2)142
John	142
John William	52,142

Shaffer, Joseph Lawrence	142
Mary Ann Gertrude	142
Sarah	142
Simon Peter	142,143
Shand, John	(2)45
Sharp, James B.	135
Shaw, Agnes	160
James	160
John	14,102
Shearer, Matthew	165
Sheffield, Benjamin	40
Sheftalls	103
Sheftall, Abigail Minis	140
Abraham	(2)139
Benj., Benjamin	33,140
Emanuel	140
Hannah	(2)140
Judith	(2)140
Levi	21,(2)140
M.	150
Mordecai	(2)9,48,64 (2)81,104,140
Moses	3,21,(2)29,55 74,151
Sarah	(2)140
Sheftall	71,95,126,147
Solomon	140
Shelly, Samuel	149
Shereman, Elizabeth	33
Martha	33
Mary Elizabeth	33
Shick, Elizabeth	(2)138
(see also Schick)	
Frederick	122,138
G.	127,168
John	6,46,50,(2)79
Peter	(2)138
Thomas	138
Shillaber, David	140
Shingleton, Richard	(2)132
Shubdrein, Nicholas	123
(see also Schubtrein)	
Shueter, Mad.	17
Shupart, Daniel	6
Sibley, Robert	54
Sigfritz, George	135
Silsby, Abigail	130,140
Daniel	130
Enoch	(2)130
Patience	130
Sampson, Samson	130,140
Samuel	(2)130
Sarah	130,140
Simmons, Elizabeth	(2)134
Frances	134
James	148
John	96,134
Walter	134
William W.	97
Simon, Claud	162
Simons, Eliza	(2)128
Eliza Susannah	128
Elizabeth	126,128
Mary Read	126
Montague	140,141
Moses	134,140,141
Sampson	140,141
Saul	140
Somerville	140
Thomas	(4)128
Simpson	18,45
Elizabeth	14
Green	58
James	14,132,134,147
John	18,124
Susannah	15
Winifred	134
Sims, Esther	141
James	(3)141
Mary	141
Rachel	141
Sarah	(2)141
William	143
William Richard	141
Singleton, Benjamin	48
Sisk, Richard	123
Sitz, Jean D.	85
Slade, Charles	96
Smart	62
Smith, Aaron	(2)132,133
Ann	132,133
Archer	4
Archibald	130,(2)141,171
Eleanor Ann	132
Elizabeth	23,(3)130 (2)141,142
Elizabeth T.	141
Helen	141
Helen T.	141
James	10
James (Mrs.)	47
Jane	140
Jane Wallace	141
John	23,(2)66,79,92 129,(2)130,(2)133,134 141,143
John Carraway	132
John Leonard Stephen	133
John Warner	47
Josiah	145
Maria	145
Mary	117
P.	133
Philip	67
Rachel	145
Samuel	111,151
Solomon B.	99
Solomon Benjamin	132
Thomas	11,159
William	11,(2)160,(2)161

ABSTRACTS OF WILLS, CHATHAM COUNTY, GEORGIA

Smithson, F. T.	6,21
Smy, Sarah	47
Snider, John	123
Solomon, Baker	157
Solomon, Saul & Co.	32
(see also Saul)	
Somerall, Margaret	29
Somers, Humphrey	156
Somerville, Ann	123,129
Edward	129
Jane	119,(2)123,129
Sorcy, Andrew	66
(see also Surcy, Saussey)	
Spahn, Michael	47
Spalding, James	131
Margery	131
Thomas	84,118,(2)131
Sparks, George	45
Mary	45
Spencer, Ann	137,139
Elizabeth	42,(2)137,144
George Basil	11,58,113
	137
George Basset	139
James John Whittendel	(2)144
John	113,139
Joseph	85,(2)110
Joseph William	117,137
Lucretia	(2)144
Mary	137,139
Samuel	137,(2)139
William	144
William H.	22,117
William Henry	(2)11,137
	(2)139,144
William J.	152
William Joseph	60,137
	(3)139
Spiers, Alexander Johnston	131
Squires, David	71
Stack, Margaret	95
Stackhouse, Mary	171
Stafford, Seth	177
Stague, Richard Mary	66
(see also Stites)	
Stallings, Esther	45
James	(2)46
James G.	55
John	82
Martha	45
Thomas Gibbons	45
Stanhope, Nathaniel	5
Stanley, Joseph	55
Stanyarne, Susannah	7
Stark, Alethia A.	71
Ebenezer	53,(3)71,75
	(2)94,99,(2)166
Starr	3
William	3,(2)152

Statham, Robert	68
Susannah	68
Stebbins, Diggins	132
Edward	131,132
Francis	131
Frances L.	139
Frances Louisa	131
Mrs.	22,132
Rebecca	131,132,140
Rebecca L.	140
Stechelys, Jacob	109
Steinert	142
Stellman, Sarah	94
Stephens, Alex.	164
C.	84
Charles	152
Charlotte	85
Elizabeth	156
Henry	42
John	42
Martha	112,143
W.	44,(2)93
William	5,9,24,(2)28
	29,30,37,58,65,77
	(2)83,84,85,87,91,93
	94,96,112,(2)113,115
	125,129,(2)137,150
	152,162
Stephenson, Sarah	11
Stevens, John	130
Martha	13
Stewart, Daniel	117,132
James	135
James W.	32,170
John	40,173
Mathew	83
Susannah	134
Thomas	165
Walten	3
William	8
Stiff, Thomas	149
Stiles, Benj. Benjamin	11,135
Jane	135
Joseph	(2)135,149
Samuel	12,(2)135
Stillwell, Joseph	68
Stirk, Andrew	58
Benjamin	(2)129,(2)135
Hannah	(2)135
John	135
John Williamson	129
Joseph	129,135
Nathan	129,(2)135
Samuel	8,20,27,114
	129,(2)135
Stites, Abraham	144
Benjamin	68
Eliza	144
Eliza Clifford	143
Elizabeth Clifford	167

Stites, Mary	167
R. M.	(3)167
Richard	76,143,175
Richard M.	24,53,61,65,68, 99,105,137
Richard Mary	66
(see also Stague)	
Richard Montgomery	144
Richard Wayne	143
Sarah	144
Sarah Anderson	143,167
StMare	146
(see also Thoison, toison)	
Stoddert, Benjamin	34
Stole (Stull), Sophie	(2)31
(see also Stull)	
Stone, Elizabeth	134
Hardeman	97
Randsom	143,169
Samuel	134,136
Thomas	(2)135
Storey, James	20
Storie, James	104
John	30,137
Margaret	(2)137
Storr, George Kincaid	139
Helen	(3)139
John	(3)139
Martha	139
Reid	139
Thomas	139
Storrs, John	64
Stort, Francis	27
Stouf, Isadore	(3)66,100, 121,168
Stow, John	7
Stradman, William	93
Stratham, Robert	5
Strickland, Samuel	114
Strobart, Abm.	97
Jacob	152
Strobell, John	109
Johanna	109
Strochacker, Rodolph	118
Elizabeth	(2)109
Stronach?, Elizabeth	21
Strong, John	20
Stuart, Ann	143
Richard	61
Stubbs, James	168
Stull, Sophia	31
(see also Stole)	
Sturdivant, Nathaniel	(2)19
Sturges, Oliver	76
Stutz, Jane Ann	142
Joseph	116,142
Sugden, John	134
Sullivan, Flor.	89
Summerocle, John	12
Surcy, Andrew	66
(see also Sorcy, Saussey)	
Swain, Eliza	3,152
Swanson, Peter	164
Swarbreck, Edw., Edward	14,61
John	61
Swarbrick, Edward	169
Sweet, George D.	172
Mary J.	145
Sym, Hugh	41
Talbird, Henry	104
Tanner, Asa	133
Tatnal, Tatnale, Tatnall, Tattnall, Claudia	92
Claudia Cattelle	(3)88
Edward F.	23,152
Harriett	152
John M.	150
John Mullryne	88,92
Josiah	60,65,76,(4)88, (3)92,(2)118,150, (2)152,160
Josiah M.	150
Mary	(2)88,(2)92
Taylor, Ann	152
David	68
J. G.	149
James	24
John Russell	139
Rebecca	97
Thomas	74,83,111, 120,126
Walter	14
William	105
William H.	65
Teague, James	26
Teasdale, John	(2)159
Tebbeau, Tebeau, Catherine	(2)151
Charles Watson	(2)151
Frederick Edmund	(2)151
James	64
John	42,45,145,150
Teider, Mrs.	60
Teissier, Stephen	148
Telfair	101
Alexander	52,55,56,67, 151,153
Edward	(2)46,50,52,55, (2)76,99,151,161
Josiah	(2)52,151
Josiah Gibbons	55
Margaret	52,55,151
Mary	46,52,55,151
Sarah	(2)46,(2)50,(2)52, (2)55, 67,(2)151
Thomas	52,55,56,151
William	65

ABSTRACTS OF WILLS, CHATHAM COUNTY, GEORGIA

Terrien, John	146
Tew, Paraclete	149
Sarah	168
Thies, Thiess, Ann	157
Jacob	103,127
Peter	30,78,103,157
Third, John	149
Thoison, De La St. Mare	147
(see also toison)	
Thomasson, P.	43
Paul P.	15,70
	(2)86,115,116,128
Thompson	45
(see also Bard)	
Claud	75
James	(2)1,89,119
	147
Jane	149
John	65,82,83,139
	(2)147
Joseph	149
Lewis B.	153
Margaret	45
Mary	(2)13
Robert	65,139
Sarah	146
William	50,127,130
	(2)146,147,149
Thomson, Harriet Cunningham	98
William	98
Thorne, Sally	20
William	20
Threadcraft, Elizabeth	152
Elizabeth Margaret	152
Esther	147
Esther Caroline	152
George	78,(3)147,152
Julia Maria	152
Mary Catherine	152
Sarah	147
Seth G.	151,152,160
Thomas	147
Throop, Throops, George	155,157
Tibbets, James	117
Ties, Jacob	11
Tighe, Francis	35
Tillinghast, Elizabeth	(2)1
Stuhley	(2)1
Tillman, John	(2)66
Timmons, Catherine	(2)57
John	57
Mary	71
Tiott, Charles	(3)151,152
Charlotte	151
Sarah	151,152
Tobler, U.	34,52,54,60
	106,140
Tobler, Ulrich	11,143,160
Toflere, Maria Susannah	138
toison	147
Tomlinson	175
G.	175
Tondee, Charles	148
Lucy	148
Peter	(2)148
(see also Jones, Champagn, Elon, Hero)	
Towers, Robert	44
Townsend, Harriot	105
Trandfield, Mary	146
Polly	146
Sarah	(2)146
Travis, Alexander	171
Trenchard, Edward	149
Elizabeth	149
Trenfield, William	124
Treo, Margaret	20
Treutlen, Catherine	146
Frederick	136,146
Margaret	146
Trevor, John	39
Triebner, Christopher Frederick	62,154
Trubere, Estevan	27
Trubert	27
Truel	85
Trushet, Charles	152
Elizabeth	152
Tubbs, Harriott Vallotton	156
Tubear, David	(2)122
Elizabeth	122
Mary	122
Susannah	122
Tubley, Tubly, Eliza	141
John	9
Tucker, Henry	(2)152,157
Thomas Tuder	134,136
Tuft, John	149
Syniston	149
Tufts, Francis	153
Gardiner	153
Jane Judith	153
Simon	134,136
Tunno, Adam	21
Turnbull, Andrew	46,94,175
Nicholas	5
Nicol	(2)15,105,150
Patrick	(2)25
Walter	(2)139
Turner, Albert G.	152
Elizabeth	148
Emeline	152
Jesten	148
John	132,(2)148,(2)150
Joseph	(3)152
Lewis	55,(2)148,(2)150

Turner, Mrs.	40
Richard	(2)55,(2)148, (3)150
William	152
Turpin, Mary	114
Twiggs, Abm.	51
David D.	100
John	51
Ullman, John	154
Ulmer, Ann, Anne	(2)154
Charles	152,(3)154
Eliza	154
Keziah	152
Mary	154
Philip	78,(6)154
William	131,(2)154
Upham, Jabez	87
Valloton, Vallotton, Volloton, Vollotton,	
Benjamin	155
D. Moses	35
David Moses	42,50,109, (2)155
Elizabeth	85,(3)156
Francis	120
James	156
Jeremiah	156
Jeremiah Oliver	155
Mary	(2)155
Moses	119,(3)155
Paul	53,156
Paul J.	85,86
Paul Jonathan	155
Vanbrackel, John	170
Vandepere, Cecile	80
Vanderhorst, John	147
VanHorne, David	128
Varn, Benjamin	170
Verdery	132
Verguen, Charles	26
Verrage, John	30
Verriere, Anthony	132
Paul Antoine	(2)132
Vertsch	123
Vessey, Abraham	155
Elizabeth	155
Joanna	155
Viaz?, L.	84
Vickers, Jonathan	67
Villards	6
Villepontoux, Benjamin	156
Frances Susannah	156
Jane	156
Maria Williamson	156
Villers, de	80
F. D. Petit de	85,128
Petit de	80
Vining, Cader	170
Violet (servant)	145
Wade, Ann	162
Elizabeth	162
Hezekiah	(2)162
John M.	162,163
Mary	162,163
Nathaniel	150,162
Nehemiah	36,162
Wagoner, S.	127
Waight, William	4
Waldburg, Waldburge, Waldburger	79,129
Anne	157
Bartholomew	(2)72,158
George	158
Jacob	9,(2)72,90, 157,(2)158
Jacob Henry	(2)120
John Alexander	157
John Bartholomew	(2)120, 157
Sarah	157
Waldhauer, Walthour,	
Jacob	(2)36
Jacob Casper	28,124
Walean, John	125
Walker, Charles	164
Joel	83,(3)164
Rachel	(3)30
William	30
Wall, Benjamin	54,118
Benjamin (Mrs.)	16
Isaac	54
James	77
Sarah	77
Wallace, Ann	173
James	11,87,128
John	41,87,93,105
Mary	131
William	12,157,(2)174
Walsh, Edmond	73
Walter, A. G.	71
Emily	96
Walters, William	33
Walthour, Jacob	35
Walton, George	(2)89,109, 135
Thomas Comber	89
Wamack, John	11
Wambersie, Emanuel	67
Wanden, John	10,134
Ward, Esther	97
John Peter	97,98
Warden, Lovell	76
Wardly, Nathaniel	25
Waring, William R.	171
Warner, Henry	147

ABSTRACTS OF WILLS, CHATHAM COUNTY, GEORGIA

Warner, Mary	73
Warnock, Abraham	147
Mary	57
Warren, Goodloe	164
Jeremiah	164
John	164
Joseph	90
Washington, William	51
Water, Peter	159
Waters, John	68,86,109
	141,151
Sinclair	109
Tamer	(2)109
Watlington, John	2
John N.	2
Mrs.	2
Watson, Charles	64
Watt, Alex.	25
Alexander	35
Richard Gilbert	71
William	104
Watters, John	22
Watts, James	38,85,158
Jane	14,(2)92
John	158
Joseph	158
Laleah H.	44
R.	84
Robert	44,84
William	158
Waugh, Thomas	87
Way, John	157
Martha	157
Moses	157
Parmenus	(2) 91
Rebecca	157
Wayne, Anthony	166
Eliza C.	144
Elizabeth	165
Elizabeth Clifford	167
Isaac	166,167
James M.	68,166,(2)144
James Moore	(3)167
Mary	144
Richard	(2)144,165,(2)167
William Clifford	167
Weatherford, John	108
Webb, Harry	65
Leddy	31
Thomas	36
Webber, Bennett	3
John M.	110
Webley	3
Webster, Mary	166
Weddall, Weddell,	
Benjamin	88,173
Elizabeth	173
Isaac	88,111
John	111
Weems, John	34
Weencoff	121
Weisenbaker, Jacob	49
Weitt, Alexander	39
Welch, Edmund	6
Wells	16
Andrew Elton	163
Elijah	16,168
James	96
Jane	(2)163
Robert	108
Welman, Francis H.	(2)16
Welscher, Elizabeth	138
Joseph	5,9,17,27,49
	(2)62,81,87,97,98,107
	114,119,137,149
Werage, Mary Ann	158
Wereat, John	52,134,(2)136
	160
West, Elizabeth	109
James	109
Weston, Plowden	71
Weymess, Mary	165
Walter Y.	165
Whelock, Thomas	(2)164
White, Benjamin	168
Benjamin A.	16
Benjamin Aspinwall	168,169
Edward	51,111,168
James	25,39,91,152
John G.	152
John Y.	62,154,156
John Younger	91
Maria Susannah	(2)168
Mary	72
Milcey S.	168
Oliver	169
Rebecca	59
S.	152
Thomas	146,168,(2)169
William	27,97
Whitehead, Benjamin	99
Whitefield	35,119
(see also Rae)	
Elizabeth	159
George	24,64,75,119
	120,162,169
(see also Johnston)	
J.	5,25
James	1,2,58,124,132
	(2)162
Martha	(3)162
Thomas	75,98,151,(2)162
	(2)169
Thomas W.	75
William	75,161,169
Whiting, Ann Lucy	150
Elizabeth	(2)150
Lewis T.	150
Lewis Turner	150
Whitlock, John	107

Whitly, John	5
Wigg, Thomas	4
Wiggins, Edmund	165
John	165
Joseph	54
Mary	165
William	22
Wilds, John	165
Wilkins, Ann	159
Archibald	151
Archibald O.	159
Elizabeth J.	159,160
Martha	159,160
Paul H.	39,91
Samuel	(2)159
Wilkinson, John B.	161
Joseph Josiah	102
Mary	(2)135
Morton	102
Sarah Ann	102
Susannah	102
Will, Joseph	(2)117
Mary	117
Willey, James	153
Williams, A.	110
D. D.	16,100,165
David D.	116
David Davies	43
Ebenezer Hills	171,172
Hannah Lorke	171
Henry	117
Henry W.	131,141
Jane	16,165
John	138
John Francis	25
Jordan	32,170
Joshua	165
Margaret C.	172
Nathan	82
Polly	157
Richard F.	172
S. S.	172
Sarah	171
Stephen	157
Stephen B.	172
Stephen S.	158
	(3)172
Thomas	142
Thomas F.	53,138,153,166,171
Thomas Francis	157
William T.	171
Williamson, John	4,(2)129
John G.	95,158,165,169
John P.	55,(3)101,105,151,(2)170
Mary Ann	170
Richard	88
Sarah	141,171
Williamson, William Henry	114,170
Willson, Caleb	168
Goodwyn	160
James M.	(2)138
Jonathan	(2)168
William	168
Willson & Young	174
(see also Young)	
Wilson, Ann Abigail	(2)166
Ann Maria	166
Benjamin	53,89
Caroline P.	49
Elizabeth	110
G.	37
George	135
Hannah	166
James	53,134
James M.	22
John	40,103,139,166
Mary M.	171
Samuel	20
Thomas	54,116,(4)166
William	(2)166
Winecoff, Ann Rosannah	168
Catherine	168
Wing, George F.	153
Winn, Banister	136
Barnard	165
John	48
Mary	41
Peter	41
Wisenbaker, Jacob	62
John	(2)62,168
Matthias	62
Winstanly, Thomas	128
Witzen, George Henrich	162
Nicholas	162
Sophia	162
Womack, Thomas	100
Wonderly, Mary	49
Wood, Catherine	(2)172
Eliza	140
Elizabeth	23
Jacob	114
James	73,172
John	9
Laleah	44
Martha	22
Mary	109,172
Woodbridge	159
Dorcas	138
Maria M.	168
Mary	138,168
Thomas M.	138,169
Thomas March	138,169
William	169
Woodhouse, Archibald	160
Elizabeth	160
George	114,160

INDEX OF PLACES

Abercorn St.	137
Acton Plantation	57
Acton, Village of	39
Africa	6,28,35
Almond St.	20
Alpes	26
Altamaha, Altamahaw River	41,51,74,90,98 117,127,144
America	43,47,65,71,75 100,107,122,(2)130,166
Amsterdam	103
Anchiries	107
Annapolis	118
Antrim Co.	100
Appleton	112
Argyle	136
Island of	28,30
Plantation on	57
Ashley Ferry	136
Asselin Plantation	66
Augusta Creek	161
Augusta, Ga.	1,11,16,25 76,89,112,(3)119,123 (3)129,(2)158,167
Augusta Road	98
Back Plantation	50,136
Back River	79
Bahama Islands	7,39,65 72,80,139,(2)159
Ballyrone Parish	32
Baltimore	12,(2)94
Baltimore Co.	121
Bank	75
Baptist Church	13,53
Bay, The	118,133,140 142,159
Bay Lot	74,75
Beaufort District	62,79 102,137,138
Beaufort, S.C.	30,(2)37 (2)43,48,99,142
Beaufort Town	4
Beech Forest Plantation	52
Belfast	90,176
Beresfort St.	141
Bergerac in Paigne	7
Berkely Co.	95
Berlin	124
Bermuda	135,155
Bern, Canton of	22
Biddo	112
Black Swamp	105
Bluff, The	29,30,48,74 93,118,130,146
Bonaventure	88
Bonaventure Plantation	150
Bonnabella	(2)66
Boston	(2)130,(2)140,(2)169
Boucher Du Rhone	26
Brampton Plantation	10,170
Branham Parish	166
Brazils	68
Bread St.	107,130
Brecon	72
Bremin	169
Bretania	17
Bretania (see also Dole de, D'hillifore)	
Brick Meeting Congregation	79
Brick Yard (Eppinger's)	75
Bristol, City of	(2)42 (2)65
Broughton St.	66,133,143 147,157,161
Brunswick	11,36,52,64,74
Bryan Co.	15,71,150,155 160,175
Bryan Creek	118
Bryan St.	22
Buckland Hall	134
Buffalo Swamp	41,90
Burke Co.	12,104,122,155 (2)158,161
Burnpot Island	28
Burnside Island	125
Caithness	45
Caldermure	18
Camden Co.	51,52,70,98 100,126,142,158,167
Camden District	104
Canada	118
Cannochee, Canonchee, Canouche, Canuche, Canuchee River	9,10,90 118,127,136
Canoe Creek Plantation	23
Carolina	96,147
Carpenter Row	68,143
Carshalton	41
Cassell	119
Cathead Creek	97
Cattel, Cattelle Park Plantation	(2)92
Cedar Grove Plantation	37
Cedar Hill	75
Champagne Parish	15
Charity School	36
Charleston District	136
Charleston Neck	10
Charleston S.C.	1,6 (2)10,14,18,21,32 36,60,85,98,103,114,118

Woodhouse, Robert	160
S.	13
Thomas	160
William	160
Woodhousen	133
Woodruff, Elias	152
G.	175
George	12,37,94
Joseph	122
Woods, Henry	132
Thomas	109
Wooley, Edward	84
Woolf, Charles	170
George	170
John	170
Penelope	(2)170
Stephen	(2)170
Woolhopter, Philip D.	77
Worthington, Charles	34
Wright	117
Ambrose	58
Ann	124,125
Benjamin	164
Edward	131
Gibion	4
James	(2)64,130,141 (2)171
Laban	33,97
Mrs.	162
Samuel (Mrs.)	25
Sarah	(2)130,141,142 171
Shadrack	124
William	125
Wul, Frederick	109
John	109
Wyensly, Bruce	82
Wylly, Alexander	64,163
Ann, Nancy	(2)163
Richard	5,(2)113 (2)163,169
Thomas	(3)163
William	39,(2)163
William C.	163
Wynne, William	108
Yonga, Mary	9
Young, Alexander	14
Benedict	96
Caroline Pooler	160
Charles	109
Elizabeth	172,(2)175
Henry	9,(4)29
Isaac	27,96,(2)173
Israel	163
James B.	18,162
James Box	75,92,(2)160
John	103,117
Margaret	175
Martha	27,(2)173
Mary	173
Nancy	96
Philip	95
Sophia	75,120,173
T. S.	160
Thomas	21,53,68,133 144,172,174,175,176
William	46,48,75,148 (2)172,173
Youngblood, Martha	15,34 106
Yromet, Gabriel	17
Zettler, Catherine	177
Gideon	177
Mary	177
Nathaniel	(2)177
Zipperer, Jonathan	123
Zitterauer, John George	124
Zuberbuhler, Bartholomew	29,48,158
Zuble, Zubley, Zubly, D.	42
J. J.	48
John Joachim	48,(2)52,120
(Mester)	48

ABSTRACTS OF WILLS, CHATHAM COUNTY, GEORGIA

Charleston, S.C. ---------
    (2)120,(2)126,(3)128,130
    134,136,139,(2)140,141
    (2)147,156,173
Charlotte Co. ------------- 164
Chatham Academy----------- 144
Chatham Artillery--------- 68
Chatham Co. ----------(2)28,43,62,82
    (2)85,(2)90,93,109,114,125
Cherokee Hill------------ 27,132
  Plantation on----------- 163
Chester Co. --------------- 167
Chester Plantation------- 118
Christ Church Parish----- (2)28
    (2)41,58,103,114,130
Churches:
  Baptist---------------- 13,53
  Brick Meeting Congre-
    gation---------------- 79
  Church, The------------ 114
  Ebenezer Congregation-- 138
  German Luteran Congre-
    gation---------------- 62
  Hilton Head------------ 31
  Presbyterian Meeting--- 30
  St. John's------------- 149
Church St. ---------------- 136
Cities:
  Amsterdam--------------- 103
  Augusta-------------1,11,16,25,76
    89,112,(3)119,123
    (3)129,(2)158,167
  Baltimore-------------- 12,(2)94
  Belfast --------------- 90,176
  Berlin----------------- 124
  Boston-------------(4)130,(2)140
    (2)168
  Bremin----------------- 169
  Bristol--------------(2)42,(2)65
  Brunswick---------11,36,52,64,74
  Charleston-----------1,6,(2)10,14
    18,21,32,36,60,85,98
    103,114,118,(2)120
    (2)126,(3)128,130,134
    136,(2)140,141,(2)147
    156,173
  Dublin----------------- (2)101
  Edinborough------------ 174,175
  Execter---------------- 139
  Fredericksburg--------- 137
  George Town------------ (2) 34
  Glasgow---------------- (2)76,142
  Halle------------------ 124
  Hartford--------------- 82
  Hull------------------- (2)139
  Inverness-------------- 117
  Liverpool---------11,65,126,158
  London----------11,18,36,(2)41,65
    72,74,80,(2)84,88,89

London-----------------(3)107,(2)108,113
    120,(2)130,(2)140
    (2)175
Louisville------------------ 52,160
Lynn------------------------ 130
Marblehead------------------ 5
Marseilles------------------ 26
Morristown------------------ 17
Nantz----------------------- 27
Natches--------------------- 55
Newark---------------------- 98
Newport---------------40,118,128,(2)168
New York --------------- 6,(2)19,60,66
    75,101,(3)113,116,118
    128,132
Oldenburg------------------- 62
Paris---------------------- 27,106,121
Pensacola------------------- 109
Philadelphia--------------- 20,67,118
    123,149,(3)167
Providence------------------ 13
Richmond-------------------- 53
Savannah-----------------(2)2,3,5,(3)11
    12,13,14,(2)15,16,(2)19
    22,(2)26,28,30,32,33
    34,(2)35,(3)36,37,(2)44
    45,47,48,52,(2)53,55,59
    (3)60,61,(3)62,63, 64
    (3)68,(2)73,78,79,(2)80
    81,82,83,89,90,(3)92
    (2)93,94,(4)95,96,(3)97
    (2)98,(2)100,101,102
    103,104,105,106,109,110
    111,112,114,115,117,118
    119,(2)120,(3)121,122
    126,128,(2)130,131,132
    (2)133,(3)137,140,141
    (3)142,143,(2)144,145
    151,152,154,(2)157
    (2)158,(3)159,(2)160,161
    165,167,168,169,(2)170
    (2)171,172,173,(4)174
    177
Sevilla--------------------- 132
St. Domingo---------------- 18,26,34,43
    54,106,147
Versailles------------------ (2)105
Vivey----------------------- 23
Warren---------------------- 3
Clapboard Bluff------------- 97
Clarendon Co. -------------- 105
Clark Co. ------------------ 85
Clarkenwell Parish---------- 23
Colerain-------------------- 65
Colerain Plantation--------- 57
Colleton Co. --------------- 25
Colonels' Island------------ 79
Columbia Co. -------------(2)55,(2)161
Conn. ---------------------- 82

Coosawhatchie	97
Coosewhatchie River	130
Copthall Court	175
Cork Co.	33
Cornwall Co.	45

Counties:
Antrim	100
Baltimore	121
Berkely	95
Bryan	15,71,150,155 160,175
Burke	12,104,122,155 (2)158,161
Caithness	45
Camden	51,52,70,98,100 126,142,158,167
Charlotte	164
Chatham	(2)28,43,62,82 (2)85,(2)90,93,109 114,125
Chester	167
Clarendon	105
Clark	85
Colleton	25
Columbia	(2)55,(2)161
Cork	33
Cornwall	45
Craven	70
Dauphin	167
Doboy	98
Effingham (Eff.)	36 43,60,(3)62,91,113 118 121,(3)123,139,154 158,177
Elbert	144
Franklin	46,52
Galloway	160
Glynn	24,41,52,90,95 152,157,169
Granville	4,25
Hanover	109
Heresfordshire	134
Jackson	52
Jefferson	52
Lafayette	137
McIntosh	(2)83,84,94 98,144
Middlesex	23,107,113,171
Montgomery	23,94
Murray	45
Ogen	162
Oglethorpe	85
Plymouth	19
Providence	13
Queens	32
Richmond	9,23,67,76,82
Screven	67,116
Suffolk	60

Counties:
Surrey, Surry	41,130
Talgarth	72
Ulster	6
Wabash	169
Warren	149
Washington	29,90,(3)118
Wayne	170
Wilkes	158,164
Wilkinson	15,16,67,172
Winton	6,19
Couree Boeufs Parish	68
Crack Tick	68
Craven Co.	70

Creeks:
Augusta	161
Bryan	118
Canoe	23
Cathead	97
Green	90
Iron Monger	14
Ociatey	97
Red Bird	136
Seneca	34
Crispinand Island	117
Cromdale	18
Crooked River	172
"Cross Lane House	155
Cumberland Island	98,100
Daber	124
Dalbeath Village	160
Dalmeny Parish	174
D'Aquea	121
(see also Quartier)	
Darien, Old	97
Daufuskie Island	84
Dauphin Co.	167
Dean Forest	64
Deverill Plantation	161
Devillare	23
Dewbury	120
D'hillifore Parish	17
(see also Dole de, Bretania)	

Districts:
Beaufort	62,79,102 137,138
Camden	104
Charleston	136
Edgefield	80
Mobile	164
Ninety-Six	1,19
Ogeechee, Little	144
White Bluff	2,15,80,115
Doboy Co.	98
Dole de	17
(see also D'hillifore, Bretania)	
Drakies	20

ABSTRACTS OF WILLS, CHATHAM COUNTY, GEORGIA

Drayton St.	140
Drury Lane	134
Dublin	(2)101
Duke St.	133
Dunane Plantation	70
Dyals Bay	104
East Indies	124
East Town	167
Ebenezer	35,62
Ebenezer Congregation	138
Edgefield Dist.	80
Edinborough	174,175
Effingham Co. (Eff.)	36, 43,60,(3)62,91,113,118,121, (3)123,139,154,158,177
Elbenrath Village	33
Elbert Co.	144
Elgin	45
Elizabeth Town	92
Ellis Square	28,63,64
Embrun, Bishopric of	26
England (Eng.)	71,75,125,(2)130,(3)139,158,166
Eppinger's Brick Yard	68
Europe	43,109,120,137, 150
Ewensbergh, Ewensburgh	36,(2)118,143,151,155
Execter	139
Ezuma Island	80,159
Farm Plantation	10,15
Fell's Lot	142
Fifteen Mile House Plantation	139
Filature	(2)142
Filature Lot	172
Florida	23,109,122,164
Foldishoffon Parish	133
Foldishoffon Village	133
Fort Argyle	10,136
Fortune	34
France	(2)7,8,15,17,22, 26,27,54,86,(2)121
Franklin Co.	46,52
Franksburg	121
Frederica	84
Fredericksburg	137
Fulham Parish	113
Galloway Co.	160
Gambria River	35
Garden, The	136
Garmency Island	123
Genes	26
George Town	(2)34
Georgia (Ga.)	1,9,(3)10, 11,(2)13,15,17,20,34
Georgia (Ga.)	(2)38,(2)60,63,65,80,83, 84,89,91,106,114,119,123, 130,133,134,(2)147, 159, 160,167,178,(2)171, 175,177
German Lutheran Congregation	62
Germany	62,(3)79,124, (4)133
Gibralter Row	130
Glasgow	(2)76,142
Glebe Lands	98
Glynn Co.	24,41,52,90,95, 152,157,169
Goodale Plantation	76
Good Hope Plantation	9
Good Rest Plantation	80
Goshen	127
Granville Co.	4,25
Great Britain	(2)57,64,75, 112,122,128,130
Green Grove	136
Green Island	135
Green's Creek	90
Greenwich Plantation	57
Grenwich	8,11
Guensey Island	91
Guillestre	26
Halifax	19
Halle	124
Halscombe	74,75
Ham Plantation	174
Hampstead	11,12,60
Hanover Co.	109
Hanover, Electorate of	162
Hardwick, Hardwicke	11, 28,30,48,64,74,161
Harleston	136
Harrisburgh	166
Hartford	82
Hassa	121
Hawthorne Lot	142
Hazzard Cowpen	167
Heresfordshire Co.	134
High gate	11
Highgate, Village of	35
Hill, The	114
Hilton Head	31,36,104
Hilton Head, Church on	31
Hog Island	57
Holborn	36
Holland	103
Horse Shoe Neck	164
Howes' Vandue Store	152
Hull	(2)139
Hutchinson Island	59, 105,120

Inverness	117	Jamaica Island	(2)45
Ireland	17,32,33,87 100,(3)119,120	James Point	136
		Jefferson Co.	52
Iron Monger's Creek	14	Jersey	92
Islands:		Jew's Burying Ground	75
Argyle	28,30	Johnson Square	63
Bahama	7,39,65,72,80 139,(2)159	Juliantown	84
Bermuda	135,155	Keall Lands	62
Burnpot	28	Killein	120
Burnside	125	King St.	36
Colonels'	79	Konigsburgh	32
Crispinand	117	Ky.	130,143
Cumberland	98,100		
Daufuskie	84	LaCroix des Bouquets	105
Ezuma	80,159	Lacrotal	22
Garmency	123	Ladies Island	4
Green	135	Lafayette Co.	137
Guensey	91	Lancester	118
Hog	57	Larne, Town of	100
Hutchinson	59,105,120	Laurel Hill	154
Isle of Hope	51,112	Leeds	59
Jaeckell	17	Leslie	76
Jamaica	(2)45,126	Leuchars	175
Ladies	4	Lezebeth Neck	109
Little	120	Liberty Co.	46,68,(2)90 (2)97,98,110,127,135,155 (2)157,158,174
Long	113,121		
Macas	8		
McKitchan's	98	Lincoln Inn	130
Nassau	65,73,139	Little Eating	170
Oatlands	99,142	Little Island	120
Onslow, Great	114	Liverpool	11,65,126,158
Pine	123	London	11,18,36,(2)41 65,72,74,(2)80,(2)84,88 89,(3)107,(2)108,113,120 (2)130,(2)140,(2)175
Port Royal	30,37,(2)43		
Portrogal	163		
Redoubt	73		
Sapelo, Sappolo	7,8,(2)17	Long Island	113,121
Savannah River	5	Louisville	52,160
Sea	60	Lynn	130
Skidaway	5,(2)29,71,82 98,110,122		
		Macas Island	8
Spring	97	Mans, Diocese and Election of	15
St. Catherine's	17,76,110	Marblehead	5
St. Domingo	54,(2)121	Market	30
St. Simon's	24,25,131 (3)152	Marseilles	26
		Maryland (Md.)	15,34,94 118
Tybee	73		
Warsaw, Wassaw	4	Marylebonne Parish	84
Great	29	Mass	5,19,110,(3)130
Little	110	Matthew Bluff	10
Watlington	139	Mauve's?, Matthew old field	23
Whitemarsh	55,62,63,148	Mayenne	17
Wilmington	15,45,136 145,150	May River	96
		May River Plantation	116
Isle of Hope	51,112	McIntosh Co.	(2)83,84 94,98,144
Italie	26		
		McIntoshville	98
Jackson Co.	52	McKitchan's Island	98
Jacksonborough	141	Medway River	117
Jaeckell Island	17	Michael's Store	152

ABSTRACTS OF WILLS, CHATHAM COUNTY, GEORGIA

Middlesex Co.	23,107,113, 171
Middle Temple	130
Mill Seat	113
Mobile, Dist. of	164
Montgomery Co.	34,94
Morristown	17
Morton Hall	46
Mortray	121
Mount Enon College	53
Mount Hope Plantation	132, 161
Mount Sterling Village	137
Mulberry Hill	47
Murray Co.	45
N. H.	168
N. J.	17,57,98
N. J. Township	148
Nantz	27
Natches	55
Nassau Island	65,73, 139
Newark	98
New Brunswick	(2)82
New England	132
New Haven	141
Newington Village	48, 50,52,55
New Leids	143
New Port	40,118,128,(2)168
New Port River	48
New Providence	72,(3)65, 73,125,139
New River Plantation	130
New Windsor	1
New York (N.Y.)	2,6,(2)19, 60,66,75,101,(3)113,116, 118,128,132
Ninety-Six Dist.	1,19
Normandie Province	121
North Brittain	107
North Carolina (N.C.)	70, 109,123
Nova Scotia	82,167
Nunnery	68
Oakland Hill Plantation	3
Oatlands Island	99,142
Ociatey Creek	97
Ociatey Plantation	98
Oconee River	118
Ogeechee	10,26,73
Ogeechee Bridge	68
Ogeechee Dist, Little	144
Ogeechee Ferry	68
Ogeechee, Great	10
Ogeechee, Little	5,7,8,28, 40,(2)72,78,97,120,157
Ogeechee Neck	94
Ogeechee River	29,60,80, 118,136,(2)163
Ogeechee River, Great	9,28, 64,89,104,(2)109,118,119, 133,(4)136,161
Ogeechee River, Little	8, 28,40,50,64,101,134,144
Ogen Co.	162
Oglethorpe Co.	85
Oglethorpe Square	74
Oglethorpe Ward	143
Oldenberg	62
Old Field	22
Old Fish St.	130
Onslow Island, Great	114
Orphan House	124
Oryza Plantation	144
Ossabo Plantation	95
Paris	27,106,121
Parishes:	
Ballyrone	32
Branham	166
Champagne	15
Christ Church	(2)28, (2)41,58,103,114,130
Clarkenwell	23
Couree Bueufs	15
Dalmeny	174
D'hillifore	17
Foldishoffon	133
Fulham	113
Marylebonne	84
Prince William	59
St. Andrews	36,48,73, 88,97,118,124
St. Bartholomew	25
St. David	41,64,90
Stepney	134
St. George	2,(2)19,36, 64,130
St. Helena	4,25
St. James	45
St. John's	91,95,(2)117
St. Luke's	61,67,84,97, 138
St. Mary's	64,148
St. Mathew's	29,36,41, 73,124,127,135
St. Patrick's	117
St. Paul's	11,44,81,103
St. Peter's	6,22,79,97, (3)114,129,130,137,157, 177
St. Philips	1,14,20,35, 39,41,64,83,89
Parsons Green	113
Pays	22
(see also Vaux de)	

Pellins Lands	62
Pembroke Plantation	95
Penn.	47,(2)167
Pensacola	109
Philadelphia (Phil.)	20, 67,118,123,149,(3)166
Piles Grove Plantation	148
Pine Island	123
Pine St.	20
Pipe Makers Briege	100
Pipe Makers Swamp	160
Placentia Plantation	88
Plantations:	
Acton	57
Argyle	57
Asselin	66
Back	50,136
Beech Forest	52
Bonaventure	150
Brampton	10,170
Canoe Creek	23
Cattel Park	(2)92
Cedar Broge	37
Cherokee Hill	163
Chester	118
Colerain	57
Deverill	161
Dunane	70
Farm	10,15
Fifteen Mile House	139
Goodale	76
Good Hope	9
Good Rest	80
Greenwich	57
Ham	174
Lachlan McGillivray's	109
May River	116
Mount Hope	132,161
New River	130
Oakland Hill	3
Ociatey	96
Oryza	144
Ossabo	95
Pembroke	95
Piles Grove	148
Placentia	88
Point	136
Providence	117
Retreat	52,170
Sana Souci	11
Scotts	4
Shaftesbury	30
Shandy Hall	(2)82
Sharon	55
Silk Hope	10,64
Skidaway	82
Stebbins, Mrs.	132
Strathboggon	97
Wakefield	60
Plantations:	
Watlington Island	139
Wayne Ham	144
Whitemarsh Island	55
Wimberly	52
Wilmington Island	150
Woodville	172
Wormsloe	73
Plymouth Co.	19
Point Plantation	136
Ponpon River	10
Poplar Forest	105
Port au Prince	105
Portrogal Island	163
Port Royal Island	30,37,(2)43
Portugal	68
Presbyterian Meeting	20
Prince William Parish	59
Prinlans	76
Providence	13
Providence, Bahama Islands	7,39
Providence Plantation	117
Providence, R.I.	13,14
Providence Co.	14
Public Road	136
Purysburg	5,9,30,79,114,129,130
Purysburg Township	10,114
Queens Co.	32
Queen's Ferry	174
Quartier	121
Rae's Hall	120
Ravensburg	124
Record Room	47,147
Red Bird Creek	136
Red Bird Lands	90
Red Bluff	142,171
Redoubt, Island of	73
Retreat Plantation	52,170
Reynolds Square	144
Rhode Island (R.I.)	3,13,52,128,168
Richmond Co.	9,23,67,76,82
Richmond	53
Ritter's Land	154
Rivers:	
Altahama	41,51,74,90,98,117,127,144
Back	79
Cannochee	9,10,90,118,127,136
Coosewhatchie	130
Crooked	172
Gambria	35
May	96
Medway	117

ABSTRACTS OF WILLS, CHATHAM COUNTY, GEORGIA

Rivers:	
New Port--------------	48
Oconee----------------	118
Ogeechee----------(2)10,26,29,60	
73,80,118,136,(2)160	
Ogeechee, Great--------	9,10
28,64,89,104,(2)109	
118,119,133,(3)136,161	
Ogeechee, Little-------	5,7,8
28.(2)40,50,64,(2)72,78	
97,101,120,134,144,157	
Ponpon----------------	10
Salcacha--------------	29
Salkehatchie----------	10,30
Saltilla, Great--------	48,52
	161
Saltilla, Little-------	24,144
	167
Savannah------------10,28,30,95	
Savannah Back----------	30
St. John's------------	82
St. Tilly's------------	41
Tombigby--------------	164
Turtle----------------	90
Wanaman--------------	147
Rope Walk-------------	12
Round O.--------------	132
Russell Square---------	84
Saggharbour Pro.-------	60
Salcacha River---------	29
Salkehatchie River-----	10,30
"Salt Kittle House"----	155
Salts, The------------	95
Sana Souci Plantation---	11
Sapelo Island----------	7,8,(2)17
Sarte, Dept. of--------	15
Satilla River, Great----	48
	52,161
Satilla River, Little---	24
	144,167
Savannah------------(2)2,3,5,(3)11	
12,13,14,(2)15,16,(2)19	
22,(2)26,28,30,32,33	
34,(2)35,(3)36,37,(2)44	
45,47,48,52,(2)53,55,59	
(3)60,61,(3)62,63,64	
(3)68,(2)73,78,79,(2)80	
81,82,83,89,90,(3)92	
(2)93,94,(4)95,96,(3)97	
(2)98,(2)100,101,102	
103,104,105,106,109,110	
111,112,114,115,117,118	
119,(2)120,(3)121,122	
126,128,(2)130,131,132	
(2)133,(3)137,140,141	
(3)142,143,(2)144,145	
151,152,154,(2)157	
(2)158,(3)159,(2)160,161	
Savannah-----------165,167,168,169,(2)170	
(2)171,172,173,(4)174	
	177
Savannah Back River-----	30
Savannah Court House----	148
Savannah Record Room----	36
Savannah River---------	10,28,30,95
Savannah River Island---	5
Savannah Town----------	154
Saverne---------------	17
Savine Grove----------	114
Scotland------------24,39,57,94,104	
117,142,160,163,174	
Scotts Plantation------	4
Scotts Trail----------	4
Screven Co.-----------	67,116
Sea Coast------------	109
Sea Island------------	60
Seneca Creek----------	34
Seneca Landing---------	34
Sevilla---------------	132
Shaftesbury Plantation--	30
Shaftsbury------------	28
Shandy Hall Plantation--	(2)82
Silk Hope Lands--------	136
Silk Hope Plantation---	10,64
Skidaway Island--------	5,(2)29
71,82,98,110,122	
Skipper St.-----------	20
South Carolina (S.C.)---	1,4
6,(2)10,13,19,22,23	
(2)25,30,(2)31,35,36,38	
43,(3)44,49,(2)63,(2)67	
(2)71,(3)72,(2)80,(2)84	
(2)85,91,92,95,96,97,98	
99,103,104,(4)105,(3)107	
110,111,(4)114,(2)120	
(2)126,128,129,(3)130	
(2)132,134,136,(3)137	
138,139,140,(3)141,142	
146,147,148,(3)156,157	
161,163,167,173,176	
South Commons---------	63
South Wales----------	72
Southwark------------	21
Spain----------------	132
Spanish Town----------	45
Spotsylvania---------	137
Springfield----------	29,43
Spring Island---------	97
Squares:	
Ellis--------------	29,63,64
Johnson------------	63
Oglethorpe---------	75
Reynolds-----------	144
Russell------------	84
St. James----------	98,161
Stamford St.---------	130

St. Andrews Parish------- 36
    48,73,88,97,118,124
States:
  Conn.------------------ 82
  Florida (Fla.)--------- 23,109
    122,164
  Georgia (Ga.)----------- 1,9,(3)10
    11,(2)13,15,16,20,34
    (2)38,(2)60,63,65,80,83
    84,89,91,106,114,119
    123,130,133,134,(2)147
    159,160,167,168,(2)171
    175,177
  Ky.-------------------- 130,143
  Maryland (Md.)--------- 15,34,94
    118
  Mass.--------------5,19,110,(3)130
  N.C.------------------70,109,123
  N.H.------------------- 168
  New York (N.Y.)-------- 2,6
    (2)19,60,66,75,101
    (3)113,116,118,128,132
  Penn.------------------ 47,(2)167
  Rhode Island (R.I.)---- 3
    13,52,128,168
  South Caroline (S.C.)
    (which see)
  Va.-------------------- 53,(2)137
St. Bartholomew's Parish- 25
St. Catherine's Island--- 17
    76,110
St. Clement's Danes------ 108
St. David's Parish------- 41,64,90
St. Domingo-------------18,26,34,43
    54,105,147
St. Domingo, Island of--- 54
    (2)121
Stebbins, Mrs., Plantation 132
Stepney Parish----------- 134
Sterling Bluff----------- 136
St. Gall----------------- 6,12,52
    143,170
St. George's Fields------ 134
St. George's Parish------ 2
    (2)19,36,64,130
St. Helena's Parish------ 4,25
St. James Parish--------- 45
St. James Square--------- 98,161
St. John's Church-------- 149
St. John's Parish-------- 61,67
    84,97,138
St. John's River--------- 82
St. Luke's Parish-------- 61,67
    84,97,138
St. Malo----------------- 8
St. Mary's--------------- 42
St. Mary Islington------- 23
St. Mary's Parish-------- 64,148
St. Mary's River--------- 41

St. Mathews Parish----------- 29
    36,41,73,124,127,135
St. Patrick's Parish--------- 117
St. Paul's Parish------------ 11,44,81
    103
St. Peter's Parish----------- 6,22
    79,97,(3)114,129,130
    137,157,177
St. Philip's Parish---------- 2,14
    29,35,39,41,64,83,89
Strathboggon Plantation------ 97
Strathie Hall---------------- (2)80,90
Strasburg-------------------- 17
Streets:
  Abercorn------------------ 137
  Almond-------------------- 20
  Beresfort----------------- 141
  Bread--------------------- 107,130
  Broughton----------------- 66,133,143
    147,159,161
  Bryan--------------------- 22
  Church-------------------- 136
  Drayton------------------- 140
  Duke---------------------- 133
  King---------------------- 36
  Old Fish------------------ 130
  Pine---------------------- 20
  Skipper------------------- 20
  Stamford------------------ 130
  Whitaker------------------ 161
St. Simons------------------- 24,25,131
    (3)152
St. Tilly's River------------ 41
Suabia---------------------- 124
Suffolk Co.----------------- 60
Sunbury--------------------- (2)20,40,68
    70,123,176
Surrey Co.------------------ 41,130
Switzerland----------------- 22

Talgarth Co.---------------- 72
Thorogood------------------- 136
Three Runs------------------ 113
Thunderbolt----------------- (2)88
Tombigby River-------------- 164
Totenham Court Road--------- 24
Towns (see also name of town):
  Beaufort------------------ 4
  East---------------------- 167
  Elizabeth----------------- 92
  George-------------------- (2)34
  Hardwicke----------------- 11,28,30,48
    64,74,161
  Julian-------------------- 84
  Larne--------------------- 100
  Leeds--------------------- 59
  New Jersey Township------- 148
  New Windsor Township------ 1
  Purysburg Township-------- 10,114

ABSTRACTS OF WILLS, CHATHAM COUNTY, GEORGIA

Towns: (see also name of town):
  Savannah --------------- 154
  Spanish ---------------- 45
  Sunbury ---------------- 70
  Willis ----------------- 167
  Yanghal ---------------- 33
Trustees Garden --------- 5,12,15,78
Turtle River ------------ 90
Tybee Island ------------ 73

Ulster Co. -------------- 6
Union ------------------- 10
U. S. ------------- 34,54,86,(2)100
             106,133,166,169,170
Union Society, The ------ 133
             159,174

Va. ------------------- 53,(2)137
Vaux -------------------- 22
Vernonburgh ------------- 3,78,122
Versailles -------------- (2)105
Villages:
  Acton ------------------ 39
  Dalbeath --------------- 160
  Ebenrath --------------- 33
  Foldishoffon ----------- 133
  Highgate --------------- 11,35
  Mount Sterling --------- 137
  Newington ------- 48,50,52,55
  St. Gall --------------- 6,12,52
             143,170
  Yamacraw ------- 3,0,41,46,81
            152,(2)169,174
Vivey ------------------- 23

Wabash Co. -------------- 169
Wakefield Plantation ---- 60
Waldsher Lands ---------- 62
Wanaman River ----------- 147
Wansford Court ---------- 174
Warren Co. -------------- 149
Warren ------------------ 3
Warsaw, Wassaw, Island -- 4
  Great ------------------ 29
  Little ----------------- 110
Washington Co. ------ 29,90,(3)118
Watlington Island ------- 139
  Plantation on ---------- 139
Wayne Co. --------------- 170
Wayne Ham Plantation ---- 144
Waynesborough ----------- 167
West, The --------------- 144
West Indies ------------- 141
Western Isles ----------- 68
Westphalia -------------- 79
Wharf Lot --------------- 74,75,93
Whitaker St. ------------ 161
Whitby ------------------ 64
White Bluff ------- 11,57,58,60,85
            102,160,174

White Bluff Dist. ------------- 2,15,80
             115
White Bluff Road -------------- 11
White House ------------------- 9
Whitemarsh Island ------------- 55,62
             63,148
  Plantation on --------------- 55
White Point ------------------- 136
Wick -------------------------- 45
Wigg's, Thomas, Lands --------- 4
Wilkes Co. -------------------- 158,164
Wilkinson Co. ----------------- 15,16,67
             172
Willis Town ------------------- 167
Wilmington Island ------------- 15,45
             136,146,150
  Plantation on --------------- 150
Wimberly Plantation ----------- 52
Windsor, E. ------------------- 82
Winton Co. -------------------- 6,19
Woodstock --------------------- 12
Woodville Plantation ---------- 172
Wormsloe ---------------------- 51
Wormsloe Plantation ----------- 172
Wovflet ----------------------- 162
Wrights Neck ------------------ 114

Yamacraw ------------------ 3,9,41,46,81
             152,(2)169,174
Yanghal ----------------------- 33
Yorkshire --------------------- 64,112,120
             (2)139,166

Zion -------------------------- 124
Zubly's Ferry ----------------- 114

www.ingramcontent.com/pod-product-compliance
Lightning Source LLC
Chambersburg PA
CBHW030553080526
44585CB00012B/368